*Mannerisms of Speech and Gestures
In Everyday Life*

Mannerisms of
Speech and Gestures
In Everyday Life

SANDOR S. FELDMAN, M.D.

Clinical Associate Professor of Psychiatry
Associate Psychiatrist,
Department of Psychiatry
University of Rochester Medical Center,
ROCHESTER, NEW YORK

New York

INTERNATIONAL UNIVERSITIES PRESS, INC.

To Ethan and Tanja, my grandchildren

CONTENTS

"But let your communication be Yea, yea; Nay, nay:
for whatsoever is more than these cometh of evil."

MATTHEW 5:37

ACKNOWLEDGMENTS

The author desires to express his gratitude to the following publishing companies and individual authors for their generous permission to quote from their publications or to use their already published papers:

The Hogarth Press, Ltd.
George Allen and Unwin, Ltd.
International Universities Press, Inc.
Psychiatry
The Psychoanalytic Quarterly, Inc.
The Bulletin of the Philadelphia Association for Psycho-
    analysis
Ciba Pharmaceutical Products, Inc.
Journal of the American Psychoanalytic Association
The Psychiatric Quarterly
Etc.: A Review of General Semantics
International Journal of Psycho-Analysis

Dr. Ernest Jones
Dr. Marianne Kris, as executrix of the late Dr. Ernst Kris
Mrs. Rose Owen Brill, as executrix of the late Dr. A. A. Brill
Dr. Hilda C. Abraham, as executrix of the late Dr. Karl
    Abraham
Dr. Karl A. Menninger

To Lottie Maury Newman, Editor of International Universities Press, I express my deep appreciation for her patience, for her conscientious care in correcting the manuscript, for her profound understanding of the subject which enabled her to make valuable suggestions and to eliminate confusions.

And last, but not least, my indebtedness to Miss Ruth Geller, Social Worker for the Rochester Board of Education, who has unflinchingly and tirelessly corrected the English and the style of this book, and typed the manuscript.

I extend my cordial feeling to friends who encouraged the author, who on several occasions was overwhelmed by the magnitude of the task, to keep up his spirit and to release the manuscript for publication.

PREFACE

In this book, I present the results of observations made on certain phenomena of speech and gestures noticeable when people communicate with each other.

The subjects of my psychoanalytic investigations were, first of all, my patients of both sexes from different walks of life; and second, all the other people with whom I came in contact. Freud once said that he had the whole of mankind as his patient. By that he meant that nobody was completely healthy emotionally or mentally. In this statement, he included himself, as do I.

On the basis of extensive clinical experience and especially on the basis of the depth of their investigations, psychoanalysts feel entitled to apply their interpretations to the majority of mankind, sick or not. In psychology, mind examines mind; therefore, pitfalls are many. Of these I am aware and because of them, I ask the reader's indulgence.

Because the phenomena under investigation are observable in our everyday life, the title of this book is justified. I thought the word "mannerism" more suitable than "language habits," "language pattern," "language behavior," "*façon de parler*" or "expressive behavior."

Rochester, N.Y., August 1957

PART ONE

Common Mannerisms of Speech

INTRODUCTION

From the beginning of life, speech and gestures are the most profound communications between persons. The mother "talks" to her baby immediately after its birth, and soon the baby will respond, first by smiles, and then by mimicry and gestures, and finally by words. Spitz and Wolf (1946) have investigated the development of smiling. Speech is necessary not only for orientation and self-preservation but also for pleasure in the relationship. To talk to somebody or to be talked to means that one *exists*, one *counts*, one *belongs* to a group, one has a *place in life*. Communication through speech and gestures is indispensable. Freud (1921) says, "Language reveals also the creativeness of the group mind" (p. 83). Hermann (1934b) comments, "Language as a social phenomenon prevents the feeling of isolation." According to Wendell Johnson (1944), "The importance of language and of symbolization generally, as a distinctly human form of behavior and as a basic factor in personal and social problems, is generally recognized."

According to Masserman (1944), the analysis of the linguistics of a person can be useful in effecting a better social and personal readjustment.

A woman patient, after having spent about thirty years in a very unhappy marriage, told, in the course of treatment, which she needed because of depressions and several other symptoms, that there is no more painful thing in life than to have one's head resting on a pillow which is shared with a husband one does not love. One could add to this that there is rarely a more burdensome feeling than that which one has when talking with or listening to a person whom one does not

3

like or in whose conversation one is not interested. It is because of this feeling that so many people have acquired the
ability to *hear* what is said and not to *know* what is said. It is
sad to see a couple sitting at a table and saying nothing to each
other; they are together by mere necessity. Usually, for some
reason, the man wants to see the mail or the newspaper; or,
because of some complex, he enjoys being at the table with a
woman whom he loves, while at the same time he must do
something other than talk to her. Sometimes such behavior is
a derivative of a child-mother relationship somewhat similar
to the habit of sitting on the toilet and reading or even eating.
Again, he may have still other reasons for his actions. To illustrate, the writer would like to recount a personal experience.

In Budapest, where, in the golden times, I spent a good part
of my life, there was a fashionable restaurant on the beautiful
island in the Danube. Sometimes it was fun to spend an
evening there. One evening, I was the guest of a friend who,
partly because of his profession, knew every bit of gossip
about the night life of the enchanting city. While sitting with
him and some others at a table, I looked around and noticed
a couple. The girl was a sort of cover-girl blonde who looked
somewhat cheap but expensive to keep. Her escort appeared
to be a very personable gentleman. Time passed, but they did
not say a word to each other. They exhibited themselves to
the public, ate, but did not talk. I turned to my friend for
explanation. He said that the man was an aristocrat who was
keeping the blonde. They never talked, at least, not in public
although they were seen for many hours each evening in some
expensive night club. When I asked my friend why they did
not talk, he said that the man met the girl in a night club and
accosted her (here we would say that he picked her up); but
he had never been introduced to her. This was a joke, and
jokes often tell more than any other kind of verbal communication.

And now let us investigate situations in which there is love,
genuine interest, talking and listening. Do people talk artic-

ulately? Do they use language to communicate correctly? Are they aware of what they are saying? Do they say what they want to say? Do they bring the listener into a position of understanding the meaning of what is being said? Do people talk well? Do parents talk well with their children; teachers, with their pupils; statesmen, with their constituents; clergymen, with their parishioners; performers of radio, stage and television, with their audiences; people on the street or at parties, with each other? Seldom. The talk is a mess. A sentence rarely has head and tail. It is broken up into fragments, and its delivery is filled with disturbing mannerisms. Such language makes genuine relationship impossible; spoils the smooth flow of communication; creates a wall between one human being and another; causes confusion, misunderstandings, suspicion, distrust, uncertainty; and is *one* of the important *perpetuating* factors in mental disturbances.

In this book, the term "mannerism of speech" was chosen to illustrate and support the above statements. Several years ago (1948), I published a paper on this subject. I will return to it repeatedly in the course of this book.

Analysis of certain characteristic habits often reveals the deepest motives of the normal and neurotic personality. In the analysis of all kinds of patients it is undoubtedly desirable to unravel the background of personally typical habits. Perhaps, it depends on the personality of the analyst whether he becomes interested in them or not. The writer has always been much interested in them and considers their analysis as belonging to the process of working through in treatment. On first suggesting to a patient that he consider analyzing his habits, one usually meets with strong resistance, but later the patient becomes interested and his cooperation is invariably rewarded by progress in the treatment. Some habits are disadvantageous to the patient and their cure is a deeply cherished secondary gain of psychoanalytic treatment. The nuclear complex (Freud) of a neurosis can be found in many of a patient's habitual actions which should be analyzed.

Freud [1914a] described the ultimate therapeutic effect in analysis as being obtained by a process of working through. The aim of this process is the aim of the treatment itself; overcoming and removing resistances. The patient inevitably encounters resistances and in the process of working through, the analyst is "forcing the patient to make the transition from intellectual to affective understanding and acceptance" [Bergler, 1945]. According to Freud, it is mainly the process of working through which convinces the patient of the existence and strength of the repressed instinctual urges, and this realization prevents him from faltering and becoming disappointed in the treatment. Working through is that part of the treatment which exerts a great influence on the patient; furthermore, it is what makes psychoanalysis different from suggestion in that it provides the opportunity to abreact in a state of consciousness without which lasting therapeutic effect cannot be achieved. Freud once compared the psychoanalytic process to extinguishing a fire in a burning house. It would be of no avail to remove only the match which set fire to the house.

Freud [1939], Rank [1932], and many others regard speech not only as a practical device for communication, but also as a creation typical of the individual, expressing the intrinsic urges and motives of man. Many personal, emotional and intellectual difficulties are reflected in certain linguistic habits [Johnson, 1944]. Glauber [1944] has proved the importance of analyzing the form of a patient's speech.

Psychoanalysts as well as psychiatrists and psychologists have recognized the importance of the way in which language is used by neurotic and psychotic individuals. To mention only a few, there are Hayakawa (1952), Jones (1920), Ruesch (1953), Szasz (1955, 1956), Loewenstein (1956), Berne (1953), and Kubie (1951). Work already done by analysts in this area will be noted in the course of this presentation. After this manuscript had been completed, Martin H. Stein (1958) published a paper in which he illustrates the value of analyzing certain clichés used by patients. To date, however, none of these men has created such a systematic and organized science of language as a means of communication as have the schools of *semantics* and *cybernetics*.

Semantics studies, besides several other important problems, the meanings of words and how human actions are influenced by thought or spoken words. The semanticist assumes that a disturbance can be eliminated by *teaching* the receiver the laws of its logic. Hayakawa (1952) says that Korzybski, the founder of semantics, offered "to psychiatrists through semantics a theoretical basis for the reeducation of patients toward greater maturity of evaluation." Ruesch (1953) states, "The psychiatrist and especially the psychoanalyst look at language from the point of view of pragmatics (what language means to the listener) and semantics, whether the speaker knows what he says when he speaks." Hayakawa (1952) mentions two good examples: (1) When talking of John Smith, it is necessary to consider whether one is talking of John Smith on Monday or John Smith on Tuesday, for the same person is not the same on Tuesday as he was on Monday. (2) When talking of the Supreme Court, one should know whether he is talking about the Supreme Court of 1950 or 1951. ". . . the same object or individual is different in each different environment." The aim of semantics is to eliminate "evaluative rigidity," to avoid "rigid adherence to systems of dogma," "eternal verities," "slogans and catchwords" (p. 250). For years, the author has been making use of semantics, and the results are very encouraging.

The influence of historical environment on the formation of language was shown by Jones (1920), who says:

> I refer to the striving insistence of the English on propriety, which is commented on not only by practically all foreign observers, but also by Americans and our fellow-subjects from overseas, not to speak of the "Keltic fringe" in our own islands. That it degenerates into prudishness here more often than in any other country, at least in the Old World, will also, I think, be widely admitted. The trait is probably to be correlated in some degree with the proneness to reserve, the ab-

sence of social gifts, the dislike of betraying emotion of any kind, and the horror of self-display, vaunting, braggadocio, gasconade, rodomontade—one sees that we have to use foreign terms to indicate attitudes so foreign to us . . . [p. 88].

Jones believes that repression of exhibitionism and historical influence were responsible for propriety in speech: "the development of the outstanding English character trait of propriety has been fostered by the peculiar nature of the English language, one resulting from the success of a Norman adventurer some nine hundred years ago" (p. 94). What he means is, as he indicates, that "the Saxon and Norman languages, after living side by side for about two centuries, gradually coalesced to form English" (p. 93). *Noblesse Oblige,* edited by Nancy Mitford (1956), is a pertinent and interesting book about the mannerisms of the English upper class.

Some psychiatrists try to apply the principles of the school of cybernetics, founded by N. Wiener (1948) and his associates, to the understanding and even therapeutic improvement of human communications. Part of cybernetics deals with the "similarities between neurophysiological phenomena and functioning of calculating machines" (Berne, 1953). An automatic machine is able to direct another and is able to register disturbances of the latter and to correct them.

Ruesch (1957) shows examples of the use of cybernetic principles in human communications. Szasz (1956), on the other hand, thinks that the application of cybernetics to *"human interactions"* is questionable. The writer claims that psychoanalysis, from the beginning, worked essentially on the principles of cybernetics: the therapist, on the basis of his training and talent, was accepted by the patient as a "directing machine" capable of perceiving (having fewer resistances than the patient) the meaning of the disturbances in the patient's associations and therefore able to correct them. Hence, the writer suggests that *in therapy, the three disciplines should be fused in one body.*

Berne (1953) rightly emphasizes that "the receiver is not interested in the information the communicant intends but in the psychological reality behind it" (pp. 190-191). The psychoanalysis of mannerisms is one of the ways through which one can reach this "psychological reality." "It is a mistake," writes Krapf (1955), "to consider only what the patient says and not how he says it: the form of linguistic expression is just as worthy of psychoanalytic research as its content" (p. 331).

In the same paper, Krapf quotes Richard Sterba (from Edith Buxbaum's paper on "The Role of a Second Language in the Formation of Ego and Superego," 1949). Sterba realized that mannerisms of speech are specific manifestations of hidden meanings.

By now the reader is entitled to know the working tools used by the psychoanalyst while he is listening to a person. Through his own training, he realizes that, in order to understand the human mind, he can effectively use Freud's depth-psychological concepts of the functioning of the mental apparatus.

Freud proposed to look at the mental apparatus from three points of view: the *topographic*, the *economic*, and the *dynamic*. These are well-known to psychoanalysts. The non-initiated reader need not be frightened by these words; he, too, will be able to understand them.

The topographic idea means that the mental apparatus is visualized as being divided into three *imaginary* localities: the conscious, the preconscious, and the unconscious. In this working hypothesis, the three, as systems, are placed into localities. The puzzling thing with the "unconscious" is that one knows about its existence not when it *is* but only when it *was*. We can perceive it only when it ceases to be unconscious. After all, if it is unconscious, one cannot know that it exists. Subjectively, the content of the unconscious comes into existence when it no longer exists as unconscious but has become, or is made, conscious. In the unconscious are mental contents which were either never conscious or, if conscious, repressed. Preconscious mental material, either with or without certain effort, can move into the conscious system. For our mental health, the preconscious is very important. After all, we cannot constantly focus our attention on all the mental contents of which we may be conscious. When we think or talk, we depend on the immense capacity of the preconscious as on a storehouse.

The economic point of view in Freud's theory of the working of the mind deals with quantities of excitations coming from instinctual bodily sources. It takes into consideration the *pleasure-pain principle*, which means that the mental apparatus (at this point, the central nervous system) does not tolerate excitations, wants to get rid of tension, and therefore tries its best to discharge, in any possible way, the psychic energy of the excitations.

The dynamic point of view comprises the *forces* which have to deal with the energies responsible for repressions, for regression (the withdrawal of psychic intensities from a more mature stage of development to a primitive-earlier one), and for resistance which may be conscious but is mainly unconscious and which bars the way of the unconscious contents striving to reach the conscious.

Another concept of Freud deals with the three *agencies:* the *id*, the *ego* and the *superego*. The id is filled, according to Freud's concept, with the energy of instinctual forces. It contains everything which is inherited, everything "that is fixed in the constitution," everything "that is present at birth," impulses, drives, and wishes in "a chaos, a cauldron of seething excitements." The ego, an agency which receives all the stimuli from the id, as well as from other sources, is capable of protecting itself against excessive stimulations. It controls voluntary movements, represents the instinct of self-preservation, makes modifications in the external world, and, according to Freud, approves, postpones, suppresses stimuli in order to avoid pain and danger for the sake of the final aim:

gratification. Furthermore, the ego takes into consideration the demands of the superego. It has to do so. The superego (or, in popular terms, the "conscience") is the agency which represents the introjected images of early authorities (parents and their substitutes), self-criticism, guilt, "order," and the demands of proper actions, inherent in nature and in our organism. We have, very emphatically, to distinguish between *false guilt*, i.e., the fear of external threats of punishment, and true guilt, the fear of self-disapproval, regardless of external threats. The id is mainly unconscious, the ego and superego can be both conscious and unconscious. Guilt feelings may be repressed but manifest themselves in symptoms. Psychoanalytic literature deals extensively with these important problems. For illustration of the above-discussed theoretical concepts, let us now turn to clinical examples. (The main body of analytic theories was construed on the basis of clinical experiences.)

A young man came for treatment to be cured of his stuttering. At the beginning of the analysis he was twenty-three years of age, but he had stuttered since the age of three. When he *intended* to speak, his face became convulsed and distorted. For several minutes, he made desperate efforts to bring out his words until he finally gave up the struggle. He could not say one single word. In the office, communication at the beginning was possible only through writing, and later partly through words and partly through writing. He had no difficulties talking with women, only with men. He could talk briefly with a man in the presence of a woman if he knew that the man was interested in the woman, that the man cared nothing for the patient and that the patient was free to leave quickly. If, in a public place, street or arena, a man turned to him with a casual remark, he could answer easily. In this case, he felt as though he were not present as a person and that he could answer automatically, like a machine. But if the man continued talking with him, he would leave the scene because he knew he would not be able to talk.

In the first interview, he was sitting opposite me, separated by a table. The table was covered with a cloth, attached to which was a circular lace which hung down to the level of his legs. His legs were crossed. As was customary at the time, he wore shoes with buttons to which shoelaces were fastened. After treatment had been agreed upon and the time of the first analytic session established, he left. As he did so, a button of his shoe got caught in the lace of the tablecloth. Though I noticed this, I paid no attention to it. When he returned for the first session, he was limping. Asked about his difficulty, he said that his foot got caught in the pedals of the bicycle he rode to the office. On further questioning, he informed me that he had ridden his bicycle for many years but that this had never happened to him before. I suggested to him that having his foot caught on two occasions might be a signal of something repressed which could not come out directly because of censorship, and that these two events might therefore be a sort of "acting out" of unconscious content. The patient then said that he had been in treatment sometime previously for about half a year with another psychiatrist. In his first interview with the latter, the setting had been the same, and his shoe had got caught, just as it did in the first interview in my office.

Subsequently, during the course of treatment, he related the traumatic event which had been immediately followed by stuttering. When the boy was three years old, his mother took him with her to the dentist. She was the patient. The boy accompanied his mother into the office, sat on a chair and watched with curiosity while the dentist worked in his mother's mouth. On the way home, the mother used an umbrella because it was raining. When they arrived home, his mother left the open umbrella on the porch to dry. The boy stayed on the porch, played with the umbrella and put the handle of the umbrella into his mouth. The handle got caught in his throat and he became frightened. From that time on, he stuttered. He never forgot this scene.

As the man considered himself adult, he wanted no other member of his family involved in treatment; he did not want me to communicate with his parents. In this case, his decision was good because we could find out much more by ourselves. The story of the trauma was neither correct nor complete. The forgotten part emerged piece by piece during the course of his analysis.

When the boy came home from the dentist and stayed on the porch with the open umbrella, he wanted to imitate the dentist who worked in his mother's mouth. The umbrella had spokes with bulbs at their ends. When he placed one of the spokes in his mouth, the bulb got caught between his teeth and frightened him. He screamed. His father came rushing out of the house and pulled the spoke-bulb out. There was some bleeding. The boy could not talk from that time on.

This case was selected as an impressive illustration of the working of the mental apparatus as far as unconscious material is concerned. It suffices to add only that the main task of the analysis was to uncover, from a large amount of material, the boy's emotional state at that time, his drives, his impulses, his relation to his parents, to his environment and to the world both inside and outside himself. We had to establish the nature of his curiosity. Why did he want to play the role of the dentist? Was it only the innate urge of children to learn, to experience? Or could it also have been due to a dim urge of erotic need and action? It was both. The inevitable "castration fear" of all men came to the fore, in our case, reinforced by the symbolic significance of teeth (Lorand and Feldman, 1955), the role of the father in this scene, the mysteries of the dentist's office, and the bleeding. Even though the boy grew up and developed into a mature man, and even though he knew enough about sex and had had some sexual experiences, the childhood scene with all its implications had not been "digested," and the conflicts involved in it manifested themselves in the painful and life-paralyzing symptom of stuttering.

The reader must wonder whether the neurosis could have developed if the man had not owned a bicycle, if his mother had not taken him to the dentist, if the doctors had not possessed tablecloths, if the patient had not worn buttoned shoes, or if it had not rained. If the reader knows that a strong "castration complex" can develop in a man without such a single and strong trauma, he must wonder how our patient or any other man betrays his unconscious complex. One cannot outwit the unconscious, it has innumerable ways to create *derivatives* of the complex. It is the task of the analyst to *see, feel,* and know how to *notice* them, to catch them, to understand them, and to make the patient do the same. Sometimes external traumatic situations are not so strong as to arouse violent emotions in a patient, but the patient aggrandizes events to the degree of trauma because he has within him a complex which causes him to react with great intensity to external stimuli.

For the second illustration of the significance of the unconscious, I have selected a man who was, so to speak, forced into analysis by his wife, who found him very trying to live with. His face was devoid of emotional expression. He *had* emotions but he denied them. He showed practically no feeling, no excitement, no affection, no passions, no drives, no aggression, no joy, no sorrow. He was neither depressed nor not depressed. He never initiated any action. He responded with anxiety and impotence whenever his wife became affectionate. In the course of time, a silent understanding was reached in order to have *some* marital relationship; each pretended that neither had any intentions whatsoever. If he yielded to a sort of reflex response, he scored success provided his wife remained completely passive and neutral. If she failed to conceal her interest, the whole thing died off. No wonder that this wife became a nervous wreck and attempted, vainly, to bury her life in work. Although the work was good, her life remained joyless. There is a limit, at least for most women, to the gratifications derived from sublimation of genital drives.

My remarks about this patient (who is discussed more extensively on pp. 204-207) will be confined to what is necessary for the purpose outlined above. Only a person who has undergone analysis can have any idea about the work which has to be done before one reaches the stage where both the analyst *and* the patient can recognize *"the nuclear complex of the neurosis,"* as Freud (1909) called it. He writes that "it is the complex which comprises the child's earliest impulses, alike tender and hostile, toward its parents and brothers and sisters, after its curiosity has been awakened— usually by the arrival of a new baby brother or sister" (p. 208).

Our man, throughout his entire childhood, suffered much from the behavior of his severe, austere and punishing father. Whenever the boy displeased his father, the latter would discipline him by depriving the boy of his toys, presents he had received, and pleasures he had been promised. The frequent loss of his cherished possessions greatly disappointed the boy, who gradually developed a defensive technique to avoid his suffering. The boy learned never to express a wish and to conceal his expectations of joyous gratification. He showed no interest in toys or pleasurable activities, particularly in the presence of his father. As time went on, this became an ingrained pattern and stayed with him, though his father was no longer alive and though the patient became independent, worked and had the means for self-gratification. We considered his buying himself a car as a first success in therapy. The events of this man's childhood were never repressed but *the realization that they affected his "total personality" was repressed*. He stuck to his defense system, *as if* his environment were the same as it had been in his childhood. The passing of time was nullified.

Sometimes, people think that they know how a symptom

came into existence, but then it evolves that all they know is the time when it was first observed but not why or how.

And now, at last, this leads us to our first example of the mannerisms of speech, to the

"By the way"—I

In a nontherapeutic relationship, a lady about sixty years "young" (as I like to think of ladies), asked me whether it was true that when the background of a symptom became known, the symptom disappeared. I replied that this was true only when we could say that it was known, whereupon our good lady retorted that, so far as she was concerned, this was not true. She knew the history of the symptom from which she suffered but the symptom remained unchanged. She volunteered to reveal her symptom, the *fear of mice*.

She loved to tell her story. When she was a young girl, she was in the living room when she heard a sudden, frightened scream coming from her mother in the kitchen. She dashed into the kitchen and saw her mother, standing frozen to the floor. "What happened?" asked the girl. (At this point, she said, "By the way, my mother was pregnant.")

The mother replied, "It was a mouse."

"At that moment, I got frightened," continued the lady, "and since then I have been horrified of mice." I did not press the issue further. At that time, I already had some ideas about the "fear of mice"—ideas which were later shaped into a paper (1949).

The mouse can be a symbol of different things, one of which is a baby in the womb. The house is an ancient symbol of the woman (one lives first in the womb). A mouse can, therefore, be compared to the child who gets into and out of the house through a hole. The activities of the mouse are as mysterious as the conception and birth of a child. One does not see how the mouse comes and goes, but one is aware of its furtive, secretive scurrying; and like the baby, suddenly, there it is. To the mind, therefore, the mouse may become a symbol of a baby. A young girl already has some instinctual feeling about sex and pregnancy. She may have partial information or complete knowledge about the causes of pregnancy. She can even talk about them to her parents or to others. But there is one aspect of the process she is supposed not to know, and that is the sensual-pleasurable part of the sexual intercourse. Nobody talks about it. The child does not want to be criticized. She conceals her interest and her own sensual drives which are stirred up by this event. She has to censor them. This is done by the censorship operating between the unconscious and the preconscious-conscious. It lies in the nature of drives that they *must* to be discharged, at least psychologically, because the mental apparatus strives to be in a state of the least tension. In order to achieve this, the drives have to be disguised in such a way as to elude the censorship and attain entrance into the consciousness. The drive has to come through despite the opposition; a compromise takes place. First, a symbol is used which satisfies the censorship; and, second, the drive is set free, at least partially. Thus, in the statement, "By the way, my mother was pregnant," the pregnancy can be mentioned only because "by the way" makes it appear to be unimportant. This unimportance is another consideration for the censorship. Still, there is a gain for the drive. Because the "by the way" has no sensible place in the narrative, it is striking and therefore attracts our attention.

When we talk about symbols in this frame of reference, we do not mean those which were *intentionally* chosen to signify an idea. Symbols about which we are talking and with which we are concerned were created with *unconscious intentions*.

There are great numbers of *universal symbols*, symbols which have the same meaning for all people in the world and which have resisted the passage of time since the first records of human culture, and still remain unchanged. In a paper already mentioned on "The Symbolism of Teeth in Dreams," Lorand and I (1955) made a survey of psychoanalytic theories of symbol formation. Since then a profound and extensive paper on this subject was written by Rycroft (1956). I would now add the following new suggestions:

The universal symbols contain the observable things of life, such as: human beings, animals, fish, insects, trees, rivers, mountains, plants, stars, wind, rain, snow, and so forth. While the baby is still too young to talk, he observes and perceives. Universal symbols are created in the preverbal period of our life and expressed in the verbal period. The process remains unconscious. To illustrate this, let us think of the two dreams of Joseph recorded in Genesis, Chapter 37:

Now Israel loved Joseph more than all his children, because he was the son of his old age; and he made him a coat of many colours. And when his brethren saw that their father loved him more than all his brethren, they hated him and could not speak peaceably unto him. And Joseph dreamed a dream, and he told it to his brethren; and they hated him yet the more. And he said unto them: "Hear, I pray you, this dream which I have dreamed; for, behold, we were binding sheaves in the field, and, lo, my sheaf arose, and also stood upright; and behold, your sheaves came round about and bowed down to my sheaf." And his brethren said to him: "Shalt thou indeed reign over us? or shalt thou indeed have dominion over us?" And they hated him yet the more for his dreams, and for his words. And he dreamed yet another dream, and told it to his brethren, and said: "Behold, I have dreamed yet a dream: and behold, the sun and the moon, and eleven stars bowed down to me." And he told it to his father, and to his brethren; and his father rebuked him, and said unto him: "What is this dream that thou hast dreamed? Shall I and thy mother and thy brethren indeed come to bow down to thee to the Earth?" And his brethren envied him; but his father kept the saying in mind.

Did Joseph know the meaning of the symbols? His brothers, eleven in number, understood it, and his father immediately interpreted it. The sun is the father; the moon, the mother; and the eleven stars are the eleven brothers. Was Joseph, who later himself became a dream interpreter and who saved his own life by interpreting the dreams of Pharaoh, so blind to the meaning of his own dreams, or was he so bold that he conveyed his dreams knowing that they revealed his strong drives to dominate over his family? The first assumption is the more probable because we notice that dreamers are unaware of the meaning of a dream; while those to whom the dream is told may understand it. An inner, silent and unconscious censorship renders a person blind to the driving forces within himself.

In the summer of 1953, I spent all my free time with my grandson. Many times during that summer, I witnessed a scene which I will describe because it is universal. The baby awakens, and his parents or others come to his crib to look at him. There they stand, smiling at the baby who beams with happiness. After a while, the baby stretches out his arms to be picked up. The infant does this hundreds of times. Sometimes his crib is placed under a tree in the shade. Then he will stretch out his arms for a low branch of the tree. When he is picked up and moved close to the branch, he screams with desirous joy, kicks his legs, and is very happy that his intentions are understood. He often grabs the branch, and he is happy when it is released. He takes hold of it again and again. In the house, the crib is sometimes placed under a lamp hanging down from the ceiling. The reaction is the same. The baby stretches out his arms as if asking to be picked up by the lamp. This happens mainly when the baby is alone. The branch and the lamp over him become identical with his parents.

How wonderful it would be for the grandfather to follow up his observations and to prove that his interpretation is correct. It could be proved if later, in the grandson's dreams or behavior, the symbolism would come to the fore. If fate does not grant the writer this joy, perhaps, the boy's parents or he himself may come to realize it.

For the infant, the lamp and the tree are not symbols; for him, the parents, the lamp and the tree are identical in their pleasure-giving gratification emanating from "above." While the baby experiences these things, he is too young to create abstractions. Later, when he can do so, they will become symbols. I believe that this universal experience prompted mankind to place its gods in high places and in heaven. From "above" comes the blessing. We look to heaven for help.

Did Jacob and the eleven brethren realize the total symbolism of the sheaves which "stood upright"? They must have. The text does not reveal this. *A symbol may be understood without one's being aware that it is understood.* The sheaf is, in Joseph's dream, a phallic symbol and expresses the powerful drives of all men to outdo sexually all other men and to have power over all other men.

Are certain symbols phylogenetically inherited? Maybe they are, maybe not. It seems to me that they can be acquired by each generation. The readiness to form symbols, however, is very strong in all of mankind. It is amazing how quickly a new object such as an airplane, train or any other new tool or device is utilized for symbolic expression. When language is learned, it has to fuse with an already present other language, the symbolic "language." It is a universal sort of communication, understood by all people, and is eternal. "For the full knowledge of the working of the human mind, the understanding of symbolic communication is indispensable" (Fromm, 1951).

"By the way"—II

In using "by the way," one wants to make believe that what he is saying came into his mind incidentally. It *can* be used legitimately when, in the course of a conversation, something is remembered that was truly forgotten and then recalled through the conversation. For example, A. mentions to B. that her father-in-law has fallen ill and is now in the hospital. Two months later, when they met again, A. mentions that her father-in-law visited her, whereupon B. interrupts, saying, "By the way, how is your father-in-law?" *But this is rarely* the case. Usually, the person who is using "by the way" knows *in advance* the content of his comment, is even waiting a while to mislead the listener as if the idea came into his mind suddenly. His aim is to pretend that what he says is not important. The truth is that it is very important to him; it may be the most important thing in the whole conversation. The "by the way" can be accompanied by the snapping of the fingers to enforce the pretense that the memory came spontaneously *only* from the stimulus of one part of the conversation, and that it is not significant.

A professional man meets his chief in the corridor of the hospital. For days, he has been struggling with himself to summon up enough courage to go to his chief's office to make some critical comment in reference to a statement the latter had made about the doctor's patient; but he is afraid "beyond reason" to assert himself. His fear is unreasonable because the chief has several times expressed appreciation of the skill of his subordinate. The latter needs treatment because of his obsessive, frightening thoughts. His fear of authoritative persons makes him overly submissive. This submission creates aggression which in turn has to be repressed for fear of repercussion. In order to be able to function and to express himself, he occasionally uses the "by the way," meaning that his statement is not important, *he* is not important, and what he says is not important. Thus the chief may be sure of his superiority and the two men need not attack each other.

Like a symptom which is a compromise between two opposing forces, such an attitude manifested by the use of the "by the way," in the last analysis, fails to achieve its goal. Both persons feel that the truth was not said. Lack of truthfulness in personal communication is disturbing for both parties. They may not consciously be aware of this, but it appears as an irritation and spoils the proper contact. It is in the nature of truth that it has to come into the open. The scientific explanation of this profound fact was discovered by the psychoanalyst Imre Hermann of Budapest. The first personal relationship, according to Hermann's theory, is the tactile contact of the baby with the mother (clinging). The body is warm. Through the skin contact, the warmth of the body is felt and the difference of temperature of both persons becomes even. This is called, then, a "warm" relationship, a "warm" friendship. A "good" relationship can be tested when two persons accept the touch of each other, and each accepts the warmth of the other's skin. One likes the feeling of a warm seat made so by a beloved person; if such warmth comes from a stranger, one dislikes it. The lack of truth *isolates* communicating persons. There is a feeling that something essential is missing, the warmth. The "by the way" is responsible for such a feeling of isolation because it is a pretense; it is not true. Our man would be better off if he would (or could) omit the use of the "by the way." If he said frankly, without pretense, that he wanted to talk to his chief, that he had something important to tell him; or if he had gone directly to the chief's office instead of chatting with him in the corridor for the same reason, he would have presented himself as a self-respecting person who expected and deserved respect from his superior. In using the "by the way," he was demeaning himself and maintaining a weakening fear. Most people will rationalize, claiming that it is important to appear timid because the chief may be the kind of man who likes others to grovel before him. This may appear to be so, superficially. Even a cruel and mean superior would distrust and disrespect weakness. He may not say so, but he will act on this basis. The chief feels and knows that such groveling invites hatred. The more one shows fear, the less he can be trusted. Animals can smell fear, anticipate an attack from a fearful person; in order to prevent such an attack, they will attack him. Frankness expressed for a good and just cause is best. It has never failed me.

Many people are afraid to remind others to return borrowed books or money. They talk about different matters; and, usually before parting, one says to the other, "By the way," "how about" [another mannerism] "returning my book or paying back the money you borrowed from me."

There are persons who do not dare to go even that far. One of my patients, suffering from tormenting guilt feelings for sexual play in his early boyhood, avoided a person who had borrowed money from him. To avoid this man, the patient walked on the opposite side of the street. It is a remarkable phenomenon that if a person feels guilty in one thing, he cannot feel right, even if he knows he is, in any other thing.

A charming use of the mannerism "by the way" was made by Freud when he wrote:

> On another occasion I had an opportunity of obtaining a profound insight into the unconscious psychic life of a young man for whom an obsessional neurosis made life almost unendurable, so that he could not go into the streets, because he was tormented by the fear that he would kill anyone he met. He spent his days in contriving evidence of an alibi in case he should be accused of any murder that might have been committed in the city. It goes without saying that this man was as moral as he was highly cultured. The analysis—which, *by the way*, led to a cure—revealed . . . [Freud, 1900].[1]

I wonder whether Freud used "by the way" in a legitimate way. He could conceivably have done so had the passage concerned itself with the process of therapy. But how could he have been using this phrase legitimately when the passage has nothing to do with therapy? I am convinced that the

---

[1] The quotation is taken from the *Basic Writings of Sigmund Freud* (p. 306; my italics). The same translator and editor, A. A. Brill, used "moreover" instead of "by the way" in the G. Allen Unwin edition.

cure of the patient was very important to Freud and was not something that deserved only casual mention.

Another, but not so charming illustration of the use of "by the way" is to be found in the case of a man who had tactlessly accused a colleague of making false statements. Sometime later, after having found himself to be in error, the man again met his colleague. In the course of their conversation, he said, "By the way, you were right about your findings in the matter we discussed a few weeks ago."

Such a person displays his weakness in many ways. In the first place, he had not checked the veracity of the statements made by his colleague before making the rude attack; and, in the second place, finding himself in error, he lacked the courage to apologize. He therefore minimized his past offense by making it seem trivial and incidental.

Very close to the "by the way" is the use of

"Incidentally"

A married man with whom I was acquainted had had a clandestine affair with a woman. His speech was punctuated with the word "incidentally." He was so filled with shame and guilt over it that he wanted to minimize it for the sake of defense. This minimizing tendency was extended to everything he said although it had nothing to do with his original problem.

A patient singularly lacking in self-assertion was talking about his girl friend in one session. He considered her a very nice girl and felt that he had helped her a great deal in many respects. He sent her to school to take courses and advised her how to straighten out her family troubles. He said, "*As you are aware*, I have helped her to organize her life and to improve her financial difficulties, and, 'incidentally,' I looked over her writing last night and I could see that her grammar had improved tremendously." The presentation is full of mannerisms which indicate how deeply this man is afraid to assert himself and to take credit for anything he had achieved. The "as you are aware" intends to apologize for his daring to know anything. In order to allay his fear, he needed to tell the listener that he does not say anything new. The credit and merit for having done so much for the girl by teaching her grammar is eliminated by the comment of "incidentally," meaning that he does not expect acknowledgment for his success. If we omit the mannerisms from his presentation, the wording would be as follows: "I'd like to mention again that I am pleased by the progress my girl friend made through my help. I noticed, last evening, with great joy, the tremendous progress she showed in her grammar. I think my help made this possible." Doesn't this sound better? Isn't it frank and true? The reader will agree that sometimes a man should be permitted to give himself credit for his work and expect others to acknowledge it too.

"Needless to say"

Freud understood mankind's resistance to his discoveries (1916/1917, pp. 246-247). He had penetrated into the deepest recesses of the mind and discovered that it contains many things of which we are not aware and that these things make us different from what we think we are or appear to others to be. He revealed man as an extremely complex creature in whom the good and the bad, the lofty and the low, are operating simultaneously. The essential parts of his discoveries, unparalleled in the history of mankind, were proved correct by psychoanalysts and by many nonmedical, professional thinkers. In spite of this proof, the resistance still exists; it must be so. It is met even in the most objective people whenever they are made conscious of something they have repressed. We all need to use repressions; but many people continue to use them after these repressions have stopped being the least bit beneficial.

Therefore, the writer expects that many of his propositions

will probably elicit disbelief, anger and doubt. He is pleading with the reader not to be too hasty in his judgment, to keep an open mind in examining the interpretations, and perhaps to see, first, that these interpretations can be applied to others, and then gradually to find that they can also be applied to himself. Certain mannerisms have become so strongly entrenched in us that it takes time and pain to alter them. It is not easy to change our minds. Our opinions *suffer* a change before we can enjoy a change.

There were two old and good friends, working in two different territories. They were nice, good, honest people who appreciated each other a great deal. Each was happy whenever the other scored success. When one of them was elevated to a very high position, socially and financially, the other, before making a personal visit, sent a congratulatory letter beginning, "Needless to say how happy I am about your promotion." The reader may feel immediately that this phrase is natural and wonder why I should find anything in it to analyze or why I should search for a hidden motive in it. Most readers would probably say that the man wished to give strong expression to his friendship. His joy about the promotion has to be taken for granted; but, in addition to this, he needs to convey his happiness emphatically.

Is he happy? Is this undiluted happiness? If it were so, would he not be able to write more and more warm words to express his feelings? He might even write that *he needs* to say more on this occasion. Suppose a man, on an extraordinarily happy occasion, sends his sweetheart flowers or a gift accompanied by a letter in which he writes that "it is needless to say" how much he loves her. Would she not be more satisfied if the man were to omit such an introduction and write that he loves her very much and is sending her a present as a token of his love and happiness?

The "needless to say" expresses an ambivalence of feelings where one of the feelings like envy or jealousy remains hidden and covered by the positive love feeling. A permanently

pure love is close to impossible. Even a mother can sometimes feel anger or even momentary hatred toward the beloved child. This does not mean that she does not love the
child; it means that she might dislike and even hate the child
on certain occasions. Hate is more likely to be pure and
undiluted than is love.

A person who has the courage to acknowledge the existence
of ambivalent feelings in him is in a better position to love
when he loves than a person who does not possess this knowledge. If the negative feeling is denied, an extra dose of psychic
energy is necessary to conceal it. Mature friends may even
understand when, on such an occasion as a promotion, one
would write the truth. For example, "We are good and old
friends. Nevertheless, when I learned about your good fortune, to my dismay, I felt a certain amount of envy. The
shock didn't last long because my liking for you was much
stronger than that other momentary, petty feeling."

A model example of such courage was shown by an
eighteen-year-old girl after her high school graduation exercises. She and her best friend, another girl of the same age,
were competing for the honor of being standard bearer. The
latter won by a fraction of a point. After the name of the
winner was announced, the girl said to her friend, "I wished
to win so that I could be standard bearer. I lost and I am disappointed; but you deserve it. I am glad for you. My congratulations." They remained good friends and both are now
successful.

"To be perfectly frank"
"To be honest"
"To tell the truth"
"Frankly, honestly"

Decades of work with many kinds of people have convinced me that the basic need of human beings is to establish a place for themselves in life, a place in which their self-

preservative and emotional-sensual needs are met and can be satisfied. If these needs are met, the inborn tendency for order in action (Hermann) will establish ethical, moral and intellectual standards, the absence of which would make it impossible to live with oneself and within a group.

Children are loved and taken care of solely because they are children. Whatever they say is charming and lovely, even if it hurts. A five-year-old boy, meeting his uncle for the first time in his life, said to him at first glance, "You look like a monkey." It was true. It was on the tip of everyone's tongue to say so the moment one looked at him; but nobody dared for fear of hurting the man. The uncle, fortunately, was an ardent and militant lover of the truth and though he hated to look like a monkey, he nevertheless deeply respected the boy's frankness. In addition, he realized that for a five-year-old boy, a monkey does not necessarily have a derogatory meaning. He knew that the child did not want to hurt him, while at the same time the boy could not lie. The child says what is true; he *is* the truth.

An adult cannot say the same kind of thing to another person. The best he can do is to avoid expressing what he feels and thinks. Otherwise, he will be considered a rude person. We are taught to conceal, even to be hypocritical, and to expect to receive from others this same concealment and hypocrisy.

A sentence beginning with "honestly" or "frankly speaking" indicates that the person is not always frank and honest. The use of these words is legitimate only if one admits that he did not tell the truth. It is legitimate when it means a *confession;* otherwise, it means that even when one says "honestly" or "frankly," he does not tell the truth. If we never concealed our thoughts, we would never need to use these words except under legitimate circumstances.

A professional man, in analysis, was asked by his fraternity to make some financial contribution to a project. In his reply, he wrote, "To be perfectly frank, I do not see a successful outcome to that project . . ."; and he did not contribute. In the very same session, he realized that, in using the "to be perfectly frank," he intended to appeal to his correspondent not to be angry with him for the refusal but rather to respect him for his frankness. He realized, furthermore, that while it was true that he did not believe in the successful outcome of the project, he had stated only a partial truth: by withholding the most important information. If he could have included the whole truth, he would have had to say that in order to be freed from his neurotic state, it would be necessary for him to sever his "attachments to the past," including his fraternity. To cover up what he concealed, he needed to impress his fellow alumnus with a "frankness" that he really did not use.

"Honest"

During the hard years of World War II, I, like many other people, had a close contact with my grocer. Everyone had a ration card; and in order to be well provided with food, he traded exclusively with one grocer. Such a relation, especially in matters of food when food is scarce, might involve strong emotions, both hostile and friendly. After the war, I moved to another house. About eight years later, I passed the store, saw the grocer, decided to go in to buy something and to have a chat with him. We were both glad to see each other again. He looked me over and said, "You look ten years younger. Honest," and made a gesture, indicating that he would be ready to swear to his statement. The grocer was about ten years younger than I but looked ten years older. When he saw me, he must have made a comparison and found a discrepancy to his disadvantage. He was in conflict. On the one hand, his observation was correct and he liked me; on the other hand, he did not like the true fact. He wanted to tell the truth, but he did not like it. Because he did not like the truth but still wanted to tell it, he felt that half of his statement was false. Since he did not want to lie, he needed to emphasize the part-truth by saying, "honest."

On the basis of the analysis of persons who were addressed by "to be perfectly honest" and similar phrases, I can claim that the second person, the listener, *feels* that the first person did *not* tell the truth. The mannerism of speech was a give-away. The mannerism damages the relationship of the two participants.

"Before I forget"

There is rarely a legitimate reason for using the phrase, "before I forget." If one forgets, he does not know about it; if he does not forget, as he does not, why does he say it? There must be a reason for this seemingly nonsensical statement.

A patient's payment is due. It is overdue. One day after a session, before leaving my office, he says, "Before I forget, there is a check for you." The patient has the obsessive idea that he might die any minute. He is afraid that he will go bankrupt, and therefore doesn't want to pay anybody for fear that he will run out of money. He wants to pay, but is afraid to pay; he *needs* to forget to pay. Through using the phrase, he is confessing this tendency to me. He needs me and wants to feel that he is liked. He feels uncomfortable keeping this tendency secret from me. Any concealment disturbs the warmth of a relationship (Hermann).

In another case involving the payment of fees, the patient's motivation was quite different. He was a very inhibited person who had difficulty in expressing his feelings. Moreover, any contact aroused anxiety. Handing over a check was, for him, a personal contact—and therefore anxiety-arousing. To avoid anxiety, he was inclined to forget the payment, so that he said in giving me the money, "Before I forget, here is the check." In this case, interpreting his actions as a desire not to pay would be incorrect.

Another motivation underlying the use of the phrase "be-

fore I forget" is similar to that inherent in "by the way."
The person wants to pretend that the matter is not important
to him even though he considers it of great importance. He
did not forget and will not forget, but wants to pretend that
he could have forgotten. This is not true.

A patient begins the analytic session by remaining seated
before assuming the customary reclining position on the
couch. He indicates that he has something to say which, in
his opinion, does not belong to the official session, and he
says, "Before I forget, I want to ask you something. It is not
my problem. My wife wants me to ask you for the name of
an analyst in another city for one of her relatives."

When I called his attention to the phrase "before I forget,"
he said he was not interested in the whole matter. He is in
conflict with his wife and he wishes to forget it; but if he
should forget it, his wife would scold him. He wants to forget
it and he wants not to forget it. But why does he say to the
listener "before I forget"? It is a form of confession that he
would forget. He wants to maintain a warm, undisturbed
relation with the analyst by telling the truth in his own way.

I myself sometimes relapse into the use of mannerisms although I thought that they had been eliminated from my
mind. The reader will probably find examples of such re-
lapses in this very book.

The motivations for the use of manneristic phrases cannot
be exhausted. Therefore, the reader may feel that this book is
incomplete and that he could write one with more examples
and additional motivations. It is so.

"And do you know what he said?"

How often, in the course of a conversation in which the
speaker has talked about what he said and did, the listener is
asked, "And do you know what he said?" There is hardly a
possibility of the listener's knowing what the absentee said.
One can imagine how disappointed and frustrated the speaker

would be if the listener were to reply in the affirmative and confabulate an answer. It is, then, obvious that the speaker wants the listener to say, "I don't know." Then *he* will tell what the other said.

A woman (but it could just as easily have been a man) tells about her conversation with a girl friend who was distressed because a boy stood her up. The girl came to this woman to relieve her heart and to get some comforting words and advice about her plight. The woman likes the girl, but she likes herself more. She likes to be interesting, to be needed, to be listened to. She needs to give suspense to the story, thus stealing the show for herself by making her own presentation of the story more dramatic.

Even if one did know "what he or she said," one would have to give a negative answer because the speaker demands that no one spoil her joy or interest in the performance. Similarly, when a person begins telling a joke by asking whether the listener has heard the one about a man and his mother-in-law, one is not supposed to answer yes. The listener must conceal any knowledge of the joke, pretend that he is interested in hearing it, and laugh no matter how bored he becomes enduring the repetition of a joke that for him already has a long beard.

"And do you know what I told him?"
"Do you know what happened?"
"Did you hear about it?"

When asked, "And do you know what I told him?" the listener is in no position to know what A. said to B.; nor can the listener find, from his knowledge of many events, a reply to, "Do you know what happened?" A frequent motivating force on the part of the questioner is to prove the other's inferiority, to make the other appear stupid because he was not clever enough to guess what the first person said or what happened.

Suppose the listener thinks he knows what A. said to B. and says so. If his answer is correct, he crushes the speaker; if he is wrong, the speaker is happy and triumphantly continues his presentation. Suppose, in response to the question, "Do you know what happened?" the listener replies that he does and says, for example, that a two-headed calf was born on a farm. The speaker would then look at the latter as though the latter were out of his mind, or would wave his hand derisively, dismissing the news with, "Oh, that. That's nothing." The speaker would then relate the thing that is really interesting to him but not to his audience. If one does not find this news the most interesting ever heard, he runs the risk of being the speaker's greatest enemy.

And what is the most interesting thing? I would again like to use a personal experience as an illustration. In Budapest I knew a woman who had the heart of an angel and was always helpful. She told me once that her son was a good runner and that he was going to participate in a contest. I did not give the matter another thought because there were so many other things on my mind. Nevertheless, she expected me to consider this a very important matter and keep it in mind constantly, but I did not. Even so, the woman would have been pleased if I had remembered to ask her how the boy made out; but I was not supposed to *know*. *She* would tell me. Life was very harsh to this woman who had once seen better days. Now she concentrates on her children. If they arouse public interest, she is pleased as a mother; but, in addition (it is very hard for me to say this), she wants to steal the show in order to excel for a few minutes, to be the center of attention for a short time.

She: "My son will participate in a contest. Do you know about this?
I: "No. What kind of a contest is it?"
She: "Didn't I tell you?"
I: "I do not remember."

Everything must be very important and everyone must know what happens to her and to the members of her family. There is tremendous resentment and frustration over her social and financial gratifications.

Often, the person employing the "Do you know what he said?" is begging for encouragement to talk. Many people are afraid of their aggressive feelings or afraid that any self-assertion will be considered by the listener as aggressive or impudent; therefore, they beg for permission to talk. *They cannot tolerate silence.* Silence means to them isolation, rejection, separation. By extracting any kind of response from the listener, they get the feeling that they are liked, wanted and listened to.

When something sad happens, people are usually eager to pose the question, "Did you hear about it?" Such was the case when the son of a prominent physician was killed in an automobile accident. The motives for asking the question are as follows:

1. Hope that the speaker will be the first to tell about the accident, thus capitalizing on it and drawing attention to himself.

2. Pleasure that something sad happened to the other and not to him. Pleasure over such a thing builds up guilt so that he must dilute the guilt by making the listener share it.

3. Gratification that the catastrophe happened to a prominent family. Gratification also builds guilt so that the speaker must make others share it with him.

4. Genuine pity and grief which make the speaker seek comfort from others by sharing the news and his feelings with them.

There are millions of frustrated persons in the world who, through no fault of their own, become narrow and crippled in their minds. They have no "self" that they can call their own. As a result of this, they need and want to engulf others in their petty interests and want to be supported in their illusions by having others consider them interesting. Most men live in petty illusions, making believe that everything is fine with them, while the sad fact is that a chicken does more independent thinking than they do. "If you make people think they are thinking, they will love you, but if you really make them think, they will hate you," said Don Marquis. (I wish to apologize to the chickens. I like them.)

"As you (well) know"
"You know"

The phrases, "as you (well) know" and "you know," are among the most frequently used mannerisms of speech and have innumerable motivations. The reader could probably add many of his own observations to the collection which will follow.

Many a speaker uses the "as you well know" for fear that he may be saying something that the listener already knows. If so the latter may become angry because he was assumed to be ignorant when he was not. To avoid an angry reaction, the speaker assures the listener that he knows the listener knows. In such a case, the use of the phrase may be wise. On the other hand, many speakers use the phrase even when they think that the listener does *not* know. In this case, the speaker wants to flatter the audience, intends to capture their hearts, wants to fool them. In using the phrase, "you know," he intends to minimize the discrepancy between his knowledge and that of the audience. In this case, the use of the phrase is hypocritical. The speaker might feel that he is too aggressive, showing off with his knowledge, that he looks down upon the audience, and that he is afraid the audience might perceive his attitude. He therefore becomes anxious; and in order to allay his own anxiety, he tries to pacify the assumed resentment of the audience. The same is frequently the reason for the use of "you see" by many speakers.

In a therapeutic session, a male patient is talking about a party he attended the previous evening. "I didn't want to drink much," he says, "the drink loosens my tongue, *you know.*" He meant that, under the influence of alcohol, he might say something that he would later regret. He has secrets from his wife, who was also at the party, and he assumes, justly, that I know about his secret (another woman) because he has often mentioned it. His use of the "you know" is partially legitimate in the sense that he is saving time. On the other hand, the phrase is used to conceal the whole secret, which, even in the safe atmosphere of the office, he is afraid to mention.

Several weeks ago, a colleague mentioned that he put in a few favorable words for another physician, whom we both know, with a certain group of importance. He later returned to this matter, inserting in his narrative the "as you know." He was on the analytic couch and he was uncertain whether I would confirm the fact that I remembered his having said this to me a few weeks earlier. He is not yet independent enough. He still needs to be reassured that he is important, liked and will be listened to. With the "as you know," he brings himself closer to the listener.

A woman patient gets very angry when somebody tells her something that she already knows. When she is talking to another person, she assumes the same, namely, that she might say something that the other person knows and that the other will become angry with her. To avoid this, she uses the "as you know." For this woman, intellect and knowledge mean everything; she is afraid to be considered stupid. This fear runs like a red thread through the history of her life. She always felt that her mother considered her brother to be much better than her.

A professional man, who wrote several books, is very unsure about his abilities. He suspects that his colleagues have no high opinion of him. I happen to know that the man's suspicions are justified. The latter likes to talk a great deal, and one feels that his intention is to convince the listener that he is a good and excellent scientist. He must know that his knowledge is deficient. He has some merit, but this is not enough for him. When he talks to a colleague who is superior to him in knowledge and talent, he makes desperate efforts to impress the other and to extract acknowledgment from him. Because he is afraid that he will not get this, he is impatient; and while talking, he uses, with annoying frequency, the "you know" or "as you know" in the hope that the listener will nod or say yes. He counts on the courtesy of the other who will not want to hurt or oppose him. Even though the patient knows full well that the other is not sincere if he does so, he nevertheless is pleased and enjoys the mutual deception. To extract such acknowledgment is a very bad thing to do. True, there is a momentary gratification, but such gratification is an illusion. It does not give him the feeling that he is good. He knows that he extracted a yes that was not sincere. He knows that essentially he made himself weaker, lowered himself in the estimation of the listener, and, in the last analysis, he is a failure.

A twenty-one-year-old girl tells, "Boys come to see my younger sister and me. They go to the refrigerator to look for food. . . . You know how boys are. . . ." Though the writer is suspicious that there may be more to the statement than there appears to be, it is possible that this is a legitimate use of the "you know." It is here used for the sake of brevity, to save time.

A male patient says, "When I was about fourteen, I liked to dive into swimming pools, swim under the water and pass between the legs of women—*you know*. . . ." Seemingly, this is a legitimate use of the "you know." The speaker justly assumes that I know what he is talking about. Why say more? But why not? Why didn't he say that it was fun? It was perhaps not necessary to give more details; but in the present setting, at least, he should have said that it was fun. This patient was an extremely inhibited person with strong guilt feelings about his illicit (he was married) sexual desires.

I know a woman who rarely omits the "you know" from

a sentence. As she uses the phrase, it sounds like a mixture of question and statement. The questioning denotes a pretense that she is ignorant of the importance of the matter about which she is talking and wishes to get information from the listener. But this is not true. She would be unhappy if the listener would answer yes to her "you know." It should be *she* alone who knows the answer. It is she who wants to monopolize the conversation. I once heard her talk uninterruptedly for a full forty minutes. Sometimes she permits the listener to talk a minute or so in order to make it seem as though both persons were participating equally in the conversation. She takes over quickly. Her husband has no chance to talk. After he has spoken a few words, she interrupts him with, "You don't say it well." Then she forces him to silence with a quick and wild flow of words. This woman's life is very frustrated, and she needs the illusion that she knows everything better than anyone else does.

The same woman, an acquaintance of mine, once began her conversation with, "As you know, I expected my sister to visit me, but she was taken ill. . . ." A few weeks previously, she had mentioned this event to me. I do not know her sister. Her coming does not interest me. There is no reason that it should. The woman knew this. Nevertheless, she expects everything connected with her to be remembered. The "as you know" means that she expects the listener to remember, or at least to say that he remembers, even if this is not true. The "as you know" means:

> You better remember it.
> I expect you to remember it.
> Hypocritically: I am sure you remember it.
> Remember, please, whatever I say.
> I would hate you if you were not interested in
>   everything I say.

In a paper written in 1948, I called attention to the analysis of speech mannerisms in therapy. Generally speaking, neuroses are caused by certain complexes. In the course of time, the "complex" invades and permeates the "total personality" and leaves its mark on the whole behavior of the person. It is necessary to unravel the effect of the complex in most of the mental activities of the person. This is called the "working through process." The analysis of the way a person uses language affords at least one important opportunity to approach the unraveling process. I am pleased to notice that Sandor Ferenczi had come to the same conclusion and had paid attention to the speech mannerisms of his patients (see Izette de Forest, 1954, pp. 28-29).

A (pseudo-) infantile professional person who often used the "as you know," meant, "I am only a child. Let me remain a child. You know everything better than I." The reader might become puzzled by the multiple meaning of the use of speech mannerisms. This overdetermination is a rule in mental phenomena. One phrase might mean different things, even in the same person; therefore, in psychology, one has to exercise the utmost caution before making a binding interpretation.

A very bright ten-year-old girl had a lizard for a pet. One day she caught a butterfly; and, in answer to my question what she would do with it, she replied that the butterfly would serve as food for her lizard. "The lizard eats butterflies," she said. "You know *that*." I did not know *that*. She made this statement in a very peculiar way. Her manner indicated that she was using a sort of affectation, showing off in a cute and charming way. At other times, the "you know" means, "You must accept as truth what I say."

Often there are vicious tendencies behind the use of "as you know." The observant reader will find many such examples in everyday life. For instance, a boss tells an employee who is at his mercy, "You are very important to us. We appreciate your work, you know." But when this "very important" employee wants something, the boss will frustrate him. The meaning of the "you know," in this case, is, "You know your hard work is very useful to *me*; you are a good worker and I exploit your energies. You need this job and you know that I know you do. If you do not work hard, you will not get a raise or, worse, you will be fired. You know these things." The employee may permit himself to think that perhaps the boss means what he says, and go on entertaining hopes for a promotion.

Another such example is that of the powerful boss of an organization who has ambivalent feelings toward younger, more talented subordinates. He likes them and needs them but is at the same time jealous and afraid of them. After he frustrated the ambition of one of the important employees, he said to him in the presence of others at a relaxed social gathering, "You know how much we love you." Seeking the motivations, we may ask a few straight questions.

1. How much?—Much?
2. How much?—Nothing whatsoever?
3. We?—To soften the hypocritical part of his ambivalence, he uses *we* instead of *I* because he knows
   that others love the person without reservation.

As a further illustration of the vicious tendencies of the phrase, "you know," there is the case of a young man who says to a girl, "You know—I love you." The pause after the phrase betrays the speaker because it reveals his insincerity. He does not love her. She, too, knows that he does not; but he hopes that he can trap her into believing what he says because he wants something from her.

Commercials are masterpieces in the art of using speech mannerisms to influence the public. To be specific, one announcer will say, "The best gift for Father's day, you know, is a watch." This announcer does not know that the listeners know any such thing. He tells them that *they know* it. He pretends that he does not impose anything on them. The listener is supposed to be pleased that he knows this and to buy the watch.

The following commercial was sponsored by a dealer of a

well-known automobile manufacturing company which we shall call Nemo: "There are many Nemo dealers in this area —as you know."

It is rewarding to examine this statement from a psycho-analytically oriented, semantic, and cybernetic point of view. Here I shall use myself as the subject.

As the listener, I observed my own reaction to the announcement. It happens that I know the location of one of the Nemo dealers in the area of Rochester, New York. I have a car, but I am not sure whether, when the time comes to trade, I shall buy a new one of the kind I now have or whether I shall switch to one of another make. I remember now that it once occurred to me that I would have a look at the Nemo. I am not sure that there is more than one Nemo agency in this area. In the event that I should decide to examine and, perhaps, buy a Nemo, I should certainly consult the telephone directory for the location of the agency nearest my home.

The announcer does not know whether the listener knows there is even one dealer, let alone two or more. He wants to take care of all the possibilities and says that we all know that there are many Nemo dealers in this area. He is using a mental trick on the listener. *He tries to make the listener believe that it is self-evident that any person in his right mind must know that there are many such dealers in this area.* If the listener does know this, he is pleased with the truth of the announcer's statement, can consider himself a well-oriented person, and will buy a Nemo car for the same reason. If he does not know that there are many Nemo dealers in this area, according to the announcer, he is supposed to be ashamed of himself, make up for his deficient information, dash out to obtain the missing knowledge, and buy a Nemo car.

The announcer plays on the listener's emotional infantilism, his passive-submissive tendency, and his desire to be liked by all means, even at the expense of intellectual integrity. On the other hand, the listener is made to feel that he will be rejected if the announcer's assumption is false and the listener does not have the requisite information. Because he fears failure, the announcer is afraid to say, "I am a representative of the Nemo Car Company. I get paid for making you buy a Nemo car. It is a good car and will do this and that for you. True, it is in my interest that you buy one; but you will get your money's worth. You will enjoy owning one and will be pleased that your attention was called to it."

In my opinion, such an advertisement would make a better impression on the listener's mind and would have more successful results. The important thing is that the announcer tell the truth. Even if the announcer's statement containing the mannerism was the truth and was instrumental in the listener's buying a Nemo car, the latter's mind was polluted and deprived of independent thinking because he bought the car for the above-mentioned reason. If the car is not good, the buyer, in addition to being mentally hurt, is misled.

What some commercials and advertisements do is "brainwashing," inflicting intellectual damage on the mind. As a result of this "brainwashing," the listener is trained to accept almost anything blindly. Such commercials cause mass infection, indoctrination to wrong concepts, and may have disastrous consequences for the mental health of the entire population.

Patients in analysis often reveal more subtle motivations for the use of the phrase, "you know." A. and B., who are acquainted with each other, are both in analysis. A. has his hour immediately preceding B., and B. knows this. Furthermore, B. has seen A. leave the office. One day, B. opens his hour by saying, "As you know from A. . . ." B. expresses himself thus because he believes that the analyst will not tell the patient what he thinks. B. thinks that the doctor has secrets from him but that the reverse is not true. By saying "as you know," B. eliminates the possibility of the analyst's having any secrets. The patient has a complex that makes him believe that people may do something against him; therefore, he must know what others have in mind. If there is no secret, he feels safe. By the same token, he could not have asked the doctor if the latter had heard the news because he knew the doctor would not tell him.

Mrs. N. has a son-in-law in whose profession music is involved. She does not like the fact that her daughter married a musician and is especially annoyed that the man is considering a change by practicing another aspect of his art. Mrs. N. makes a statement to the analyst. In order to secure the acceptance of it, she says, "You well know that all musicians are tense." She wants to trap the doctor by hoping that he will not denounce himself and that he will be pleased that she considers him more expert in these matters than she is. If the doctor falls into this trap, she may then use his agreement to support any provocative statements that she makes, at home to her daughter, and to her son-in-law.

Another patient begins his session with, "As you know, the hospital is planning . . . A meeting will be held . . ." He was interrupted by my question: "Why do you begin with 'as you know'? You are right that I know about the plan. Why don't you begin your statement without 'as you know'?" After a brief pause, he says, "Before I say anything, I need to make sure that I am liked. Beginning with 'as you know,' I first draw you close to me. I make sure that I am liked and won't be criticized. If I don't do this, I become anxious." These remarks reflected one of the most important complexes which had affected his life since childhood. He used this technique as a defense against being criticized by his mother. The patient became fully aware that the analysis of this speech mannerism helped him to work through and master a strong complex.

On the other hand, "you know" may sometimes be used legitimately. Mrs. E., who was somewhat depressed and had difficulty expressing herself because thinking and talking used so much of her energy, was talking about the kind of lights that she had in her store. She said, "The bulbs were hanging

on a cord from the ceiling—you know." In saying this, she
acted as though she would have difficulty in explaining and
wished that I would figure it out by myself.

"I don't care"

Every reader must be familiar with the speech mannerism,
"I don't care." The phrase is frequently heard, and the reader
himself probably employs it too. Its use is rarely legitimate.
It is legitimate *only* when it is meant sincerely and when it is
important to communicate the feeling that one does not care.
Let us see one classical example.

One of my female patients' main trouble is that she is very
easily hurt. In conflicts with others, she always feels innocent.
Her sensitivity continually causes her much irritation, dis-
illusionment in her "friends," and sleepless nights. The moment she gets hurt, *she immediately denies* the feeling by
saying, "I don't care," or "I don't really care." Her tremendous pride does not permit her to admit that she can be
hurt because only an inferior person can be hurt and she is a
superb human being. She knows that she is a fine person, but
she also knows that she is not a superb human being. She
would be such a person if she could admit that she feels hurt
when she does. But why does she not admit this? Why must
she constantly emphasize to herself and to others that she is
superb and that she is not vulnerable, when actually she is
more vulnerable than others? The core of her trouble is her
need to be superb. Whatever she has—her friends, her books,
her plants, her pet animals—they must be superb. If the
speaker at a meeting is considered prominent, our lady laughs
aloud at any witticism he makes, utters loud comments like
"That's wonderful"; in short, she demonstrates to the whole
audience how to react. She is a nuisance, but nobody dares to
tell her so. She forces everybody to agree with her. They do
not want to hurt her and they pretend to agree. If somebody
flatters her, that person is most wonderful, competent and

great. If a competent person disagrees with her, she will try to discredit him at the first oportunity. If she does so, she is afraid she will fail because the person is considered competent. If she meets resistance, she withdraws, gets depressed, and tries to ingratiate herself with the powerful person by pretending that she respects him when she does not. She neither respects nor disrespects anyone in the true sense of the word. She does not get to this. The only thing that counts is her own complex. All her judgment depends on it. She has a wonderful education, perfect command of the language, and is very alert; but all these qualities are misused for an irrational purpose. Because she knows the truth, she is unhappy. It cannot be otherwise. It is not true that she does not care. The truth is that she cares more than is necessary. She did not realize for a long time that from early childhood and throughout her college years, she attempted to make up through illusions for the love, indulgence and prominence that she could not and did not receive from her parents.

Even if the "I don't care" were true, there is seldom any valid reason to say that one does not care. If a person were asked whether he cared, he may answer with yes or no or, "I won't tell you whether I care or not." If a person says that he does not care, without being asked, then he does care and will not gain anything by denying his feelings.

The use of the "I don't care" affects all of our professional, social and amorous relationships. Its effect is pernicious and spoils the mutual communication between people.

"Am I right?"

This chapter, too, may arouse criticism, attack, or even ridicule. Many readers might ask, "What is wrong with asking whether one is right?" A great many patients who were, at first, irritated by analyzing the hidden motives of this mannerism later became very grateful and reported that the understanding of its meaning and consequent disappearance of the phrase from their vocabulary gave them relief and made them happier. Similar reports were given by a few friends who took the pains and had the patience to listen to my reasoning.

Somebody presents his case, his views, and his opinions to another person. The two people face each other and look at each other. The speaker frequently interlards his narrative with, "Am I right?" What is the position of the listener? Does the speaker expect to hear the reply, "No. You are wrong"? Does he consider the *listener* an expert from whom he wants to *learn*? If this were the case, he would ask the listener's opinion in a different way and in a different tone. He considers *himself* the competent person; it is *he* who is the authority. He is using the listener as a "yes man." He expects to be told that he is right; and if he is not, he is hurt and annoyed. He who is sure that he is right does not need such flippant confirmation. If he knows that he is not right, he should not feel right simply because he is told that he is. He might even ask if he is right when he *is convinced* that he is. He asks because he lacks the courage of his convictions. He needs approval in order to dare to continue his speech.

Sometimes, a man says, "you are right." In *this* case, he agrees *only* because he thinks the same thing regardless of whether he is right or wrong. His judgment is emotional and not based on objective verification.

When two people are trapped in a conversation in which one consistently uses the phrase, "Am I right?" both are losers. If the listener declares the speaker to be right, he loses because he is deprived of the joy of saying spontaneously what he feels and thinks, and therefore loses because he lies. If the listener disagrees, he loses because the speaker is hurt and disappointed. On the other hand, the speaker loses because he needs to be told whether he is right or not. He should know this himself. The speaker is loser when he hears an affirmative answer because he cannot be sure that it was meant. He also loses if he is told he is wrong, because he has unfairly dragged the listener into a painful reaction.

This and all the other mannerisms have their roots in the core of the personality. As I see it, personality means the type of reactions with which a person meets all the situations in his life. Personality depends on the vicissitudes of life affecting the instinctual drives in an individual's specific environment. In many cases, a deep analysis is necessary to discover when and how the personality was damaged in the course of its development. It takes enormous work to determine why and how the "ego weakness" originated. Even then it is extremely difficult to "work through" and correct irrational responses to different life situations.

Some people might have corrected their "weaknesses" through experiences in life, but unfortunately they again become involved in circumstances in which the complex is revived. Then one wonders whether by some (unconscious) devious ways, these people did not select a situation identical with the one in which the trouble originated.

A patient in analysis uses, both inside and outside the office, the "Am I right?" He is married. He thought that he was being married to a loving, considerate woman who would create a warm home for him. Instead, after a few weeks of marriage, his wife displayed her unfortunate "nature." She became domineering. She acknowledged her husband's professional excellencies, but *only* the professional ones. In the home, she laid down the law in every matter. Whenever he expressed an opinion, he was yelled at, flooded with abusive and degrading invectives. This went on for years until this man thought and felt like an idiot. Finally, he did not know, so to say, whether he was a boy or a girl. His sad and crippling experiences in his maternal home rendered him putty in the hands of a woman who, for her own reasons, needed to subdue an able man. These experiences led to a grave neurosis in the man and to his frequent use of the "Am I right?"

There are many talented and successful men who fall into

the habit of saying, "Am I right?" mainly in conversations with their wives. The wife need not even be familiar with the topic of her husband's ideas or the area of his performances, but it is important that she approve. Such men are proved to have been "mamma's boys." Some wives or girl friends do not mind assuming a mother's role; they might like or even exploit it. In other cases, a woman's doing so leads to serious trouble, even to divorce, because she wants a strong man who is sure of himself and does not need her to be his mother.

Maria Lorenz, one of the outstanding workers in the field of psychiatric implications of the use of language, found that the "language habits" and "language behavior" of a person reveal "something of his basic attitudes, drives and general orientation toward the self and the external world" (1953, p. 278). The reader will be rewarded by reading her original paper in which, among other things, she mentions a patient who, in four sentences, used "see what I mean" four times and "you know" twice (p. 281). Lorenz also discusses (on the same page) the meaning of the elaborate use of "so," "therefore," "because," "since," "as a result of," 'because of," and 'in consequence of."

In another paper (1955), the same author reports that she succeeded in showing that certain language patterns (Freud would call them "caprices in the use of language") are characteristic of certain "reaction types," for example: hysterical, obsessive-compulsive, manic, and paranoid schizophrenic.

Glauber, one of our experts in speech disorders, considers speech as "one of the chief component tools of the ego: resembles the ego closely" (1944, p. 18). In his paper, he does not deal with manneristic phrases but with speech characteristics of patients. He describes incidents, for example, when the "speech was profane, bubbling, emotional, high-pitched" or "sharp, witty, biting, melodramatic at times" (p. 25). Glauber succeeded in showing that speech characteristics are specific to the stage of libido development where the patient was arrested. Neumann and Mather (1938) examined the voice and language of manic-depressive patients and others with affective disorders and observed "loose and broken sentence structure . . . this feature of language may be indicative not of any particular syndrome, but of the severity of the disturbance."

The reader might already have become aware of the fact (and this awareness will grow stronger in the course of our discussion) that I deeply appreciate the views of Lorenz and Glauber. My aim is not to categorize people according to their speech mannerisms, but to show the hidden motives behind the mannerisms regardless of the category of classification into which the patient using such mannerisms would fall.

"Of course"

"Of course" is another phrase that needs examination and discussion. Let us begin with the most frequent and popular "of course." A wife asks her husband, "Do you still love me?" If the husband replies, "Of course, dear, I love you," the wife will not be satisfied. The answer does not seem to be bad, but it only seems that way. She might not oppose it, and she might even make a show of being pleased; but she is not. A simple "yes" would be a more satisfactory answer. The husband cannot say "no" because that would not be quite true, and he cannot say "yes" because that would not be true either. The wife wants to know whether her husband loves her in the same blind way he did when he was romancing her. A simple "yes" would mean to her that he "*really*" loves her; that only she, and no other woman, attracts him; that he is interested in her in every way; that whatever she does is charming, thrilling, incomparable; that she is brilliant, enticing, interesting; that she is always in his mind, waking or dreaming; and that she is the greatest treasure of his life and will remain so until his dying day—in a word, that he is crazy about her. The "of course" tells, in a thinly veiled way, the truth: "I love you but no longer as in our romantic days."

It cannot be otherwise (only in exceptional cases, "of course").

A young doctor, after returning from his honeymoon, resumed his practice. As he was leaving the house, his wife pleaded with him to stay home with *her*. "Do you love your patients more than me?" she cried. "Of course, I love only you, dear, but . . . etc., etc." The young wife confused her husband's feeling of duty with his love for the patients. She wanted him to care *only* for her. Had he been wise enough to stay home *once, she* would have sent him to work. Women *expect* men to work; but first they have to make sure that the men would rather stay home with them.

Another doctor said, "I saw a woman in my office for the sake of examination. She undressed. Besides having a beautiful face, she had a perfect figure with well-developed breasts. I looked at her professionally, *of course*." If he says this, he did not look at her professionally. If he had, he would not have needed to analyze his activity.

A woman patient came to pay her bill; and in doing so, she told the doctor that her husband had asked her to see whether the doctor would consider making a reduction in his fee if neither the husband nor the doctor included the amount in the declaration of their incomes for tax purposes. When the doctor asked what the patient thought his answer would be, she said, "Of course, you wouldn't do it." If she already knew what the doctor's answer would be, why did she ask the question? She could not forget her conversation with her husband. If the doctor refused her husband's proposition, the husband would get the entire blame. In phrasing her question the way she did, she neglected to tell the truth: she omitted mentioning her own interest in the matter. If she had told the whole truth, she would have said that both she and her husband were interested in knowing whether the doctor would consider reducing his fee under certain conditions. As the doctor remained silent when the patient said, "Of course, you wouldn't do it," the entire matter was dropped.

A male patient in analysis said: "You know what I am referring to, of course." The man said "of course" as if to indicate that he was sure that I remembered everything even though there was a doubt or uncertainty about this in his mind. He wanted and demanded the analyst's undivided attention. The "of course" is a self-assurance in order that he should not need to ask whether the doctor remembers or not. Such a question, he feels, might hurt the doctor; and if the latter does not remember, the patient will attack and criticize him. He is afraid of doing so.

Another male patient, a general practitioner, was in treatment for a certain type of neurosis. He was afraid to be examined lest his neurosis should turn out to be a "fatal organic disease." In his office, this man was examining a patient in whose abdomen he found a mass. He suspected cancer. The man's family had several cancer cases. The doctor said to the analyst, "I felt sorry for him, of course; but I suspected that my apprehension for him was a projection of my own fear or an identification with him." True, he felt sorry about his patient's grave troubles; but *now*, in his present condition, the doctor can feel apprehensive only for himself. The "of course" is an apology to pacify his conscience for his self-centeredness.

A young lady was going steady with a boy when her present husband made his appearance. She fell in love with the latter, married him, and continued to have a happy life with him. A few years after her marriage, the name of the first young man came up, and she permitted herself a mental play. What if she had to choose between the two men *now*? Whom would she prefer? "Of course," she said laughingly, "I would choose my husband." The "of course" means that there is a chance that she might now prefer the first man; but, being happily married, she does not want to face the other possibility. If she were absolutely sure that she would still choose her present husband, she would not have needed to say "of course."

"Naturally"

The word "naturally" means the biologically inevitable. The "natural" is in the genes. It must come out and is bound to appear under all circumstances. "Naturally" is meant to be the strongest confirmation of a fact.

Let us see what happens to this word in our everyday talking relationships. It is very close to the "of course" which has just been discussed.

A brilliant surgeon related, in analysis, a conversation he had with another doctor who had referred a patient to him for an operation. For the patient, the decision to submit to surgery meant life or death; for the doctors, it meant emotional, ethical, professional and social responsibilities and consequences. I knew his patient and knew that the surgeon's first interest was the welfare of the patient. All other motivations were secondary with him. He was a *doctor* in the true sense of the word. There is every reason to assume the same about the other doctor who asked the surgeon whether his patient should be operated and if so who should perform the surgery, the analysand or a surgeon in another city. In the course of his narrative, my patient said, "Naturally, he [the referring physician] was concerned about his patient . . ." He meant that the referring doctor's position was easier than his because the former had only to find the right surgeon; but the analysand might have to operate, in which case his own responsibility would be the greater. He who has the lesser responsibility is in a better position to follow his "natural" inclination and think *mainly* of the patient's interest; but he who might perform the operation also has to deal with the other forces involved.

"It is not that . . ."

In an analytic session, a physician patient said, "It is not that *I* am such a good doctor but, in my opinion, Dr. X is not a good doctor at all." The patient *is* a very good doctor, and it happens that he is right about the other one. What he wants to say is, "I am a good doctor and he is not good at all." Why does he not say what he feels? The cause for the suppression in this case lies in this man's having been subdued in childhood by his mother, and in adult years, by his wife. Both women admit that he is good in his work. He brings money home. In everything besides his work, these two women consider themselves absolute authorities in making judgments. The patient is supposed to leave any decision to them. In addition to this, society demands that men make a show of humility to the point of being false, insincere and hypocritical. Humility should come, not through being forced upon us, but through the acquisition of increased knowledge which persuades us that the more we know the more we can see our limitations.

"I don't want to hurt you, but . . ."

There is rarely a person, including myself, who has not used the phrase, "I don't want to hurt you, but . . ." Since realizing its meaning and recognizing the damage it can do, I have abandoned its use and call upon everybody else to warn me whenever I happen to relapse into using it.

When A. says to his friend B., "I don't want to hurt you, but you made a fool of yourself at the discussion," we are inclined to believe that A., for the sake of his friend, *has* to convey something unpleasant which, he assumes, will hurt B. In order that B. should not think that A. wants to hurt him, A. assures B. that he intends *not* to hurt B., but that he wants merely to correct the latter for his own sake.

Clinically, this kind of mannerism was observed long ago and was theoretically explained by Freud (1925). His explanation fits almost all forms of speech mannerisms. "Now you will think," says the patient to Freud, "I mean to say something insulting, but really I've no such intention." We see at once that this is a repudiation, by means of projection, of an association that has just emerged. Again, when a patient is asked who the person in the dream might have been, he says, "It was *not* my mother." We emend this to mean, "It *was* my mother." In our interpretation, we take the liberty of disregarding the negation and simply select the subject matter of the association. It is just as though the patient had said, "It is true that I thought of my mother in connection with this person, but I don't feel at all inclined to allow the association to count." The explanation of Freud (1925) is that *"thus the subject-matter of a repressed image or thought can make its way into consciousness on condition that it is denied"* (with the exception of "denied," my italics).

Mark Antony's speech in Shakespeare's play, *Julius Caesar*, is full of mannerisms, as is the speech of Brutus. "As Caesar loved me, I weep for him; as he was fortunate, I rejoice at it; as he was valiant, I honour him; *but* as he was ambitious, I slew him" (my italics).

In the course of time, the human mind became a very complicated and, we have to admit, tricky machine. We think first of ourselves. Only when we are taken care of can we afford to think of the other fellow. The devil selfishness is always with us; and we have a hard time checking and controlling him. It can be done only after a long, hard struggle and *only* when we can be and dare to be aware of the existence of such selfishness.

First *we* want to be safe. We measure our safety by positive and negative means. The positive is the measurement of our own safety; the negative is the measurement of our safety by the misfortune of others. This is a primitive way of thinking, a childish one. The child persists forever in most people. We are more interested in bad news than in good news. Sometimes, we have an outburst of goodness; but it is only an outburst. After its explosion, it disappears. We like to look over death announcements. If a reader of such announcements is fifty years old, he reads with satisfaction of the death of an octogenarian, thinking he still has thirty years to go. He reads with equal satisfaction of the death of a thirty-year-old whom he has survived by twenty years. The reader is in trouble when he reads of the death of a man of fifty whose age is identical with his. What will he do? He will try to forget the latter case or figure out some method of self-deception.

A. *is* in conflict when he tells some bad news to his friend B. He does not *want* to hurt his friend; but the devil part of him *needs*, and therefore likes, to hurt him. To fend off the reproach of his conscience (which is the representative of truth), he tells B. that he does not want to hurt him. If this is so, he should remain silent; or he should say what he intends saying without the introduction, "I don't want to hurt you." The friend will get hurt and A. should trust that B. will be mature enough not to accuse him. If B. does become angry, A. should take the punishment and be satisfied that he accomplished his task.

It is more dignified to admit the tendency to malicious joy at another's misfortune (*Schadenfreude*) than to deny it. I was deeply moved by the courage of an analyst-colleague, J. C. Flugel (1954), in writing a paper "On Bringing Bad News" (1925) on the occasion of getting the news of the death of a highly esteemed analyst.

"I don't want to burden you, but . . ."

A burden is a burden and nobody likes to have one. For a decent cause, we accept a burden and feel good about having done so. Because of our self-love, we expect that nothing should be a burden to another when *we* want something. We want to be so important to others that they should be glad to do anything for us.

A male patient said during an analytic session, "I don't want to burden you by telling you the whole story"; but he *did* tell the whole story. He wanted his analyst to assure him that it would be a pleasure to hear the whole story and that he would not be burdened by it. In *this* case, as in so many others, the mannerisms can be traced back to childhood. He was told that "children should be seen and not heard." He was afraid to say what he wanted. He was afraid to assert himself. This and other attitudes of his parents affected him so deeply that they caused severe impairment of his sexual and other functions.

It is possible that more boys than girls are affected by verbal inhibition. It was again Flugel (1925), who called our attention to the close psychological connection between tongue and penis and between speech and sexual power.

Even the letters of the alphabet can symbolize the person himself. The clinical proof of this was furnished by Dr. Karl A. Menninger. In a letter to Menninger, a man with a strong homosexual trend misspelled the word "fairy," changing it to "fary" wherever the word was used. "It was easy," writes Menninger (1924), "to elicit the fact that by omitting this 'i', he was, so to speak, leaving himself out of the accusation of being a fairy, a well-known vulgar expression for a homo-sexual man."

I can confirm the findings of Menninger by another striking example. A male patient who wrote and spoke German per-fectly always misspelled the word *"ich"* (which means "I" in English), making it *"cih."* For a long time, as a child, he slept between his parents. Then he was removed from the middle position and placed beside one of the parents. He wanted to be between them. The letter "i" represented him-self.

In Menninger's paper, there are also interesting examples of the unconscious meaning of the letters "U," "Z," and "B."

"I am not boasting"

A patient, in talking about his vacation, said what a won-derful relationship he now had with his wife. "I made love to her more often than at any other time during our marriage. I am not boasting; I am only reporting." Can there be a single male reader who believes that he was not boasting? Even the patient realized this.

He was a premature child. He won a beauty prize in a baby contest and his mother did not miss an occasion to show him off and make him feel that her pride in him was her most important joy. He also remembered that she was extremely proud of the fact that when he urinated, he stood in such a way that the urine would go directly into the pot and not drop outside of it. Whenever he spoke or made love or did anything at all, he visualized, in back of his mind, the pride of his mother.

"It is not my business, but . . ."

A male patient asked, "It is not my business, but is the young lady whom I have seen a couple of times in the house your daughter?" (My office and residence are in the same house.) He was right about the identity of the young lady. He easily admitted that he entertained the idea of becoming my son-in-law.

A married woman asked a man, "It is not my business, but are you married?" If it is not her business, why does she ask it and why does she say that it is not her business? We do not always declare our disinterest when we are not interested. She must have some sort of interest, but this interest is denied.

Persons who use this mannerism are in conflict. Either they should be mature enough to bear frustration or be frank about their curiosity.

Another female patient, a case of grave character neurosis, never admitted to herself or to anybody else that she had any personal or emotional interest. There was inhibition and denial of any instinctual drive. She claimed that her interests were only intellectual and sociological. This was a self-deception. Only a dead person can be uninterested. She used a whole gamut of mannerisms which betrayed her. She sharply criticized anyone who, in social conversation, mentioned money, parts of the body or sickness. One should live in a refined, spiritual atmosphere. Her philosophy was a gross exaggeration of fine manners. It is, if not fake, worse, self-deception. In another case, that of an aesthetic male, there was a strong preoccupation with excremental matters and functions.

"I cannot tell you how much . . ."
"I cannot find the words to describe . . ."
"It is beyond words . . ."

Grandmother is asked how she likes her newborn grandson. She rolls up her eyes, turns away her body and shrugs her shoulders, indicating that this is an impossible question to answer. Then she begins. She cannot be stopped from telling all the wonderful details. She is eloquent, finds all the words to express her enthusiasm, joy, pride and happiness. In such cases, when at last the words are found, the introductory denial expresses an overwhelming feeling which, for a few seconds, throws the speaker back into the preverbal period during which emotions were expressed by bodily manifestations. Furthermore, the grandmother knows that the listeners cannot be as emotional as she is and she scolds them for not being able to identify themselves with her.

Everybody should be able to find a way to express his emotions, effectively and impressively, in a few simple words, if the feelings are genuine and he is sincere. "I cannot tell you how much . . .," "I cannot find the words to describe . . .," and "It is beyond words . . ." are mannerisms, phrases frequently used in order *not to* express one's feelings or to betray that one has no feelings. People who cannot find the words are reluctant to do so either because they are envious, jealous or lazy or because their inability to find the words betrays the truth, a lack of feelings.

"I only . . ."

In his book on dreams, Freud (1900) illustrates the hidden tendency in the word "only" (p. 488). When a person has a dream concerning something about which he would prefer not to think, he protects his sleep and the impact of the undesirable thought by saying, "It is only a dream." He is therefore able to continue dreaming, reassuring himself that there can be no possible reality to the dream. Sometimes a thought that would be censored even in sleep slips through. In this case, the censorship finds it too late to retrieve its powers of suppressing the undesirable thought which then continues to be articulate in the sleeper. His last recourse of self-protection lies in minimizing the impact and in denying the reality of the uncomfortable idea by saying, "It is only a dream."

"Only" may be used legitimately on rare occasions. In most cases, it is used for the defense of guilt feelings. A wife is preparing a soft-boiled egg for her husband. He breaks the shell. The egg is stone-hard. "It cannot be hard," she says. "I only went upstairs for a second to fix my hair for you." But the egg is hard, and she knows that she has been gone for more than a second.

A husband pays too much attention to a lady at a drinking party. His conduct is atrocious and damaging to the reputation of his wife who is also present. When she calls him to account, he offers a very poor explanation, introducing his defense with an "I only." The "I only" is used extensively by children who learn this sort of hypocrisy from their parents, in the street, school, from movies or in the homes of other children. They are very keen in spotting the weaknesses of adults whom they copy for their own pleasure purposes and interests.

I once heard the following joke. Two Jews went to a rabbi to confess that they had broken the fast earlier than permitted on Yom Kippur, the Day of Atonement. "You have to atone and be punished," said the rabbi. He turned to A. and asked what he liked most. A. replied that he liked most to be with his wife. "You have to sleep in another bedroom and be separated from your wife for six weeks," said the rabbi. Then turning to B., he asked, "And what do you like most?" B. replied that his greatest joy was smoking his pipe.

"Your punishment shall be," said the rabbi, "giving up your pipe for six weeks." Both men accepted the punishment and explained the situation to their wives. A. slept in a separate bedroom; B. put away his pipe. On the third night, A.'s wife knocked on her husband's door. He awakened, understood that his wife was knocking and exclaimed with a voice of desperation, "But, dear, it's only the third day. We still can't share the bedroom."

To this his wife replied, "I only wanted to tell you that B. is already smoking his pipe." "Only?"

"It goes without saying"

A. asks B. to lend him some money. "It goes without saying," says A., "that though we are friends, this is strictly a business transaction between us." If "it goes without saying," why does he use these words? If he wanted to assure his friend, he could say that he would return the money on a certain date. The important point, from a psychological point of view is A.'s suppressed or repressed intention, *not* to repay the money, on the basis of friendship.

This intention has been revealed in the analysis of many persons. I believe that B. would feel more certain of getting his money back *without* the reassuring words. It has already been emphasized that we all have within us a wonderful seismograph which immediately registers the slightest stimulus in our mind: the unconscious of each person communicates with that of the other.

"I just"

The phrase, "I just," is legitimate only when it refers to time, for example: "I just met Joe, who told me . . ." It is legitimate if it is true that he met Joe just now. Otherwise, it is not legitimate; it is a mannerism which intends to conceal something. Often, it is identical with the "by the way," for example: A. tells B. that something "just came into his mind" when the matter had been there all along. It was probably the most important thing on his mind. If a person says that he "just could not fall asleep," he means that he cannot find out why he was unable to do so.

Someone asks, "May I borrow your car for two days?" If the listener were to ask indignantly whether the speaker was crazy, the speaker would cry out defensively, "I just said it." With this phrase, he is trying either to minimize his words or to fool the other person into believing that the request was not important. In either case, communication is spoiled.

A fellow analyst who had heard about my interest in speech mannerisms explained that he wanted to test my findings. In order to do so, he asked a woman patient why she always used the phrase, "I just said it." Her response was, "I thought you weren't interested in me."

I was invited to lunch by a couple who had two children, a girl of eleven and a boy of eight. During the meal, the usual talk and conversation went on. The children played the main role.

The girl: "Billy exercises on me every morning."

I: "What do you mean?"

The girl: (pretending that she is annoyed although she smiles and laughs, indicating that she likes it): "He awakens me each morning by coming to my bed and spanking me."

I (addressing the boy): "Why do you spank her?"
The boy: "I *just* do it."
     (This is concealed sex play.)

A male patient stated that his wife left him because he subjected her to such humiliating things in their sex relations that she could no longer endure them. A few weeks after the separation, as often happens, he again became interested in his wife. A good part of his interest was morbid because he became sexually stimulated by the idea of seeing his wife dating another man. (Both the man and his wife were highly intellectual persons with honorable views and philosophies of life.) For neurotic reasons, he spied on his wife. "Last night," he said, "I just drove around the place where my wife is living." By "just," he could not mean time; and he did not mean time. "Just" means here that his actions were without any specific reason. This was not true. He had very strong feelings and impulses to spy on his wife at a time when he could expect to see her with another man. If she had been with another man, he would have felt not only jealous but *also* stimulated. Furthermore, he was ashamed to admit his renewed interest in his wife because he had previously spoken of her with disparagement.

"I had a silly thought"
"I was just kidding"
"I was just joking"

For reasons already presented, we should not make the mistake of using in our communications such mannerisms as "I had a silly thought," "I was just kidding," or "I was just joking." Whenever some persons make a proposition which contains strong wishes, and there is a possibility of rejection which they are reluctant to face, they protect themselves by creating the way for withdrawal. They introduce such a proposition with the "I had a silly thought." Or, later, after having dared to utter the proposition which has met with rejection, they use the "I was just kidding." The use of these mannerisms is even worse when the person who is using them himself believes that he is "just kidding" when he is not. This is self-deception; it is like a drug which may lead to addiction and damage the person's self-esteem.

In some cases, a person uses these phrases as trial balloons. He hopes that the second person will *not* consider his proposition "silly" or "joking" or "kidding" but will understand his intensions and agree with them. The first person is fishing for encouragement. In the long run, this is the wrong way to operate even if it sometimes works. It is not good to make a habit of using mannerisms. In certain situations their use may be catastrophic. For example, if a man were to make a proposal of marriage, saying, "I just had a silly thought. Would you marry me?" a girl would later regret having married a man who, on such an important occasion, was unable to behave sincerely. In accepting the proposal and marrying the man, the girl would be ignoring his weak points in order to gratify her desire to be married.

Many hostile and aggresive thoughts are expressed and discharged under cover of the word "just." One may think that it is good, after all, to be able to release drives in a "kidding" way and at the same time prepare the way for withdrawing from an angry response by using the word "just." True, both parties, in order to avoid a fight, may accept such a settlement of hostility; but, in my opinion, this method of settlement is not constructive. It would be better either to control oneself and say nothing or to settle serious matters openly, frankly. To do so means one has "emotional dignity."

Adults inflict a great deal of undignified and stupid kidding and joking on children. When this practice has gone so far that the child cries, the adult is unable to comfort the child by saying that he was "just joking or kidding." Children are justified in their crying because they feel the aggressive or indirect sexual tendencies of the adults. They cry because they did not give cause for aggression; and if the kidding contains sexual elements, the children do not know what to do with the stimulation. They are not yet ready for it. The same is true of teasing, as has been shown by Brenman (1952) and Samuel J. Sperling (1953).

"Don't be ridiculous"
"This is ridiculous"
"You make me laugh"
(On ridicule and fear of being ridiculed)

The manneristic phrases, "don't be ridiculous," "this is ridiculous," and "you make me laugh," are used, as a rule, when the second person (the ridiculed) makes a serious statement or a weighty suggestion, or expresses a desire, a wish, an expectation, an apprehension or a concern. The first person (the one who ridicules) opposes the words of the second with "don't be ridiculous" or another of the above-mentioned mannerisms; but he does *not* laugh, although he intimates that he *could* do so. He may act out a laugh; it is a forced laugh. There is some irony and sarcasm in it. Under certain circumstances, the laugh is a hearty one. The first person may or may not have the intention of hurting the second. In either case, the second person feels hurt. As a matter of fact, the pain of the second person, the humiliation he feels, is one of the deepest a human being can experience. The ridiculed person can not and never will forgive an insult inflicted through ridicule. He may blush, become angry or furious, or even cry. He is thrown out of countenance, will brood for a long time. The memory of the injury comes back time and time again. The more the ridicule aims at reducing self-esteem, the more it hurts. In describing the history of a patient, Loewenstein (1950) shows the deep effect that the mother's laughing had on a small boy who, when he attempted to walk, fell on the floor in front of her.

An employee asks for a raise, a promotion. The employer ridicules the man and refuses to consider his request. The request is denied, for no monetary reason, in such a manner as to indicate that the employee is not good enough or not worth enough *as a person* even to think of an advancement. *What* the employee asks is not so ridiculous as the fact that *he* could even think of an advancement. This thought is considered to be so out of place that the employee's self-appraisal has to be completely destroyed and his idea ruthlessly eliminated.

Take the case of a person who feels that he has a good reason to be jealous. He expresses this feeling to his mate who is the only one to know whether or not the jealousy is justified. In either case, the accused will feel that the most effective method of dealing with the accusation is to ridicule the accuser. The ridicule will hit the mate. It will convince him that the jealousy is absurd, preposterous, morbid, insane, and crazy.

The nature of laughter was studied by many scholars from various fields. I shall discuss the phenomenon of laughing only as it relates to speech mannerisms. It was Freud who gave us the deepest information about the circumstances in which laughter is evoked (1905a). Analyzing the structure and the dynamism of jokes, Freud found that the saving of repressing energy elicits, from the listener, laughter in response to a joke. He means, very briefly, that in the joke a drive is brought to the point of discharge in such a way that neither the joke-teller nor the listener can be accused of the objectionable drive because that drive is not openly expressed; it is only suggested. The joke, seemingly, attracts both persons by its mechanism which allows that the repressed drive can break through into consciousness. I have elaborated on this subject in two papers (1932a, 1941a).

There is a situation in which ridicule is, in my observation, frequently resorted to: when a girl tells her parents or others that a man has proposed to her, she often will openly ridicule the man. I came to know a medical student, who was a young,

attractive, and rich girl. She was being courted by a young
doctor. She had told me that she was pleased by the man's
affections but that the man did not suit her, did not live up to
her expectations. I asked her how she would react when her
colleague proposed. "I would tell him," said the girl, "that I
am very much honored by his proposal, but because I am not
in love with him, I am sorry to say that I cannot accept his
proposal." I then asked her, anticipating her reply, in what
form and manner she would convey the event to her mother.
She replied, "After he leaves, I shall burst into laughter, run
to my mother and tell her what has taken place." I asked what
kind of laugh this would be. She answered that it would be a
laugh of ridicule. "Why would you ridicule him?" was the
next question. She said, "It is ridiculous that such an ugly
man could even imagine that it would be possible for me to
consider a proposal to become his wife." Further question:
"Would you ridicule him at the moment he made his proposition?" "No," she replied. "It would be the wrong thing to do
because he would be mortally hurt." "Would you have any
further thoughts?" I urged. "Yes, well, I would," she answered; "but I would not like to tell you." She laughed and
looked peevishly at her interrogator, who suspected that she
visualized love-making, beyond kissing, with her rejected
suitor. I conveyed this suspicion to her, and she confirmed it.

A whole series of emotions are evident in this event. Let us
examine the situation of the girl. She is young and knows that
she is very pretty; she is very well off and has definite possibilities of making a "good" marriage. She is sure to find the
right man. Furthermore, she feels superior to the above-mentioned man, who is rather unattractive and only slightly older
than she, which to her means he is too young and immature.
The sense of superiority is her first gratification. For all these
reasons, she does not permit herself to respond sexually to the
man's sexual intentions, but she can play with the idea without
feeling guilty. In females of the somewhat prudish upper-
middle class, to which she belonged, "lust without guilt"

(Stekel) is important. She is free of guilt. After all, she is not pleased; she is *ridiculing* him and his intentions. Another gain is that she can run to her mother or to her girl friends to show them how much she is sought after and to let them see that she is in a position to refuse a man, and that she is confident of receiving more proposals from which she can choose.

This, as well as other cases in which the *fear of being ridiculed* is prominent, points to the probability that one ridicules a person in order to indicate that he is not fit to find a sex partner because he or she is still like a child. There is hardly a more painful feeling for a human being than to have insufficient power, strength, importance, maturity, and physical appeal to attract the opposite sex.

A shy patient, a young law student, made a sexual proposition to a pretty woman some years his senior. She refused, telling him, in the idiomatic language of the rural folk of Hungary, that his semen was not mature enough. She did not mean that the man's semen was not good enough to impregnate her; she meant only that she wanted a more mature man (more mature semen) even though she dreaded to become pregnant.

In ridicule, there is a great amount of irony. The ridiculing person can also discharge and enjoy aggression. Therefore, in order to prevent being ridiculed by others, many people *ridicule themselves*. "Oh, how ugly I am today," say many women when they meet others. They thus "vaccinate" themselves against the real blow. Such psychic "antibodies" are ego defenses.

"I think"

Suppose one enters the office of a colleague friend and, finding him in his chair doing nothing, asks, "What are you doing?" If he answers, "I am thinking," then, from our point of view, the answer is correct. If the question should be, "What do you think about the patient whom I asked you to see?" and he quickly answers, "I think this and this . . . ," the "I think" can still be legitimate, though one wonders whether he could not have omitted the "I think" and yet have made an articulate, clear statement. One wonders whether the "I think," in the last instance, is not the same as the "well" or the "er . . . err . . . er," which will be discussed later.

There is an essential difference when the "I think" is used at the beginning or at the end of a statement. When, for example, a husband asks his wife, "Where are the car keys, dear?" the proper answer would be, if she is sure, "The keys are on the kitchen table." If she is not sure, she should say, "I think they are on the kitchen table"; and not, "They are on the kitchen table—I think," inserting a pause before the "I think." The latter is not correct because the wife *pretends* that she knows where the keys are; but, in the end, she betrays the fact that she is not positive. Either she is sure or she is not. The improper use of the "I think" disturbs the "noiseless" relationship between the two persons. The harmony is spoiled.

One of the most delicate relationships is that between a patient and his analyst. In the analytic situation, through the so-called "transference," the analysand's past relationships are revived, discussed, and "worked through." This statement means that through numerous examples and events, the relationships are deeply understood. The analysis of past relationships in the transference situation is an excellent opportunity to show the analysand how many elements of the old relationships are transferred to the present relationships, not only in the relationship to the analyst but also possibly to *all the patient's relationships*. The transference relationship thus creates the opportunity for correction and readjustment of the analysand's relationships. This is a very delicate process, and there are many pitfalls. It is, by no means, sufficient that the analysand reaches an intellectual understanding of his problems, although such understanding is important. It is far more important for him to reach an *emotional understanding*.

To achieve this, it is necessary to observe, to become aware of all "resistances" which interefere with this emotional process. Some of the many resistances can be noticed in the speech mannerisms. For example, there are patients, and others who are not patients, who, instead of talking in a straightforward manner and associating during the sessions, say, "I was thinking that . . .," instead of omitting this phrase and saying *what* they were thinking. If they do not say what they think, they are talking about themselves in the third person instead of the first person; they split themselves off emotionally from the verbal content.

A girl would immediately sense that something was wrong with a man who would propose by saying, "I was thinking of telling you that I love you and want to marry you," instead of saying, "I love you. I want to marry you."

A female patient very frequently used, at the end of a statement, after she paused for a few seconds, the "I think." We realized that this mannerism pointed to the basic conflict of her troubles. She had a severe, disciplining mother who incessantly criticized the daughter's doings and sayings. Gradually, the latter adopted the habit of using, after her answers or statements, the "I think" in order to decline responsibility. The phrase meant that she "only" thinks and she is willing to change her ideas in case her mother should oppose her. In adult life, she looked at mankind as at a million-headed monster; everybody became a dangerous beast. This feeling isolated her from all people, but she still had to be with people. She had to work, and it was inevitable to have bosses and other people around her. She often was mortally hurt by the attitudes of people, cried, and withdrew more and more. This withdrawal created a marked social anxiety, examination fear and deficient sexual responsiveness.

Another woman, in talking about a party she attended, said, "They are such unusually nice people—I think." She had experienced their hospitality and knew that they were nice people; but she had to say that she *only thought* they were nice in order not to be afraid of them in case she should be nice and kind to them and they should not reciprocate. After all, she only *thought* that they were nice; she did not *state* that they were. This was a defense. The understanding of the mannerism contributed to the effectiveness of the "working through" process.

In the course of the sessions, a male patient often said, "I am thinking," or "It ocurs to me," instead of saying what he was thinking or what occurred to him. This man had been secretly meeting and having an affair with a woman before his marriage. After that, he did not see her any more, but he thought and fantasied about her. His wife, who did not know about the affair, was a jealous woman. The patient felt very uncomfortable when his wife asked him what he was doing while he was away at work. Besides the affair, he had nothing to hide. On the other hand, he was afraid that he might betray himself in some way or other. Therefore, his answers were vague, uncertain, so that he could retract them in case he should be trapped by his wife's scrutinizing "examinations."

"It wouldn't be too bad"

A happily married man, in analysis, felt sexually frustrated because of his wife's pregnancy. Her husband was a man of high and healthy ethical and moral standards. There were good reasons to assume that he would never be disloyal. Nevertheless, he felt frustrated; and the devil never sleeps. The man became attracted to a well-built girl who worked in the same building with him. He said, talking spontaneously, during an analytic session, "It wouldn't be too bad to sleep with her."

One immediately senses that he means it would be very enjoyable to have relations with her. Because he is afraid to express his desire in a straightforward way, he omits any word which would indicate pleasure. Instead he uses the word "bad," though he qualifies it by saying that "it would *not* be bad," and, moreover, that "it would not be *too* bad." The "ego" of the man is the field of a violent battle between opposing forces; and in this mannerism, a "compromise formation" takes place through omission, condensation and reversal, "turning into the opposite," mechanisms observed, discovered and described by Freud.

"Do you want me to tell you something?"

There are marriages in which the wives have more intelligence than their husbands and those in which the wives *think* they have more intelligence than their husbands. In either case, there is trouble.

A glib-tongued housewife, full of spark and intelligence, does the planning and talking for the family. She expresses her opinion about a certain important matter. A week or so later, her husband asks, "Do you want me to tell you something?" Getting her approval (what else can she do?), he tells as *his own* exactly the same thing *she* said to him some time ago.

The husband "ignores" that he learned something good from his wife. He liked what she said. Being the "Man" of the house, he must, at least sometimes, say something good.

"Bye-bye"

The phrase "bye-bye" indicates greater closeness to a person than does good-bye. Women, particularly young ones, use the "bye-bye" when parting from men with whom they do not but wish to have a close relationship. They think, by using the phrase, that men may accept the familiarity graciously. Sometimes, however, the person to whom the "bye-bye" is addressed finds the phrase irritating because he is uncertain whether he should allow himself to be trapped by the "bye-bye" or whether he should maintain his authority and stick to the "good-bye," thus indicating to the woman that she is in no position to say "bye-bye" which means more closeness.

"I am asking you a great favor, a very great favor"

The sentence, "I am asking you a favor, a very great favor," is unfair because it is blackmailing. In using it, the speaker wins the first round because he has trapped the listener who has to give him permission to go ahead with his request. The speaker also wins the second round because he can argue that the listener granted him permission to divulge the content of the request. In giving his consent to the other to talk, the listener is forced to be good and grant a favor against his own best interests. Watch out!

"In a way"

A woman patient who was in treatment because of deep depression would not commit herself in any way. To any statement she made, she affixed the phrase, "in a way." This mannerism could be traced back to her childhood and girlhood during which time she had been criticized and reprimanded by a very strict mother. The latter found fault with the girl for not doing or saying things or for doing or saying them poorly and incorrectly. In this case, the "in a way" is a defense. It allows her to retract any statement which may be challenged because her use of the phrase kept her from being direct. Her retraction of her statement, including "in a way," is another way in which she can please her critic.

Some insistent people

On a nice spring day, a man is invited to the home of a couple for lunch. While dressing, the prospective guest becomes aware of his weakness in choosing the proper color combinations in his clothing. In viewing the end result of his efforts, he is certain that he has made the wrong decisions. He considers his friends experts in the matter of clothing and decides to seek their opinion and advice. He arrives and the meal is served. In the course of the luncheon, he asks, "Is this combination all right?"

They reply, "It is awful. How can you wear this shirt with that tie?"

The guest replies, "I know it is awful, but . . ." In spite of this remark, the host still goes on and on until he is satisfied that he has exhausted his feelings on the subject. Only after the host has satisfied his aggression will he give the requested advice. The guest feels that it is more important for friends to criticize than to give help. Watch out!

"What if"

Though "what if" never sounds musical, it is tolerable if it is used to gain time. Even so, it is an affront, an insult, to the marvelous instrument, language. He who is in love with language will not use the "what if."

Let us illustrate the use of the phrase with a hypothetical example so common that one can observe it hundreds of times daily. A wife prepares to go shopping and asks her husband what kind of bread he would like her to bring from the grocer. The husband wants black bread. The woman asks, "What if the grocer is out of black bread?" She probably wants her husband to make a decision and direct her what to bring in such a case. Should she bring another kind of bread, no bread at all, or what? In this case, the use of the "what if" appears to be legitimate because it saves time. Nevertheless, one might raise the question, "Why does she sacrifice the harmony and beauty of the language to gain time?" Is she in such a hurry? Would she not use the "what if" even if she had plenty of time? Is it laziness? Why then is she lazy? Is it sloppiness? Why is she sloppy? The use of language in such a sloppy, neglectful way reflects the whole personality of the user. The sloppiness which appears in the language will be discovered in all her activities, in her gait, principles, morals, ethics, total intelligence, love attitudes, relation to her children, friends, community, and country.

A highly educated person, in analysis, whose wife had a grave disease, said one day, "I thought to myself, yesterday, 'What if my wife should die?' " He dropped the subject but was interrupted by my asking what he meant by the "what if." The man had a happy marriage that had lasted for many years. He was devoted to his wife and they were sexually compatible. "All right," he replied. "You got me at the right time again." Then he admitted that he thought of the tragic possibility and wondered what he would do in the event of his wife's death. Should he enjoy his freedom and have many affairs? There were some women who, in the course of time, had attracted him. He discarded them. He loved his wife. When he is free, he may take advantage of this freedom before he gets married again. He cannot live without a woman; he needs a wife. Whom would he like to marry? These were his thoughts.

"All right," the angry reader might say, "granted that you are right, what good does it do for anybody to be aware of the hidden thought behind the 'what if'?" The reader may suggest that it is good to "forget," to repress such thoughts. To this I would say, No, no. The repression fails. Those feelings maintain their strength despite the attempted repression. They become indestructible *because of* the repression. Because of the repression, one avoids the proper settlement of a problem. The repressed feelings will exert their influence on all the actions of the man, lead him to wrong actions and decisions, and prevent a healthy choice of a love object. He cannot be master of his emotions when they are not at the disposal of his consciousness. *Emotions can be controlled only when they are attached to their ideational content and both become conscious; otherwise, they become independent and the person is helplessly influenced by them.*

I have previously described the following case in my paper on "Mannerisms of Speech" (1948, p. 363). A woman patient, who suffered from anxiety hysteria and compulsive neurosis, very frequently used the "what if." She had an intimate friend, a girl whose social position, wealth, and especially attractiveness, she envied a great deal. She tried to hide this envy from herself because she was ashamed of it and would have liked to be a good friend without envy. The two women attended lectures together. Once, on her way to class, the patient noticed her friend's car parked in front of the building. At the same time, she noticed a policeman coming out of the building. Immediately, the thought flashed through her mind: what if her friend had had a fatal accident and the policeman were here to investigate? She realized that the "what if" meant that she was wondering whether she would feel joy or sorrow if the friend had suffered a fatal injury. By using the "what if," she omitted the thoughts that counted. She continually used this phrase which represented and colored her whole condition and was strongly allied with the basic problem of her neurosis.

"That's nothing!"
"No"

Who has not met and become irritated by characters (is the reader one?) who ruin the telling of any story by cutting in on the narrator with, "That's nothing"? Who has not met the kind of wife who, when her husband begins to describe an event witnessed by both, cuts in with an emphatic "no"? Her interruption means that his story is not so, that he does not tell it well. *She* will tell how it was. People, especially wives, who do this are usually not aware of what they are doing. They do not know what damage they are inflicting on others, nor how much hatred they create in the person whom they have "cut" down. The reaction of the person thus "cut" down is as deep and as grave as it is in the person who is ridiculed. The wound, especially when it is inflicted in the presence of others, is mortal. The "that's nothing" brutally says that the speaker does not tell his story well, that the scene he witnessed is nothing by comparison with what the other saw, and that the joke he just told would be effective only if the critic told it. The single "no" does not bother to indicate even that much. The single "no" eliminates, liquidates, destroys the speaker completely, makes him nonexistent, and erases him from the surface of the earth. The single "no" orders, without explanation, that the speaker stop abruptly, cease talking. Such injuries are not forgotten. Whether it is admitted or not, they may even put an end to marital happiness or to relationships with friends. When one is the target of the phrases under discussion, he would be wise to ignore the remark when it occurs and discuss it with the offender at a more opportune moment.

On the basis of my experiences, I would conclude that the causes of behavior revealed through the mannerisms are the following.

1.   One of them is a feeling of omnipotence stemming from the very early period of infancy. A child wants everything. For example, if one brings presents to two children, aged three and five, each child, regardless of sex, will immediately look at the present of the other to see whether the latter received more than he did. Sometimes a child will even begin to stutter because he thinks another who stutters has something more than he has. A child may notice an adult's dentures which he, too, would like to have and he tries to take out his own teeth. The reader will probably be able to supply many other examples.

There is an anecdote which tells about a mother who took her little girl to a candy store to buy a chocolate doll. When the mother asked the child whether she wanted a boy doll or a girl doll, the girl answered that she wanted a boy doll because there was more chocolate on it.

2. Another cause is aggression, one of the strongest forces in humanity. Aggression is denied, repressed, and is therefore forced into other channels, like "that's nothing," "no," and many others. From our point of view, it is irrelevant whether aggression is considered as a primary, innate force, in which case the mannerism is used for the gratification of an aggressive instinct itself (Hartmann et al., 1949; Bak, 1954), or whether it is used as a reaction to deprivation and frustration (Montagu, 1955).

3. If a man "cuts" down another man, the act represents the strong tendency in all men to eliminate all other men from the surface of the earth in order to be the sole possessor of all females or to put all men into their service ("castrating tendencies"). Men may also try to create in women contempt for a rival.

4. If a man "cuts" down his wife, he may be expressing his contempt for her because he considers her an unsatisfactory sexual object. In this way, he indicates to other women that he is dissatisfied with his wife and available to them.

5. If a woman "cuts" down a man, she reveals her tendency to castrate him. This tendency is strong in women in whom, for some reason or other, there is a strong "penis envy." I believe that, essentially, every creature could be happy with the anatomy with which it was born. But it is not always so; there are periods of life in which a woman is not satisfied with having been born a female. A woman who was able to overcome her resentment of being a female is a well-balanced, healthy individual and will feel happy in her feminine role. Freud (1937) says, women's "strongest motive in coming for treatment was the hope that they might somehow still obtain a male organ, the lack of which is so painful to them" (p. 356). Women's resentment of their femininity is strongly presented by Simone de Beauvoir (1953).

The penis envy of women is expressed in different ways. One of the many is presented here by the use of the mannerism in "cutting off" the men when the latter tell a story. The reader who desires to know more about the psychoanalytic concept of the castration complex is referred to Freud's original writings (1905b) and to Sterba's book (1942).

Sexual frigidity with the aim of frustrating the man might be caused by the "penis envy" of the woman. Or, there is the (usually attractive) woman who makes a man fall in love and then demands so much from him that he finally commits criminal acts, even murder. The girl then goes to the prison and gives the man the "death kiss" before he goes to the electric chair.

Women also expose their husbands through "cutting" them down, thus indicating the sexual indifference of the husband toward them, or revealing the sexual weakness of the husbands. In addition, the use of this device could be a method of encouraging the courtship of other men, because the woman thus shows that she is frustrated and available.

6. If it is done by a woman to a woman, the woman who does the "cutting" reveals inferiority feelings, envy, jealousy and rivalry.

In all cases where "that's nothing" or "no" are used, the user intends to "cut" someone down to size, that is: to make him small, to render him a child. In many cases, it might be caused by deep-seated, repressed, latent homosexual tendencies.

"It surprises me"

Over a period of years, on several occasions, I have found myself fascinated by the phenomenon of surprise. Though I knew of Theodor Reik's book on the subject (1937), I abstained from reading it because I wanted to arrive independently at my own conclusions. After mentioning my theory of surprise to my students, I *then* read Reik's book. To "my great surprise," I realized that Reik and I had arrived at the same conclusions, namely: that in surprise, something expected but suppressed or repressed comes into consciousness. I am well acquainted with Reik's brilliant writings and agree with him on many matters. Knowing that Reik had written a whole book on the subject of surprise, I must have thought that our ideas might be identical, as they had been in many matters. Therefore, I intentionally suppressed my desire to read Reik's book. When I eventually did so and realized the identity of our conception of surprise, I "became surprised."

Let us now examine under what circumstances people, in their everyday life, use as mannerisms the "it surprises me" and the "you surprise me." Usually, these phrases are expressed in ill-concealed anger and annoyance. There is a great difference between one's having the feeling of surprise and merely saying that he is surprised though he is not. What interests us now is the hypocritical use of the phrase. The person who says "it surprises me" is *annoyed* but says that he is surprised. Without knowing it, he betrays that he *expected* the comment or the reaction of the person to whom he is talking *but pretends* that he did not, that he expected the other person to behave or react as the speaker *wanted* him to do.

There are persons who cannot tolerate an opinion contrary to their own. They want and expect everybody, *especially their friends*, to agree with them. They demand that the friends behave, think, and feel as they do. For example, Mr. X likes to vote for political party A, while his friend believes in party B. When the latter learns of his friend's preference for party A, he says with serious (mostly hypocritical) concern and disapproval on his face, "I heard with surprise that you are for party A." With this remark, he brings his friend to trial in which he is the supreme judge. He is not surprised; he *only says* he is. He is angry and disappointed. On the other hand, he is also right, because he must have expected this possibility as he did not know which party the other supported.

A woman born and raised in the South was visiting, with her adolescent boys, the other members of her family who

still lived there. At a family gathering, one of the aunts commented, indicating either by her facial expression or her tone
of voice, her surprise, "Your children have strange views.
They think that the Negroes are the equals of white people.
Did they get these views from you?" On receiving an affirmative answer, the aunt retorted, "Don't forget that our grand-
fathers were slave owners." The aunt, though she held firmly
to her prejudices, must have suspected that her sister had
changed her attitude about colored people after having lived
for many years in a place where people felt different about
Negroes. The aunt *expected* that her sister might feel different.

Mrs. A. meets Mrs. B. and they stop to chat. They are
neighbors.
Mrs. A.: "Have you heard about Mrs. C. [another neigh-
    bor]?"
Mrs. B.: "What?"
Mrs. A.: "She has a lover."
Mrs. B., who is my patient, does not say anything.
Mrs. A. (unable to rest and egging Mrs. B. on for a reac-
    tion): "What do you say to this?"
Mrs. B. (feeling she must react): "This is not my business."
Mrs. A.: "Would you associate with that woman?"
Mrs. B.: "She [Mrs. C.] is a nice woman. I feel sorry for
    her, but I would talk to her."
Mrs. A. (surprised and annoyed): "I certainly would not."

Mrs. B. has no lover and does not need or intend (even if
she should need) to have a lover. It is most probable that
Mrs. A. does not have a lover either; but the reader may
surmise that Mrs. A. entertains the idea of having a lover, that
she is suppressing such a desire, and that she *expects* the same
of all other women. She is not surprised; she only pretends
that she is.

Answering a question with a question
"How are you?"—"How am I?"
or
"How are you?"—"How should I be?"

There was a large, happy, close family in which the adult children were devoted to their aged parents. When the father died, the children showed even greater affection and devotion to their widowed mother. One of the sons was especially conscientious about telephoning his mother every day in addition to paying frequent visits. The following is a telephone conversation between mother and son:

Son: "How are you, Mother?"
Mother: "How should I be?"
Son: "What do you mean?"
Mother: "What do I mean?"
Son: "I am asking you how you feel?"
Mother: "How should a widow feel?"
Son: "I know this, Mother, but we all love you. You have a nice apartment, a comfortable living."
Mother: "Comfortable living; I am alone."
Son: "You are not always alone, Mother. We often visit you and I was there yesterday."
Mother: "Yes, yesterday, for half an hour."
Son: "We were all together the day before yesterday."
Mother: Yes, the day before yesterday."

This man knew nothing about analysis. He was sad, bitter, and angry. Finally, he burst out, "I wish she were dead." Mothers, do not do such things to your children or to yourselves even in such a sad situation.

A woman patient in a psychotic episode was transiently negativistic. She repeated every question addressed to her. To the question, "How are you?" she replied, for example, "How am I?" She thus acted out, instead of remembering, a period in which there was complete distrust of her mother. The patient was never sure that her mother talked to her out of loving interest or out of a desire to get something for herself from the girl. Sometimes the patient would say, "You are the doctor. You know better how I am." In this way, she transferred her distrust from her mother to the doctor. When she felt that the doctor's interest was genuine, her confidence was restored and the "echolalia" (echoing the heard words) ceased.

Other causes for this phenomenon are:

1. Repetition betrays a kind of stage fright. The person behaves as if he is left alone without emotional support and has to take care of himself. There is no contact with the other person. The need to repeat the question is a sort of crutch. It is, in the last analysis, a clinging (to mother). This can be observed in pure culture in children who like to get attention from others; but when such attention is offered them, they either run away (and soon return) or, if mother is present, cling to her for reassurance while they communicate with the other person.

When my daughter was about two and a half years old, we took one of our cherished and habitual walks. We passed a house which she often visited because it was the place where one of her girl friends of the same age lived. On these visits, she was accompanied by one of her parents or by a familiar member of the household. The house was not far away. Once I asked her: "Could you go to your friend's alone?"

"No," was her reply.

"You know the way. It is close to our house. You could do it," I encouraged her.

"No," she said. "I cannot reach the bell." (The house was in the middle of a large garden, surrounded by a fence which opened by a door in front.)

"Let's see. You *can* reach the bell," she was told. She tried and she could reach the bell.

"You should come with me," she insisted.

"Why?" I urged.

"When I ring the bell," she explained, "the janitor will hear it. He won't know that it is I [the janitor knew her from previous frequent visits] who rings the bell."

"That's true," I admitted, "but when he comes out of the house, he will notice you, recognize you and greet you." She still was not satisfied because she said:

"He won't smile at me until he recognizes me. For a while, he will not smile." I felt that she was still too young to be independent and accompanied her to the house. As she grew, she became independent, very much so.

2. Another reason for the repetition is the wish to gain time in order to think over and decide whether one should tell the truth or not.

3. The repetition is to a slight degree legitimate *if* the question is difficult to answer. Even in such a case, it is better to say that one needs time to answer instead of repeating what one has heard.

"I would be more than happy"

A doctor patient, a general practitioner, talked about a patient who came to him for advice. After his examination of the woman, he advised her to consult a psychiatrist. When the woman asked him if he would contact the psychiatrist for an appointment for her, he replied that he "would be more than happy to do so." I stopped him by asking what was more than happy. The patient said, "That's silly. There's nothing more than happy." He went on to explain that he used the phrase to be polite and that it was just a phrase he was in the habit of using. I asked whether the woman believed that the doctor would be "more than happy" to make the contact for her. I also suggested that he would sound more convincing if he said, simply, "I will do it."

Exuberant politeness may be pleasant momentarily; but,

in the mind of the receiver, an impression is created which, in my opinion, is felt by the communicant and plants the seed of distrust.

On making a vow
To swear
To promise

"Again, ye have heard that it hath been said by them of old time, Thou shalt not forswear thyself, but shalt perform unto the Lord thine oaths: But I say unto you, Swear not at all: neither by heaven; for it is God's throne: nor by the earth; for it is his footstool; neither by Jerusalem; for it is the city of the great King. Neither shalt thou swear by thy head, because thou canst not make one hair white or black. But let your communication be, Yea, yea; Nay, nay: for whatsoever is more than these, cometh of evil."

Matthew 5:33-37

In Hungary, a young, married business man of high standing made a vow that if Hitler were defeated, he would stop smoking. His family, friends and acquaintances knew about the vow and were very much pleased that he was able to carry out his vow. The writer knows the man. He does not smoke.

In everyday human relations, one can often observe that individuals, in order to give strength to their words, say, "I swear on my life," or "I promise." Parents make their children promise to do or not to do certain things. Adults give their "word of honor" as if to underline that they will live up to their promises. A host of people committing a grave and serious offense, sexual or otherwise, vow to discontinue or never to repeat the offense by attaching the clause to their vow that they should die if they violate it. Moreover, some people, to make their vow still stronger, add to the clause that their children should die in case of a violation of the vow. The latter means that if the man does not keep his vow, he will be responsible for the death of his children.

The pages of the Bible as well as the history of mankind are full of pertinent examples.

No person other than a psychoanalyst may be in a position to unravel the psychological background in a person who makes such a promise or vow and to follow up the consequences.

A woman of high moral standards, under the influence of her childhood experiences, committed what she thought a grave offense which she deeply regretted. She made a vow that she would never do it again, and kept it. After making the vow, she gradually developed a grave neurosis. Both the therapist and the patient realized, in the course of treatment, that one of the forces which stubbornly maintained the neurosis was the fear that she might violate the vow. I explained to her that a *vow is an insincere or weak decision;* if she sincerely *decides* not to repeat the offense, she is more secure than if she makes a vow. A vow permits a person to continue to entertain, at least, the pleasurable though offensive idea; a decision does not.

I believe that the same is valid for a promise, a word of honor or an oath.

A vow, a promise, or an oath indicates that the person uses self-threat or is submitted to threat, while a decision indicates an independent, automatically functioning and integrated force in the personality. A vow makes us insecure and leaves open the possibility of repeating an offense. A decision is final. If a decision does not work, it was *not* a decision; it was a vow. The inability to make a decision indicates a neurosis. The reader may realize that psychoanalysis, by helping a person to build up a "true superego," helps him also to achieve the most basic ethical character of humanity.

Telling more than asked for

There are persons from whom it is impossible to obtain a straightforward answer, a "yes" or "no." They tell more. The causes differ and are sometimes very touching, as in the case of my late mother. In her late years, she became a widow. Only one of her ten children was living with her, but several others lived in the same city. She was a model of the "grand lady," an inexhaustible fountain of kindness, love, and wisdom. All who knew her loved her.

I called her often on the telephone but could afford to visit her only once or twice a week for about an hour. It is the lot of an analyst that he has not as much time for his mother as he would like to have. She was the "button-holding mother" about whom I wrote a brief chapter in the already quoted paper on "Mannerisms of speech" (1948), from which I take the following excerpt:

Convincing evidence that words or gestures may be habitually employed because of fear of separation and of being left alone was furnished by an elderly woman, the mother of ten children. When the children grew up, and went their ways, she developed certain habits when talking to them, which later, especially after she was widowed, extended into her relations with everyone who came to visit and talk with her. After arousing her listener's interest in her story, she would abandon it and talk about other things. In this way, she kept her visitor pinned down for a long time until she finally came back to the subject and settled it. Another of her habits was to grasp the hand, the arm or the garment of the person until she released him. When this was called to her attention, she said smilingly: "I am a lonely woman. Who wants to talk to an old woman? Nobody. Sure, people and my children like to come to see me; but only for a short time; after all they all have their own lives and are busy. I handle the situation by keeping them and forcing them to spend time with me" [p. 366].

On one occasion when her son visited his mother, the following conversation took place:

Mother: "Do you know Mr. A?"
Son: "No, Mother, who is he?"
Mother: "He is living in town X."
Son: "And . . ."
Mother: "He has a daughter."
Son: (already with some impatience): "And . . . , Mother?"
Mother: "She is married to a Mr. B. Do you know him?"
Son: "No, Mother, I do *not* [irritation rises] know him."
Mother: "The daughter of Mr. A. is married to Mr. B."
Son: "And . . . ?"
Mother: "Wait. Don't be so impatient. I'll tell you."
Son: "Ye-e-e-es?"
Mother: "The grocer told me yesterday that he bought new mattresses. This reminded me that my mattresses were worn out. I talked about this to my grocer and during the conversation, it turned out that he bought the mattresses from Mr. B., and the grocer told me also that the father of Mr. B. is the Mr. B. who was your father's student. So, I went to Mr. A's shop and he sold me, with a discount, beautiful mattresses."

After many conversations of this kind, the son understood his mother's aim; and when he visited her, he listened patiently and enjoyed hearing his mother begin each new story like the heroine of *Thousand and One Nights*.

In a certain session, a patient was speaking about his son. When I asked about the age of the boy, the patient, instead of giving the age, paused and concentrated for a while and then gave an *exact* date, August 7, 1945. He gave the birthdate and not the approximate age of the child. He knew full well that, at this point, such exactness was not warranted. Why did he do this? He was always afraid that he did not have much to say; therefore, he seized every opportunity to talk more than necessary whenever anyone asked him a question. But this was not all. The man had important things to hide, especially from his wife, and thought that he had to be extremely careful of what he said and how he said it because his wife was very smart and suspicious. When talking to his wife, he preferred to talk "mechanically," to avoid entering into long conversations, and to stress data which, he felt, could not give him away.

Similar, though not identical, compulsiveness was shown by another patient. This young man once went on a business trip and returned to his town at 12:05 A.M. Next day, he met a friend who asked him when he had returned, to which question he answered that he had come back the previous night. No sooner had he parted from his friend than he realized that he had not returned last night but today since he had arrived at 12:05 A.M. He could not rest; he felt the need to correct his "mistake," but he also felt that he could not do so because he would be ridiculed for his foolish exactness. Therefore, he found an excuse to meet his friend, talked about different matters and, at one point, he said, "By the way," and told the exact time of his arrival.

A man in analysis talked about a couple, each of whom was married for the second time and each of whom had children from the first marriage. I asked the patient whether they had children from the present marriage. Instead of saying "yes" or "no," he went into lengthy details and explanations which had nothing to do with our aims. I call this kind of response *"resistance-free-association"*; and this resistance, too, should be subjected to analysis. It turned out that this mannerism was characteristic of the patient and stemmed from a deep complex, hidden in his mind. As the aim of this study is to present only those parts of the history that are pertinent to the description of revealing mannerisms, it suffices to say that this man was very much pleased whenever somebody talked to him. This otherwise very intelligent, talented and successful man was afraid of everybody, especially of self-asserting persons. Because of this fear, he became submissive to the point of a passive-homosexual tendency, which he repressed (it was latent). Telling more than necessary meant giving himself up to the other person, even at the expense of his masculinity. This latent homosexuality did not affect his sexual functions, but it crippled his self-esteem which then burst out in neurotic symptoms.

I once called up my friends, a couple who are very nice people. The wife answered the telephone and I asked whether I could speak to her husband. Instead of saying "yes" or "no," she went into a lengthy story which she had to tell before giving me the answer I wanted.

Another time, she asked a simple favor of me which I was glad to confer, first, because I was generally happy to do so, and, second, because this couple would go out of their way to do whatever is possible for me or for anyone else. They are "suckers." She apologized for the necessity of asking me this favor.

This lady was never in analysis; but from impressions and information gained by personal contact with the couple, I feel entitled to surmise that with her, too, there is a great need to lengthen the conversation in order to give her the gratification of being listened to, considered, accepted and appreciated. Because their status and social situation changed for the worse, they were frustrated; and she had to make up for this by using different mannerisms, one of which was not to talk to the point but to say more. The apologies she made were caused by a fear of failing or boring the listener.

Another important factor in garrulity, in many cases, is "oral eroticism," manifested in the intense pleasure of speaking. "The longing to experience gratification by way of sucking has changed in them to a need to *give* by way of the mouth," as Jelliffe and White (1917) put it.

In many other cases, talkativeness, loquacity, aims to avoid the issue. Ferenczi (1915a) noticed that superficial talk during a session is a sign of resistance in order to avoid talking about essential things.

A woman patient has some house guests about whom she has ambivalant feelings. She says that they are all right, but she feels burdened by them. Later, when the analyst asks whether the visitors have left, the patient replies in the affirmative but continues talking. She does so because she thinks that the analyst will be suspicious.

In the analysis of the mannerism, it was found that this woman's relations with her mother were bad. Whenever the mother came, she stayed only for one day. The patient always thought that other people would be curious as to the reason the mother did not stay longer with her daughter and the grandchildren. Because the patient did not have the heart to tell the truth, she talked more and more, thus creating suspicion. Even though, in this instance, the mother had not been visiting, the patient, who did not want to tell the truth, used the same technique. She did so in every relationship.

Many "sales talks" are, therefore, annoying and fail to achieve their aims because the customer understands the tendency, becomes suspicious and feels insulted by being held stupid.

I once had a cook whose husband, a poor, sick, alcoholic creature, often came to the house to call for his wife, to get some charity food, to earn some money by doing odd jobs around the house, and to borrow money in emergency. He always received the money and "worked it off." He was very loquacious, whether he wanted money or not. He considered himself "as belonging to the family" (to use his own words). One day at lunch, I found him again in the kitchen. After his customary greeting of "Hi, doc," he began the following conversation:

Joe: "Do you know Mrs. Smith?"
I: (reacting viciously and feeling guilty for his attitude): "How much do you want?"
Joe: "Wait, doc. Do you know her?"
I: "Why? I do not know her."

Joe: "I met her and she asked me how I am. I told her that I am in trouble. She asked me what trouble I was in and I told her that tomorrow is the deadline to pay the remittance for my life insurance, eight dollars, and I haven't got the money."

I: (already feeling my estate diminished by eight dollars): "And. . . ?"

Joe: "She asked me who I work for and I told her that I am working for Dr. Feldman. She said, 'Oh, Dr. Feldman? I know that he is a good man. I am sure that he will give you the money.' "

He does not have the "ego strength" to ask directly for the badly needed money. He is afraid to come out straight with his request. He first needs to bolster up his "ego," by hiding behind someone else.

Evasive speech, as a form of resistance, is a frequently observed phenomenon in patients in analysis. Evans (1953), in a penetrating paper, has described this form of resistance. It manifests itself, according to Evans, in the frequent use of "maybe" or "sort of." I agree with Evans that pompous phraseology and high-sounding words also belong to evasive speech and that "in this type of evasive speech, words are used primarily to convey not meaning but rather an impression of gravity and importance" (p. 553).

The importance of oral eroticism in speech was emphasized also by A. J. Westerman Holstijn (1932), who said that indulging in "grand words" or in the habit of "talking big" made, not the content, but the speech itself important, as in mania.

The aggressive element in loquacity (logorrhoea) i.e., to pin the listener down for a long time with a flood of words, is mentioned by Bergler (1947).

Making long introductions before getting to the point, talking in minute details, is a characteristic and revealing mannerism of many people. Two examples from analytic practice will illustrate the background of *circumstantiality*. Both patients used this manner of talking not only in my office but also in their communications with other persons. One was a male intellectual who took about thirty minutes to say what he could have said in two sentences. He was a compulsive neurotic with many rituals and ceremonials in his daily activities. He adopted circumstantial talk as a defense technique against his father who was dreadfully controlling of him and who demanded of him to be excessively exact. Furthermore, he was afraid, at the age of eighteen to twenty, that he might be caught by his father in having sex relations with the maid. He had to be very minute to be sure that there were no contradictions in what he said. Therefore, in addition to being circumstantial, he talked carefully and slowly.

The other was a female patient with remarkable intellectual abilities and a sharp mind; but the way she talked was a torture to the listener, who hardly had a chance even to make a single comment. I understood that this sabotage was a symptom, called her attention to her manner of speech, and emphasized that this was a sign of strong resistance to revealing something essential. She agreed and became quite interested in the analysis of this phenomenon. Her attention was frequently called to this mannerism; and in response to this urge, she had a dream. The dream was revealing and characteristic of her, being again circumstantial. (In my experience, certain analytic patients bring to the session several lengthy dreams, even written down, so that their recital takes up the whole hour, leaving no chance for getting to the possible dream thoughts which are the most essential part of the dream analysis. In such cases, I temporarily suspend the presentation of dreams as a therapeutic measure.) The dream of the patient was as follows:

There was this woman—in front of me—a little to my left and higher up as if she were floating on air. She was dressed in a severely tailored tweed suit. I especially remember her sen-

sible shoes—large bag and her severe hat. Yet she was faceless
—had only back really—seemed to have no figure on top in
front; and yet I was not disturbed by it. It seemed natural that
she should look that way and she was familiar. She was talking
to X [the man she loved]—talking down—as he was on my
right and a little lower than I. I did not really see X clearly in
the dream either; but again, it was because he was so familiar.
I knew it was X. That's why I did not have to bother to picture
him. So the woman spoke. I did not see her speak nor hear a
word; yet she spoke. And then, she turned around and walked
away—upwards—disappearing into the air. And suddenly, I
had a revelation, "Let her go." I called to X, "Don't you see
that she was jealous? The poor thing is jealous and does not
even know it." And then, it was as if suddenly a light had gone
on and a weight had fallen off and, with laughter and happiness, I almost shouted, "Why, that was me. Don't you see that
I was that woman? I was jealous and I did not know it." And
I went on to say to him that the reason she spoke so much and
in so much detail was that she had an inferiority complex, not
believing she was good enough and interesting enough to be
listened to if she were to tell just a plain tale. But if she could
prolong it and make it sound real impressive, she could make
people listen and believe. And then suddenly, I wasn't talking
any more, but thinking and racing after my thoughts, and
talking again quietly stumbling along—as if a door had suddenly opened and this was my chance to see everything and
I must not let it slip away; and I raced on and on and said
now I see everything. The reason I always talk in such detail
is to make it sound interesting; otherwise, I do not believe
myself worthy of attention and the reason I repeat and repeat
is that I want to impress the fact that it's really so—or they
may not believe and then I thought, "But I always knew that
but what I did not know till now was that I wanted to belong;
I wanted to be part—that in silence I could be shut out but
if I wanted to be part of a group, I could talk my way in. I
could convince them to like me." And then there was the
counter feeling—suddenly, I realized how right you were. I
did talk down to people—not really talk down—but take over

—race away with the subject—make people feel inferior. I interrupt. I stick to my theme, my way of thought and talk no matter what—I have to bring home my point. I did not want to hear what the other had to say. I wanted them to listen to me, and while they talked, I was preparing what I was going to say and I would take over again and monopolize. I had to show off, just plain show off—impress the other person with my knowledge and wisdom. Again because I wanted to be liked and admired and the more I went about it that way, the less I succeeded—and the harder I tried. I did not listen to the other person and learn—but no matter how amazed and impressed I was, I was too busy trying to bring home my own point, as soon as I could interrupt to tell the other person how well I thought of what he said. And all the time the thoughts or words [she wrote worlds] rush in and tumble out after one another. I have the feeling that now where I know— that I can change it all with application and work and that everything will be all right. Even about the feeling of jealousy, I felt that once I recognized it, I shall be able to conquer it.

This was the amazing dream which speaks for itself. The faceless woman in the dream represents the dreamer herself, the part of her personality she resists knowing. Usually, this feature of the dream work appears in sexual dreams when a man makes love to a woman whose face or head is either covered or appears as if in a cloud, not recognizable. The love object is not identified. Such a dream always means that the man entertains a desire to make love to a forbidden object, usually an incestuous object or its derivative, a representative of it.

The incapacity to get "to the point," circumstantiality as such, was studied by Hart (1953). Taking the genetic approach, he succeeds in tracing circumstantiality to three stages of psychosexual development (Freud). As far as the oral influence is concerned, Hart says that "Time and reality are ignored by the prolonged oral pleasure of circumstantial talk. This also holds true for the babe at the breast. The pleasant

flow of words is equated with the pleasant flow of milk . . ."
(p. 271). In circumstantial talk, the talk is a mess, a sign of
regression to the infantile stage when making a mess with the
bowel content was a pleasure (p. 276). And last, Hart mentions urethral eroticism. He refers to the papers of Sharpe
(1940) and Abraham (1925). The urinary flow through the
urethra is also experienced as pleasurable. As a character derivative, this might appear later as pointless talk (p. 278). My
own clinical experiences confirm the findings of these authors.

"As you remember"
"As you may remember"
"As you may recall"

The analytic situation (by virtue of the prolonged contact
with the therapist) is especially conducive to the use of such
phrases as "as you remember," "as you may remember," and
"as you may recall." Some patients use them with the same
frequency in their communication outside the analysis. And
listening to the manner in which people talk, the reader will
experience this habit with many people from all walks of life.
Another condition favorable to the use of these phrases is
created when the listener is considered by the speaker as a
superior or an authority.

Everybody, whether he is aware of it or not, considers himself very important and wants to be so considered by everybody else. There was a time when prime importance and the
feeling of prime importance was given to us, when we were
babies. When a baby gives a sign, a cry, or a sound or makes
a gesture, the environment, first through the person of the
mother, understands the signs and acts to gratify the baby.
The "baby" is beautiful, wonderful, clever; every bit of
progress he makes is admired, appreciated, noticed. This is the
"megalomania of childhood" and the "period of unconditional
omnipotence," as Ferenczi (1913) called it. This feeling of
absolute importance has to be abandoned under the pressure

of reality. It is hard to accomplish this task. The extent to which the feeling of omnipotence operates in humanity can be seen by the frequent use of such manneristic phrases as "as you remember" and "as you may remember" as well as other similar expressions. One of the outstanding signs of being important is to remember everything one has heard, noticed, observed or experienced in connection with another person. In love relations, it is absolutely mandatory that one remember all these things. If he fails, the other person is hurt. A person must remember the birthday of his wife and the anniversaries of his friends; he must remember what his love object wore when he met her several decades ago; he must notice (*and he does* when he "really" loves her) a new hat, a new belt, or the slightest change in her hairdo; and it is especially important to remember what she has said. The same is true to a lesser extent in every relation. There is a constant fear of revealing that one does not remember all that he is expected to remember. The manneristic phrases used by so many persons serve the purpose of dealing with the afore-mentioned controversial wishes, demands, defenses. They are begging for attention; express hope that the listener remembers; beg for confirmation of the fact that he does remember; threaten a person in case he does not remember; intend to deny such a threat; and they contain an apology for wanting one to remember.

"And you don't know this?"

Men are more ambivalent toward each other than are women. There is a solidarity between women to the extent that they acknowledge the beauty and other good qualities of each other, even if they are rivals, more easily than do men. Men do not; they seize every opportunity to "cut" each other down. Even when they are friends, on several occasions, the desire to eliminate each other breaks through. Every man would like to be the only male and possess all women.

This vicious aggression manifests itself in many subtle ways. It exists in all of us, and it takes us a long time and causes us a hard struggle before we can recognize and overcome it, "de-aggressivize" it (Hartmann), and turn it into constructive aggressiveness: to help, to teach, to learn and to be firm. In many persons an erotic element is attached to aggressiveness: a pleasure to hurt, to cause pain, and to inflict physical and mental misery, torture on the other person (sadism).

Since my very early childhood, I have loved to study and to learn. I have some specific and some general knowledge, yet I often realize that I do not know certain things that a man of my professional standing should know; but I know it not. Therefore, I ask those who know more than I do. Once I asked a brilliant young scientist for some information. Before giving the requested information, the young man said, "And you don't know this?" Obviously, I did not; otherwise, there would have been no sense in asking. The scientist knew this. Because he was frustrated at the time and considered me a successful man in my field, he probably needed to cut me down and make me realize, before answering, what an ignorant person I was. I told the young man that I had asked a question and was entitled to an answer and not a humiliation. The scientist is not the only one who does this. The readers, I trust, have had such experiences, or have themselves done the same thing to others.

Referring to a third person in order to prove that one is right

In scientific papers or discussions, it is legitimate to refer to a third person or persons in order to prove one is right or to refer to other workers who have had ideas similar to one's own. The aim of so doing is to pay credit to them and to gain support for oneself through them. This chapter, on the other hand, concerns itself with the use of the mannerism of referring to a third person for support in everyday conversations. Even in the latter case, it is legitimate to refer to an *authority of knowledge*, whether this authority is a book or a person, when one wants to verify the truth of a fact which was expressed. The use of the mannerism is not legitimate when the communicant has an *emotional* need for the support of the authority and hopes that the listener has the same need and will blindly accept the statement. For example, one woman who could never express what she thought herself always referred to the group. It was her habit to say, "The girls [her bridge group] told me . . ."

A woman who had a very unhappy childhood always sought the friendship of other women to replace her mother who had frustrated her. She found solace in the companionship of a sort of sister. There were a series of subsubstitutes for mother. It was impossible for any man to satisfy her because she behaved like a problem child and men could not "understand" her. The girl friends she had chosen were themselves unhappy and frustrated; they exchanged their grievances and this kept them together and cemented a lasting relation between them.

One day, this woman received a letter which hurt and upset her. In answer, she replied, "The content of your letter upset me. *I showed the letter to X.* [a close girl friend], *and she couldn't believe it.*"

Another time, she was happy about a certain event. She reported this to a friend and added, "*I wrote about it to my sister.*" She always had to cling to somebody else. She had to connect anything that happened to her with another person. Therefore, there was no thought, no emotion, no affect which she could have felt as hers because she would rather have given up her identity than to be independent. To be independent meant aloneness to her. She complained that she was not wanted as a child. She felt herself to be unimportant and to be one who does not count. She had to replace herself by another person because she thought that any other person would count. Sometimes, she displayed a defensive self-love, considering herself the most clever, the most attractive, the most talented person who did not need to learn because she knew everything herself. She was clever; she was attractive, but she still felt empty. She could not love; she loved only herself; she wanted only to be loved. But even if she were loved, she could not be happy because the love was needed only to compensate for her frustrations. Everything was "as if": sorrow or happiness. She was a classical example of the "as if" persons described first by Helene Deutsch (1934).

"Do you see what I mean?"

In the paper published in 1948, I mentioned the following cases:

> The main complaint of a female patient was that she had a strong, undefinable feeling of guilt which had persisted from her early youth and from which all her symptoms seemed to spring. From the time of her mother's death she had a recurrent nightmare in which, coming home to where she lived with her mother, she realized to her great horror that she had completely forgotten her for many days, that she had not prepared food for her, and that her mother was starving. Often, after awakening, she felt that the events of the dream were real and she had to assure herself that it was only a dream.
>
> Her mother had been an invalid for many years. All her children were deeply devoted to her and had done everything for her comfort, as had the patient who, indeed, considered herself and was considered by others to be a most devoted, self-sacrificing daughter. But it was not an easy task to gratify the mother's demands. The patient had always a tense awareness of caring for her mother. Her own sense of well-being was dependent on whether she felt she was doing enough for her mother. It was a great relief to her, whenever, for a short time, arrangements could be made which pleased the sick mother.
>
> One day, in association to a recurrence of the nightmare, the

patient described an incident in which her mother had expressed dissatisfaction, and the patient had gone to great trouble to provide more satisfactory living conditions for her. She thought she had solved the problem for some time and that she would have now an opportunity to devote herself without worry to her own affairs; however, hardly a day had passed before the patient found her mother in the same dejected and complaining conditions. At this point the patient exclaimed: "My heart sank into my shoes; I was dejected and in despair"; then, raising her arms and dropping them to her sides in a tragic gesture, she said: "Do you know what I mean?" At a similar point earlier in her narrative she used the expression, "Do you *see* what I mean?" The writer replied: "I know what you mean but I wonder whether *you* know what you mean." At this point the patient raised her voice and with resignation mixed with desperation said: "I know what you want me to say; you want me to say that at that time I had the feeling that I wished my mother should die. Yes, I did."

If the patient had not been led to her own interpretation of "Do you know what I mean?" the opportunity to bring her to the source of her underlying unconscious feelings of guilt could have been missed. When a patient whose statements are articulate and coherent still employs "Do you see what I mean?" then it must have some meaning which, in correct analysis, has to be verbalized.

A male patient had an impulsive urge to look conspicuously at women's legs or low-cut blouses (including the women in his family), and at men's trousers. He started one session with: "I saw your daughter on the street. It wasn't the first time that I have seen her. I am interested in her, not only and mainly because she is a pretty girl, but because she is your daughter! Do you see what I mean?" Why does the patient need to ask when he says it so clearly? It is because he omitted something, because he is repressing something important. At this point the ego is split into a part which wants the analyst to understand only as much as he says, and into another part which, for the sake of the cure, hopes that the analyst will see the repressed content. At this stage of the analysis his passive latent homosexuality was under investigation. Looking conspicuously at women serves as an identification with a woman for homosexual purposes, masked by the seemingly heterosexual interest. In a second layer the analyst's daughter substitutes for the analyst's wife and refers to the primal scene experienced in early childhood [pp. 358-359].

[The term "primal scene" denotes the observance of parental intercourse at a very early infancy, as described by Freud (1918).]

Since completing the foregoing paper, I have collected several other examples of the mannerism under discussion, some of which will be presented subsequently.

Is there ever a legitimate reason to ask a person with whom we speak, "Do you see (know) what I mean?" Does the speaker expect an answer? If so, is he prepared to hear a "no"? Will the listener answer honestly? If the listener is convinced, he will readily say "yes"; but even if he is not, he might still reply with a "yes" either because he does not want to disappoint the speaker or because he is afraid to say "no" when he would otherwise like to say "no."

A woman became aware that her husband, though he loved her, was seemingly more interested in females of ill repute who were less attractive than she. She complained, "I noticed lately that he does not sleep in our bed as before, but makes his bed on the couch in the same room, giving different reasons for his strange attitude. Do you see what I mean?"

The analyst asks, "What do you mean?"
The patient replies: "He is impotent with me and doesn't want this to come into the open."

In this case, "Do you see what I mean?" is used to avoid mentioning the painful facts.

During a session, Mrs. X. talked about a man. She said, "I don't like him. He gives me the impression of being a 'fairy.' It is not conspicuous, but he has a way of doing such little things, gestures, and so on. Do you know what I mean?" The use of the question here seems to be legitimate as the patient had difficulty finding the words for adequate portrayal. But even in this case, we have to take into consideration that Mrs. X. is a very good speaker, has a rich vocabulary, and expresses herself very well on all matters; furthermore, she was for a while homosexually involved, and we are looking for subtle signs of this tendency in her. The difficulty could have stemmed from this source.

Sometimes, the "do you see what I mean?" expresses the speaker's superior attitude toward the listener: "Are you able, you stupid one, to understand what I, the brilliant person, am telling you?"

A grown girl worked in her father's small business. When she came into the store, her first action was to look into the cash register to ascertain whether it contained enough money *for the day*. (Her father came to the store earlier than she and had already done some selling.) When in her narrative she reached this point, she said, "Do you see what I mean?" Behind her use of the mannerism was a characterological trend, namely, that with her everything *always* has to be perfectly good; otherwise she does not accept life. From early youth, she felt, in comparing her lot with that of the other children in her family, that she had been cheated and expected life to make up for this deprivation for all her remaining years. Furthermore, she felt cheated because she was born a girl and not a boy. Freud realized that the "exceptions" are mainly among women. He writes, "As we learn from psychoanalytic work, women regard themselves as wronged from infancy, as undeservedly cut short and set back; and the embitterment of so many daughters against their mothers derives, in the last analysis, from the reproach against her for having brought them into the world as women instead of as men" (1915, p. 323).

A physician patient, in analysis because of severe depressions, often used the phrase, "Do you see what I mean?" His father, who did not believe in him, often said that, in his opinion, the son could not do anything well. For this reason, the patient felt inferior, and therefore wanted to make sure whether he spoke clearly or not and whether the listener understood him.

The reader, by this time, can realize that it would be a forced attempt to make completely distinct classifications and to establish clear-cut types in persons using one or another of the mannerisms. As has been previously mentioned, some writers believe that they can, to some extent, make such classifications. Even if it were possible to classify persons into certain constitutional groups on the basis of their different environments, the classifications would have to change because people become different. But, on the other hand, Freud found the libidinal basis for the choice of neurosis (the libido theory of Freud).

"You see"

The "you see" is not the same as the "do you see (know) what I mean?" The "you see" is not a question; it is a phrase which comprises statement, encouragement, self-confidence, confidence in the listener, self-encouragement, pleading, threat, superiority and the like.

It is used by many teachers and lecturers. They may use it out of a fear that their listeners are not interested in what they have to say. In other cases, it is used because of the need to cling to the listener. Talking means self-assertion, assuming independence with all its responsibilities. If the speaker is afraid of responsibility, he reverts to clinging (as to a mother), and achieves this through the use of the phrase, "you see." Or, when the speaker does not take the time necessary for his presentation, he wants to say the least and still be understood.

"Is something wrong, dear?"—"Nothing."

Friends, most married couples, agree to meet and have a nice evening. They go to a pleasant restaurant. Everything is fine. When it is time to leave, the members of the party rise but stand around the table for a while. In the group is a recently married couple. Suddenly the young wife bursts out in a bitter cry. The husband, who was not sitting near his wife, rushes to her with, "What happened, dear? Is something wrong, dear?" Either there is no reply; or she says coldly, bitterly, resolutely, "Nothing." Behind this "nothing," there is everything which is emotionally important. Friends try to comfort her, urging her to tell the cause of her upset. At first she refuses, but soon she tells what troubles her. She is reluctant to tell it to her husband; but it is finally revealed that her husband, for the first time since their marriage, "forgot" to help her with her coat. If there is a strong affect, there must be an appropriate ideational content belonging to it (Freud). The wife is right; her husband's attention is not so strong as it was before his "forgetting"; and she cannot tell him of her misery and its cause. If she does so, he will be *intentionally* careful and attentive (in order to avoid trouble); and she will never know for the rest of their lives whether the attention is genuine and spontaneous or a defense against being scolded, nagged at, and punished.

Mrs. T. is building a house. As in all such cases, difficulties are encountered but overcome; and the building goes on. Mrs. T. meets a woman "friend" in front of the house.

Friend (with a concerned look on her face): "Is anything wrong?"

Mrs. T.: "No, nothing is wrong."

Friend: "You can tell *me*. I am sorry that something is wrong."

Mrs. T.: "But nothing is wrong."

The friend shows an expression of being peeved and disappointed. She expects and wishes to hear that something is wrong. Under the guise of promising to feel compassion for Mrs. T., the friend wants to extract from the latter an admission of some trouble that she would like to hear. The friend envies Mrs. T.

The reader may be angry with the writer who, although probably right, may be doing harm by unraveling the meaning of a drive that people need to use in their plights of life. What harm can there be in using such innocent little things as crutches in love tiffs and other social interactions and communications?

Yet, in my experience, these mannerisms are harmful. At the time they are used, they serve a purpose—the same that any other symptom serves: solving a conflict. But such a solution, in the long run, causes harm because it keeps the ego in an inferior, immature condition.

"I say—he says"
"He says—I say"

It is extremely irritating to listen to a speaker who makes excessive use of the mannerism, "I say—he says; he says— I say." A case invented on the basis of many true experiences would sound like this:

> I said to myself I am going to go and ask Joe to be a financial partner in a business undertaking. I said to him, "Look, Joe," I said, "this can be an excellent opportunity to make quick money," I said; and Joe said to me, "Look, Jim," he said, "I have to ask my father," he said; and I said to him, "Look, Joe," I said . . .

The use of this nauseating mannerism can be observed even in professional and well-educated people. There must be a strong complex behind this phenomenon, as there was in the case of a physician who used this mannerism to excess.

To him, conversing with someone, the personal relation, *was more important than the content*. The "I" and "he" relationship was laden with anxiety; the ego was struggling with two opposing tendencies: to keep himself submissively close to the other, while at the same time freeing himself from the listener.

The following case is quoted from "Mannerisms of Speech" (1948).

> A man of about forty used these phrases several times in every sentence. He was impotent with women, masturbated, had polymorphous-perverse tendencies. Outwardly, he was aggressive, self-sufficient and an effective businessman. In his social and emotional relations he was full of ill-disguised fears, especially of men. There were classical features of oral and genital fears of castration. When walking in lonely places he was afraid of being attacked by men who might consider him homosexual and misuse him; when walking with a girl he feared he might meet a gang of "tough" men who would take the girl from him . . . One might say that this patient was afraid to assert himself but, nevertheless, compelled himself to do so. The effort elicited anxiety from which he sought immunity by rituals of speech. He used "I say" and "He says" indiscriminately; moreover, he rendered "I say" erroneously as "I says." In this he was often corrected, but no matter how hard he tried to say it correctly, he always failed. His rationalization was that he came from a place where this error was habitually made, but he realized that his education and his conscious efforts could have rid him of it. In the writer's opinion, "I says" was for him less assertive than "I say" [pp. 362-363].

"Er—er—er"

It is the habit of many, many persons to exhibit a sort of moaning noise before they begin to talk to another person. In most cases, this noise is not restricted to the beginning but continues and persists throughout the whole conversation. The moaning-like "er . . . er . . . er . . ." is annoying, draws the conversation out to great length, and makes the listener, who is far ahead of the speaker, wait.

In "Mannerisms of Speech" (1948), I discussed a girl who was a victim of this speech habit. As a child, she thought that she meant a great deal to her mother; but certain events "convinced" her that she did not, that her mother was selfish, and that her mother's love was not genuine. She craved a "real" motherly love. She fantasied herself as a cocoon, living in the mother's womb. When she talked to another person, she did not want to talk like an adult. Through the "er . . . er . . . er," she clung to the listener like a child to its mother's apron strings.

A male patient whose speech was characteristically dotted by "er . . . er . . . er's" made use of this mannerism only when he was talking with a kindly listener and never when he was angry and dared to show his feelings. This man was very much under the control of his mother whose domination he considered it futile to oppose as he would lose anyhow. In order to suppress his anger while talking with his mother, he paused and filled the pauses with "er . . . er . . . er's." This attitude was later transferred to any other person with whom he was talking. Sometimes, when he had an outburst of too much accumulated anger and aggression, the mannerism was absent.

In general, one can say that whenever this mannerism is used for one reason or another there is anxiety present. This anxiety is handled, in the speech, by pauses which are filled by "er . . . er . . . er." The mannerism is a crutch. Often, the reasons for hesitation in speaking fluently are conscious, as in the case of the speaker who hesitates before deciding what to say, how to say it, or whether to say anything at all. In many other cases, the speaker is not conscious of the use of the mannerism. Then its motivations must be unraveled. Such an attempt may reveal that the "er . . . er . . . er" was originally used in childhood, in situations when the child was afraid to

speak and disclose what he wanted because of the presence
of the father or of another authoritative person.

"As usual"

When one sees a sign saying "business as usual during
alterations," one has the feeling that the text is legitimate
because it conceals little or nothing.

A male patient said, "I met my girl friend, as usual, Tuesday." Here, the "as usual" is partly legitimate because it is
information, and partly not because he has told this several
times. In repeating the information, he conceals his concern
that his analyst might have forgotten it; and he, like everybody else, desires that he and what he says should be remembered. To him, remembering means not only that the analyst
is competent, but also that the analyst likes him.

In cases like the following, the mannerism conceals or conveys a drive, a tendency, which, though not frank or out-
spoken, is still perceived by the reader or listener.

A father is irritated by the fact that his son needs psychiatric treatment for which the father has to pay. The son,
who is not a patient of mine, talks bitterly about a letter his
father wrote. The father lives in another city and sends his
son a monthly check. In the particular letter about which the
son complains, the father wrote, "Enclosed, *as usual*, you will
find a check for $ . . ." (italics by the author). Both father
and son know full well that the father sends a monthly check
which defrays the expenses of the treatment. Why, then,
does the father write the "as usual"? It is an oblique attack
against the son. Instead of writing frankly that "the check is
enclosed" and either expressing his annoyance or omitting it
completely, he interlards the message with "as usual" for a
purpose, which is that the son should *perceive* the father's
anger but should not be able to criticize him for it. The father
is, thus, in a position of asserting that he *"only"* writes the

"as usual" to register the facts and that his son is wrong in assuming that the father has ulterior motives in using those two words.

"Don't worry. It will be worse"

"Don't worry. It will be worse" is used by two communicating persons who are close to and sympathetic toward each other or who pretend that they are.

A. talks to B. about his apprehensions, about sad things which have already taken place, and then adds to the story, "Don't worry. It will be worse." The mechanism of this mannerism is delicate and complicated. It can be broken down into the following thoughts:

"Worry. It might become worse."

"Don't worry even if it does get worse."

"Don't worry. It will not become worse."

"Worry with me even if it does not become worse."

"Worry. I worry too."

There is a tendency to overcome the worry by creating an unexpected contrast which draws the interest away from the worry and brings relief. The speaker compensates for the worry by being interesting and witty.

"Hi, stranger"

A man visits his friends who resent or pretend to resent his not coming to see them for a long period of time. They greet him with a happy, smiling face and the words, "Hi, stranger." It is understood that they recognize the visitor, that he is not a stranger; but they are angry and resentful against him for neglecting them. They need not have missed him tremendously. They are resentful that *he* did not come, and that it is *he* who did not want them. *They* want to have the privilege of accepting or rejecting the visitor.

"Hi, lucky"

A group of able and successful doctors, working in the same place, often congregate at meetings, for discussions, in the elevator, at the lunch table, or in the parking lot. They are all about the same age and at the peak of their careers. They are all hard-working people who want to be financially secure when they get old. Besides having different kinds of insurances, they play the stock market and engage in several other kinds of business enterprises. Though they talk somewhat cautiously (as most people do concerning money matters) about their business activities, something always leaks out. Dr. A., one of my patients, made an investment which appears to be lucrative. He meets Dr. B., who greets him with a loud-sounding, "Hi, lucky."

Dr. A. has positive knowledge that Dr. B. too has investments, perhaps more than he himself; but Dr. B. never talks about them. He prefers to remain silent on the matter though he anxiously fishes for information on what the others are doing. He is probably afraid to miss an opportunity, and he is envious of the successes of the others. Moreover, he would like to be the only successful investor. He is afraid of the envy of his "friends," and tries to make believe that he is a poor, naïve guy, while the others are lucky.

In listening to patients, one observes such fears frequently. It is always an encouraging sign when, in the analytic situation, one characteristic of which is mutual confidence, the patient, instead of saying *only* that he "made a nice profit" or that he "got a nice check from father" will tell the sum of the profit or the amount of the check. They have the amounts in their minds and are supposed to say everything that occurs to them. If they do not, it is close to impossible to make them say what is repressed if they are afraid to say what is not repressed.

"Hello, Professor"

In Europe, one lost his case if one did not address a medical man as "Professor" when the latter had a right to this title. In our democracy, this is not done among medical men. They are all "doctors." In their official capacity, under certain conditions and in certain exceptional situations, they might use the title, "Professor." Even a first year medical student addresses a Nobel-prize-winning medical man as "doctor."

While preparing myself for immigration to this country, in 1939, I took English lessons for a few short months from a Hungarian man who had spent several years in the United States, working in some capacity at a Hungarian consulate. When I arrived in the United States, I had to forget everything I had learned from this teacher. The latter, besides being a poor English "teacher" (he liked to be called "Professor"), was a fool. When he came to my house, he made a deep bow and very reverently said, "How do you doooo . . ., Professor." Even though he was asked not to say "Professor" (I had not yet earned the title), he insisted not for the *pupil's* sake but for *his* own. He considered himself great when he was teaching not a simple "doctor" but a "professor."

Arriving in this country, I realized that I knew nothing, nothing whatsoever about English. I learned English in a school for immigrants which I attended for about ten months. The teacher was a wonderful woman who had the task of conveying the English language to a great number of pupils, from different countries, ranging in age from ten to sixty or more.

Before acquiring some knowledge and practice in English, I had to settle problems of licensure. For this I needed an interpreter. Although my mother tongue is Hungarian, I was once very familiar with German. I received help from a colleague, with the title of professor, who sacrificed his precious time to go wherever I had to go. (This colleague was older than I was). He considered me German because I spoke German. The interpreter must have been impressed by the demigod status of European professors. In spite of the fact that he knew I was not a professor, he nevertheless consistently addressed me by that title. At that time, I had nothing; I could not speak English and had neither money nor license, nor practice. Although the man liked me and did a great deal for me, because he had a kind heart, he also needed to find a scapegoat. He felt deep resentment against the Germans and against the haughty German professors with whom he had once studied in Germany. For him, European doctors were all Germans.

A friend who came from Germany and is now a very successful business man always addresses me as "professor" in spite of all objections. Whenever he introduces me, besides calling me "professor," he gives a short *curriculum vitae*, mentioning only the items of excellency. He loves to have socially prominent persons as friends. For this reason, he elevates them or points out their "brilliant" faculties, believing that in this way he himself will rise in his friends' estimation.

I was astonished to be addressed as professor by some of my professor colleagues who are not themselves addressed by this title. These men are all native Americans who like and respect me. They know where I came from. Applying my experiences to explain this phenomenon, I concluded that a strong ambivalence is here in operation, exaggerated respect existing simultaneously with resentment against the newcomer, a sort of "sibling rivalry." I face this ambivalence with equanimity; it is inevitable. If the positions were reversed, my own reaction would probably not be very different.

"Did you hear the radio talk of your friend Hitler?"

I have often heard one Jew asking another, "Did you hear the radio talk of your friend Hitler?" Both were persecuted and victimized by Hitler. They hated him intensely. Why, then, does one say "your friend Hitler?" Why does he not ask, "Did you hear the threatening speech of Hitler?"

We have an easy answer ready. He means just the opposite of what he says, "Did you hear the speech of *your enemy* Hitler?" Or, "Did you hear the speech of *our* enemy Hitler?" It would be good if the phrase meant only the opposite. Unfortunately, this is not the case.

Our children whom we brought over from Europe were very much disturbed by anti-Semitism in the old country. My little daughter, who was nine years old at the time, came home with tears in her eyes, complaining that the other children at school stopped playing with her. Twice she came home crying because the other children had drawn a swastika on the back of her coat. Our children wanted to deny that they were Jews when they came to the United States. We heard that they presented themselves to other children, both Jews and non-Jews, as "Hungarian Israelites." One boy, about eleven years of age, told me that if he had been born a German and non-Jew, he would have become more of a Nazi than anybody else. He identified himself with the strong brutal enemy. Some adult Jews blurted out that if Hitler had not made a racial issue in his "philosophy" but a cultural issue, they would have ardently supported him.

Bearing all these statements in mind, the reader may agree with my interpretation of the "your friend Hitler." The speaker would love to be Hitler's friend and follower if he were permitted to do so. But this wish is impossible; he is ashamed of it and has to repress it. The repressed, however, has to come out in some way or another. He permits enough of it to come out in the phrase "friend Hitler" but not *"my* friend Hitler" because this would be too dangerously close to the truth; therefore, he says *"your"* friend Hitler.

"Your friend, this s.o.b., Dr. X."

A male patient, a student, burst out with, "Your friend, this s.o.b., Dr. X." The patient knew that my contact with Dr. X. was of such a superficial nature that he could hardly be called my friend.

The patient hated his father, and therefore all authorities, no matter how kind and tolerant they were. He claimed that the only exception to this hatred was his analyst; but this was not all true. His analyst was, for him, an authority also in the analytic situation. But the hostility was concealed: he made the analyst a friend of a person whom he dared to hate. If the analyst has a friend whom the patient hates because the friend is a s.o.b., then this hatred reaches everybody who is a friend of the hated person. Any authority is a s.o.b., including his "respected and beloved analyst."

"But, darling, you are terribly wrong"

Probably all readers have witnessed heated arguments between married couples (or have themselves participated in such arguments), who otherwise love each other. In these arguments, one or both of the mates get angry and hateful and sharply contradict, refute and criticize each other. The aggressive party injects, between the harsh words, the mollifying "darling," indicating that no matter how angry he gets, no matter how much he hates the mate at that moment, he still loves the other person.

It is impossible to love an otherwise beloved person at a time when one is angry with and hates him. One may anticipate, with good reason, that when he cools off, *he* will *again* love the person he cannot love at this moment. So it is with husbands, wives, parents, children and friends. The attacked person may be somewhat comforted by the fact that the other, even in a state of anger, can find sufficient energy and will to say "darling" when he cannot mean it.

My late father often interviewed and put certain people through tests and examinations. As a child, I often witnessed such "examinations" and gradually learned to foresee the results of interviews which my father would begin with: "My dear friend. . . ." The man thus addressed was, in the end, rejected. The "my dear friend" was needed to muster up enough courage for the aggressive step and to put balm on the wound my father had to inflict on the other person.

Transient disbelief at hearing good news:
"No"
or
"That's not true"

An exclamation of a loud "no" upon hearing bad news or upon being suddenly exposed to a repulsive sight when the opposite was expected or hoped for, has a simple explanation; it is a denial of the painful facts or perceptions. The mannerism needs explanation when the converse is true. When one suddenly hears good news or when, after a long time, he takes a first glance at a person whom he remembers as unattractive and who now appears as a stunning beauty, he may, for a split second, be taken aback and say loudly, *"No!"* or *"That's not true,"* or something of the sort. Only after this "no" can one permit himself to enjoy fully the good and cherished fact.

"Really"

"Really" means that something is true, that it exists, that it is no falsehood, that it is not make-believe, that it is deep rather than superficial, and that it is neither an illusion nor a hallucination.

The word "really" is used in thousands of circumstances,

legitimate and illegitimate. It is the latter with which this chapter is concerned.

A guest is offered a drink by his host. The guest replies, "Thank you. I don't want it now. I really don't want it." He means that he often refuses a drink for other reasons *though* he wants it. This time, it is true that he does not want it.

A mother is talking about her son's sickness. She says, "His temperature was 99. I got scared. The next morning, the temperature went beyond 104; then I got *really* scared." She was anxious when the temperature was 99 degrees, but even more anxious when it went beyound 104. Both "scares" were "real." The difference was only in the intensity; therefore, her anxiety was more real at 104 than it had been at 99.

A staff member of an institute is doing some excellent work. He rarely meets the head of the institute; but on one occasion, they do meet, and the chief says, "Did I tell you how much we appreciate your work in our institute? I really mean it." They have worked together for many long years, and the chief *did* express his appreciation two or three times. It is impossible that he could have forgotten that he had done so. He *pretends* that he is uncertain because he is jealous of the other's work and needs to stress the fact that the whole matter is unimportant. After finishing the first part of his sentence, he pauses for a short time and then says, "I really mean it." He means it and does not mean it. Two forces are struggling in his mind: one means it and the other does not want to mean it. If there were only the first force, it would not be necessary to say that he really means it because he does; but because another force opposes the fact that he really means it, he has to say that he *really* means it. There are two facts present: meaning it and not wanting to mean it. The ambivalence is revealed in the mannerism and in the pause. The truth forces itself to expression.

A grandmother, in talking about her recently born grandchild, says, "He is *really* cute." She wants to say that all grandmothers feel that a grandchild is cute whether he is or not. Her grandchild is cute on the former basis; and besides that, he would be cute even if he were not her grandchild.

Women, notably wives, often torture their husbands with "really." A wife asks her husband, "Do you love me?" If he says "yes," she will be interested in still further investigations: "I know that you love me; but I want to know whether you *really* love me." The underlying motives were discussed in the section dealing with the "of course."

A married man tells that at about the age of ten, he stole pennies from his mother's drawer. "I did not consider this as being too bad," he said, "because it *really* didn't harm anyone." Asked what he meant by "really," he said that it was only a few pennies. At first glance, this may appear to be a satisfactory answer. It was not. He deceived himself by this rationalization; and because of this self-deception, he permitted himself in later years to tell what he considered to be "white lies." A lie is identical with stealing and cheating; *one steals or cheats the truth*. Such an attitude has grave, though not immediate, consequences. If, shortly after swallowing a handful of needles, one gets cramps, he easily realizes the causal connection; but the consequences of lies, being subtle, come later. Lies, thefts, cheatings disturb the warmth of relations with everybody, including wife, children, friends, and all the other people in the world.

Following the propositions of Freud (1930) and Hermann (1934b, 1940), we realize that there are two kinds of consciences: a false and a true one. The false conscience is based only on the fear of *external* punitive consequences and *the imitation of the group;* the true conscience, the true "superego" will give disapproving signals even when there is no possibility of external repercussions.

A surgeon said to a patient, "I do not really think that an operation should be done." Asked what he meant by "really," he replied, "It means that I have doubts." Discussing the matter further, he agreed that the correct statement would have been, "I have doubts."

For many years, I myself lived with a mixed, false and true superego. It was an unhappy condition. I had to struggle hard before I could change. Such change is a lifetime job in this tough life. "Ideals can be pursued but not achieved"; not completely.

Sharpe (1940) had a patient who very often used the word, "really." At first, she thought that its use was a habit of the patient, but gradually came to realize that its use had deep meaning and "revealed the core of a profound psychological illness." Sharpe continues, "I found the following. Whenever he was surprised into saying something critical about me, my belongings, or the analysis, he put up his hands in a beseeching way and said in an apologetic deprecating voice: 'Really, Miss Sharpe . . .' I correlated these transference affects with the underlying infantile and childhood emotional situations . . . and they included: the appearance of a new baby, the awareness of parental intercourse, when he slept in the parents' room, the sight of the female genital, the sight of menstrual blood." According to Sharpe, one can put the word "really" where it belongs:

"Another baby, really?—Really."
"Made by father and mother, really?—Really."
"A person without a penis, really?—Really."
"Is that blood on her nightdress, really?—Really."
"I think she is dirty. Is she, really?—Really."
"I feel like killing, really?—Really" (pp. 211-212).

"I wouldn't do it for a million dollars"

He would. In all of us there is a constant struggle between temptations and conscience. Many people like to argue with themselves about what they would do in case they should find some money. They wonder whether they would keep it or return it. Often the decision in this hypothetical problem is a compromise. If the money were to belong to a poor man or to an employee who might lose his job, they would return the money; but if it were to belong to a rich man, to a bank or to the government, they would keep it.

Two of the greatest temptations are money and sex. I have heard several men say that they would not seduce a virgin—not for a million dollars. But if somebody else had the nerve to do it, they would not mind being second best. Or, they say that they would not violate ethical or moral codes—not for a million dollars! The fact that they express the thought, even though negatively, betrays that they are toying with the idea of committing the wrong if not for one, perhaps, for more millions of dollars.

It is advisable to realize that one cannot fool the conscience. Nothing helps. Truth and conscience will be the victors in the end.

"I have sixteen million problems"

We like to exaggerate. Exaggeration stems not only from the need to impress the listener but also from a persistence of a childish attitude in certain persons.

A four-year-old boy coming home after a spending his first day in kindergarten says to his mother, "There is a boy who is a hundred times bigger than I."

Mother: "But, honey, a hundred times?"

Child: "Yes, mother, even three times."

Before coming to this country, I made what was probably my last visit to my native town which I had not seen for twenty-seven years. Recalling my home I had the image of large rooms with wide windows. What I saw was two small rooms with tiny windows. When I had seen them previously, as a child, the rooms and windows were comparatively large. This "relativity of percepts," as I would like to call this phenomenon, is responsible for the error in memory. One should bear such a possibility in mind in order to check one's objectivity.

Another reason for exaggeration is the fear that people will not believe us. Therefore, when we relate an exciting event, we are tempted to say more than what actually happened in the hope that the listeners will believe part of the story which was correct. This kind of tactic fails because even a slight distortion of truth will cause suspicion and doubt in the listener, even about the part of the story which is true and correct.

Presentation through the opposite
"I had a wonderful week"

When a person calls or meets a friend with whom there has been no contact for a few weeks and asks him what is new, the other replies, "I had a wonderful week." One is prepared to hear pleasant things; but it takes only a few seconds to be disillusioned, for what is heard is nothing but misery. The mate had a cold, the brother-in-law died, a brother lost his job, and so on and on.

A colleague who has returned from a tour of inspection of other institutions for the purpose of incorporating some of the good points in his own place is asked, "How was the trip?"

He answers, "What a neat organization I saw there." He then fills in the details of a dismal story. The place was anything but neat.

Investigating this mannerism, I found that the persons who use it are afraid that the listener will not be interested in hearing good news, and they intend to trap the listener by making him believe that good news will come. Then they tell the bad news. As the listener's attention has already been aroused, it is difficult for him to turn away. Furthermore, the contrast is, for the moment, startling. The listener is caught by surprise. People have a strong craving to be found interesting. They take advantage of every situation that allows them to be so. This technique also compensates for the pain they had to suffer through the bad events.

Securing praise by minimizing the merit

Some people when praised add further evidence to the praise. Others minimize the praise by telling about flaws and faults. For example, on being told her hair looked very nice, one lady said that the hairdresser could not do it well, that she had trouble with the curls and that the hair was not well-dried. In this case, the lady was displaying her distrust of the speaker. She might have suspected that her hair was not perfect but that the other would not say so. She did not want the speaker to think that he fooled her into accepting undeserved praise. She preferred that it should be *she* who told the truth and *then* she was safer. She could then consider the statement of the other to be, at least, partially true. The truth must come out one way or another.

One tells a friend that his talk was a great success, and the latter will minimize the praise by telling that he was not well prepared, that the speech was not well organized, that he left out important things, and that he had really not felt well while talking.

What makes people do this? They do not trust anyone's sincerity in praising them. First, they themselves do not often tell the truth when they praise others and cannot help thinking that others do the same with them. Second, the person praised knows that everything is not perfect and needs to reveal the flaws in order to be able to enjoy what is true in the praise. This proves again and again that truth is the greatest power in human relations. The slightest deviation from truth causes tension, uncertainty, suspicion.

One of Freud's patients, a young woman, always criticized herself and minimized her intelligence. According to Freud (1913), the cause of her behavior was her desire to indicate that she was stupid but attractive.

Success-securing pessimism
Optimistic expectation by pessimistic prediction

Somebody faces an important examination; he predicts, "Sure, I will fail." In planning a trip which necessitates good weather, he predicts, "Sure, it will rain." If his prediction turns out to be right, he says with a sort of gratification, "I told you"; if he was proved wrong, he smiles with an expression on his face which seems to say that fate made an error.

Pessimistic prediction is caused by one of the most profound worries of all mankind: that one's success will create envy and evil wishes in others. One has to feel this because the same happens *in him* when others are successful. This feeling of envy, and the assumption that it is present in others, is projected outward as "*fate*," fear of evil spirits; or it appears as a primitive conception of a jealous God.

In my early youth, I lived in a community in which nothing, but nothing, was done without referring to the Lord, making some magic gesture or saying some magic formula in order to avert evil. When a letter was written, the phrase "in the name of the Lord," was noted in abbreviation. I still have a vivid memory of one of the letters my late father sent me when I was serving in the war as a soldier: "My dear son (you should live a hundred years), we were very happy to hear that you are well (thank God). Your mother (she should live long) will go (if God permits it) to see her sister (her candle should light) . . . etc." Every step was considered as an aggression against some authority; every success, as a tendency to rule over others. Everything good was considered dangerous because it might arouse opposition, enmity against us. The Lord was fancied as a jealous, cruel being who always has to be feared, flattered, and influenced in our favor. We imagine Him to be the kind of being that we feel *we* are. The conception of the Lord as truth, good will and the essence of love is still strange to the human mind.

"You must read it"
"You must see it"
"You must hear it"

When we read, see or hear something pleasant, thrilling or touching, we feel the need to share our experience with others. There is a similar need when the experience is painful or horrifying. There is a need in us to give to others from the warmth of our own experiences or to receive from others comforting warmth to mitigate our own suffering.

This sharing is more complicated when a person forces us to hear a horrifying story because the speaker obtained a perverse pleasure from the experience and intends to gain a new pleasure by relating it or making his audience share the guilt he has because of such pleasure (assuming that the listener may have the same pleasurable reaction).

The foregoing statement, as proved by Freud, is definitely so when somebody urges us to listen to his jokes.

To illustrate the forced sharing, there is the case of A., who has an idea to which others object. A. adheres to his idea, not because he is convinced of its validity, but because he is convinced of its error. He denies this knowledge to himself and insists on the idea because it serves his complex. Now, when he sees, hears about or reads a book in which he believes his point is stated by somebody else, he becomes enthusiastic about the book, praises it highly and forces the listener to read, see and hear about it.

To illustrate further, there is the case of Mrs. N. who gives a party. One of her guests is a famous baritone who, during the evening, graciously and spontaneously, sings for the assembled company. Later, another guest arrives. After a greeting, the hostess says to the latecomer, "Mr. C. has just thrilled us by singing his latest recording. You must hear it." In spite of the singer's reluctance and the guest's embarrassment, Mrs. N. insists that the celebrity repeat the performance. This performance is accompanied by strain and tension because both the guest and the performer feel that they were trapped into acceding to an imposition.

The hostess was motivated in her insistence on an encore by her need to receive all the credit for the success of the party. But her "success" will soon be followed by a hangover because there is in each of us a seismograph that indicates any error we have made, usually, through anxiety.

"You are nervous"—"I am nervous?" "You are jealous"—"I am jealous?"

People become irritated when they are considered "nervous" or "jealous." Unless they go to a therapist for help or if they can no longer deny these conditions that are obvious, they oppose being told about their nervousness or jealousy.

Mental illness is still considered a stigma. To be nervous or jealous means that one is weak, that he has no control over his drives, that he does not master situations, and that he has failed to deserve a proper place in the group.

The defense against being tagged by these two words is greater when it is true, when it hits home, than when it is false.

It often happens that the accuser is nervous or jealous and projects his condition onto the accused. Even when the accuser is right, he likes to emphasize his statement. He is teasing because it gives him superiority over the other, especially when it is *he* who is the cause and source of the latter's nervousness and jealousy. The accused is afraid to admit the validity of the charge because it renders him, at least so he thinks, helpless. He becomes subservient to and enslaved by his accuser. These reactions can often be observed in love relations. There are justified affects in certain situations. There is and can be justification for nervousness or jealousy. In such cases, it is advisable to admit that one has these feelings because admission and frankness make exploitation difficult. The admission can become one's strength instead of his weakness. Anyway, one cannot conceal strong emotions. Denial renders him weaker because he does not have sufficient courage to admit the truth.

"I"—"I"—"I"—"I"

It is distressing to realize that the whole world is one big "I" Club. Most people come together with a tacit agreement that they do so solely for the purpose of giving each other an opportunity to talk about themselves. If, while dining in a restaurant, one volunteers the information that he likes some particular food, it serves him right to be accorded the privilege of hearing a similar recital of what his "friend" likes. Whether the subject of consideration is a book, a dress, a writer, a place, a sport, perfume, drinks, sleeping habits, anything, the main need will come out: the "I" from one and then from another. Such a relation cannot be satisfactory. It is superficial and hypocritical, though it serves a transient gratification of a need.

To have a delightful and constructive conversation, it is not necessary that one be well-educated or brilliant. It is enough to be oneself and talk about oneself only when asked and if the inforamtion serves the *common interest of the group,* even though the group consists of only two persons. To know the facts correctly is the main interest of the group. It should not be important to know who said this or that; it is important that what is said be correct.

"Stealing the show"

There are hundreds of variations of a certain mannerism or, if one prefers, "behavior pattern" in which a person reporting and presenting an observed scene, an experience, is able to do so in such a way that the audience loses interest in the story because the narrator steals the show by putting himself in the foreground. This mannerism is irritating. The listener feels cheated, put upon. The storyteller loses because he has made his listener resentful. The first person drives himself into a narcissistic trance and becomes the victim of self-deception, believing the listener to be impressed. The listener is not.

Analyses of people who use such mannerisms reveal that they, in the course of their development, justly or not, developed an "inferiority complex," conceived the idea that they were not important, not loved and not wanted. I have seen tragic examples of this mannerism in people to whom life was harsh and to whom the environment was unloving, caused suffering and dealt traumatic blows. Sadly enough, the victims of such experiences treated the injury in the wrong way: putting themselves in the limelight when they were not asked to do so, when the listener was interested only in the story and not in the narrator.

These people can be divided into two groups. One exaggerates the emotions experienced when observing an event; the second describes the observed scene theatrically.

First type: "When I say this (or heard this), I almost screamed (or fainted or melted). I almost died."

Second type: In addition to a verbal description of the experience, they shout, shriek, slump into their chairs, and pretend to faint.

It is a sad picture. These people bring the listener into conflict. The latter does not know whether to yield to the feeling of anger or of pity. In everyday communications, we do not want theatrical scenes.

False scolding

A woman patient who had gained weight decided to lose many pounds. She stuck courageously to her reducing diet. Another woman, who belonged to the same club, watched the process. Whenever they met, she was asked how much weight she lost. One day she was asked by a fellow club member how much she had lost in the last week. She answered truthfully that she had lost nothing, whereupon the "friend," assuming an angry face and voice, strongly scolded her.

"You are terrible. You are just no good. You are lazy. I am giving you a week and if you don't lose at least three pounds, I won't talk to you." The latter behaved as if this matter, her friend's interest, was very close to her heart. The patient was positive that the friend did not care at all and was, on the contrary, pleased with the patient's unattractiveness.

A true friend would be sorry, would have a few encouraging words, would not scold, at least not so strongly, would not get angry, and would not use false threats.

A. is on friendly terms with B. A. is a man who, for certain reasons, is interested only in his own welfare. Nevertheless, he likes to show at least some interest in others, as he does in B. He advised B., at the latter's request, what kind of stocks to buy for investment, not for speculation. B. got certain "tips" and bought two kinds of speculative stocks for a small sum. When he told A. what he had done, A. burst into a long, furious rage scolding and repeatedly admonishing B. for having made the investment. In this case, A. did not want B. to lose money; but it was not true that he was so upset as he appeared to be. It was a small matter for A. to show himself to B. as a good friend and good fellow. When the motivation was brought to A.'s attention, he could not accept the interpretation.

"You cannot fool people all of the time." As a matter of fact, they very soon find such things out. They may not even be aware of them, at least not right away. An immediate feeling-reaction to the hypocrisy is there; and it will show up in the relation of A. and B. sooner or later.

When A. discussed the matter, he offered the following explanation for his tirade. Being friendly with B., A. was concerned and would feel guilty if his suggestions were to come out wrong. This would upset him and he displaced the upset from the original matter to the present one. A.'s interpretation is acceptable. A phenomenon can contain different, even contradictory interpretations. Freud's clinical finding, i.e., that one phenomenon can have a large number of contradictory motivations, has been verified innumerable times. Bearing this in mind, one can avoid being confused by psychoanalytic propositions. For the variety of different interpretations made by analysts, the unconscious is solely responsible. Psychoanalysts can, nevertheless, make errors.

"I am sure"

From its beginnings, mankind has craved for evidence of something "sure." To date, the greatest minds of humanity have failed to gratify this craving. On the other hand, in our everyday life, we use the "I am positive," "I am sure" frequently and with the greatest ease. Millions of people accept dogmas because the acceptance relieves them from painful uncertainty, from the frustrating "I don't know."

A patient, a young married woman, borrowed one of my books. A few days later, she apologized for not yet having returned the book. She said that her husband had taken possession of the book, and she had not yet read it. She observed, furthermore, that her husband handled the book sloppily (by her compulsive standards). She said to her husband, "I am sure that Dr. Feldman is very finicky about his books."

She does not know whether I am finicky about my books or not. She is afraid that I might be, and she will be embarrassed to return the book soiled or damaged. *She needs* to be sure in order that she will feel right and thus warns her husband to be careful. Furthermore, she is safer if the lender is not finicky, in which case she would not need to scold and warn her husband. Not knowing my habits, she prefers to assume that the lender is finicky and forces herself to be "sure" and to act accordingly.

A. says to B., "I am sure that you will understand my request." A. cannot be sure about this. It is more probable that he is afraid that B. will *not* understand or appreciate his request. There is, in this mannerism, a mixture of aggression and pleading with B. not to disappoint him.

A husband says to his wife who is in analysis, "I am not sure that I like your going to this psychiatrist." He means he is sure he does not like it. He is motivated, in his statement, first, by a fear of causing an argument with his wife, and second, by the legitimate feeling of his indecisiveness about her being in treatment.

Mrs. X. says to her husband, "I am sure that you are better than your brother." She is sure of the opposite. She gives her husband false encouragement with good intentions.

A patient, another young married woman, said during an analytic session, "I am sure that you are familiar with Michelangelo's 'David.' " She had good reason to assume this, but she could not be sure. She wanted to say two things. One, "I wish that my analyst were familiar with it, because he should be well informed and educated in order that I should have complete trust in him." Two, "I would like to be sure whether he knows this or not. I wish that he does. To make sure, I have to ask him; but he might be hurt that I assumed that he did not know this, and he will be angry with me. Furthermore, it is possible that he might say that he does not know this or even mislead me into thinking that he knows when he does not. I better force myself to be sure, though it is an illusion to do so, and get out of the trouble." On the other hand, one can see that the lady gets into more trouble by permitting herself to indulge in such illusionary assumption. She creates a wall between herself and the other person. She spoils her reality-testing faculty by lending herself to an assumption. She misses an opportunity to enforce her intellectual and emotional courage. She creates distrust in the listener. She might impose such an attitude on her children. She is weakening her chances to see and face things correctly.

The most important aims of analytic treatment are to face facts and to see and accept the truth. In my opinion, the analyst is missing a chance to remove resistances when he permits the patient to indulge in such a travesty of truth. It is close to impossible to "work through," therapeutically, a complex without the analysis of mannerisms.

A male patient frequently used the "I am sure" because he did not dare to be sure about anything lest he create opposition in others. He was, therefore, terribly frustrated and vainly wanted to force himself to be sure. The source of his fear and weakness could be traced far back into childhood. He had been made to feel that any definite statement on his part would result in losing the love of some important member of his family. First, he did not dare to say what he knew; later, he did not dare to know what he knew. This led to painful troubles, disturbances, including polymorphous-perverse sexual activities.

Reacting to praise with indignance

One can observe a peculiar phenomenon in communicative relationships in which persons who, when praised, display a manneristic attitude. Instead of showing that they are pleased, some persons behave as if they had been criticized or accused and become indigant. They get into lengthy and ardent explanations which try to convey that they did not have any other choice and that they had to do what they did. The listener is puzzled. He wants to be appreciative; but, instead, he finds himself considered a prosecutor.

The probable cause of this phenomenon may be an inhibition of exhibiting, displaying one's feelings, emotions, joys, and gratifications. Many people even blush when praised. They feel as though they are in danger when they are put into the limelight. Since my two previous papers on blushing (1922, 1941b), the results of further research work indicate that a woman blushes because she is ashamed to show that she is a woman, and a man blushes because he is ashamed that he (unconsciously) desires to get attention, as does a woman.

Defending oneself without being accused

In two cases, I succeeded in unraveling the meaning of the strange phenomenon, defending oneself without being accused. Both were patients in analysis for the purpose of gaining help and liberation from severe neuroses. In both, the phenomenon appeared primarily outside of the analytic situation. When, for example, somebody said to them, "It is a nice day," they reacted with, "I didn't say that it is not a nice day." Or, if they were told that a play was very good, they replied with, "I didn't say that it wasn't good."

One of these patients was a young intellectual, with strong masochistic trends, who constantly fought against the alleged cruelties and injustices of authorities. Sexual stimulation, for him, could be achieved only through fantasies in which he was forced to endure sexual seduction by strong women who overpowered him physically and forced him to an acceptance of the seduction. In his social life, he was an ardent perceiver of injustices and indulged in a frustrating fight against them. The moment there was a chance to rebel against an authority, he did so. No matter what the situation, he behaved as if he had been accused and put up a fight. Even in analysis, the patient reacted to interpretations as though they were accusations.

The other patient was a young married woman who felt very guilty about an extramarital love affair. She submitted to the most extreme sexual perversions and humiliations by a perverted domineering lover. The woman loved the man. She would do everything for him. She tried to rationalize and justify her humiliating perverted submission to the man. Nevertheless, she still felt guilty. On the other hand, she wanted to be rid of her guilt feelings, or at least neutralize them by making every attempt to be right in everything.

When she was told that it was a nice day, she immediately perceived the statement as an accusation and set about to prove her innocence, even though she had not been accused.

"I did this"—"I can do this too"

One takes a walk with a friend or acquaintance and, without any ulterior motive, he makes a statement like, "I can tie my shoelaces so that they never get loose." The companion immediately says, "I can tie them well too." There are innumerable such examples of this mannerism in everyday life. I would accept the interpretation a patient made about a man close to her. She said the man displayed this mannerism very conspicuously. It was an infantile trend. Even in childhood, the man wanted to impress his parents and prove to them that he could do whatever the other children did. This trend remained in him. It annoyed his wife a great deal.

"Isn't she pretty?"

One of the basic characteristics of human beings seems to be the need to share emotions with others, with the expectation that the others will have the same feelings. If there is no response, the feeling of frustration follows. This trend is not equally strong in all persons, but the trend is universal. It probably begins with the mother who shows things to the child, who in turn likes to show and tell everything he knows or experiences to his mother. It is possible that this practice may be the *emotional basis of learning*. Many adults, not only children, can study only when somebody works with them.

H., I and a pretty young niece are together in a room. H. turns to me and asks, "Isn't she [the niece] pretty?" H. does not dare to tell the niece directly that she is pretty. He tells her this through a medium.

The spontaneous and genuine sharing tendency which manifests itself by calling upon the other with "isn't it beautiful," "isn't it terrible," is frequently marred by deceit, hypocrisy, and several other ulterior motives.

An attractive woman introduces a man, in whom she is very much interested, to another equally attractive woman. She says to the man, "Isn't she pretty?" I happen to know that this woman considers her girl friend a rival. It is obvious that the other woman is pretty. The man is cornered. He has only one answer, and he has to say that she is pretty even if she were homely. He is brought into the somewhat embarrassing position of being immediately and emphatically polite to the other woman whom he has just met. And last, but not least, he has an "instinctual feeling" that the introducing woman is motivated by something not quite right. The latter, *sub rosa,* has the following intentions: to take the initiative away from the man who might voluntarily say that the other woman is pretty, and to make it appear that the man was *forced* to make the flattering comment. She covers up her jealousy by bringing up something she hates to be true. She conveys to her rival that the latter is *not* so attractive as she herself; believing herself to be so much more attractive, she can afford to be generous, because she cannot be the loser in the contest. She prevents the man from making the first pleasant comment.

The same attractive woman likes to give parties and to invite men. She enjoys being the center of attention. She cannot avoid inviting women also, but she is very careful not to include any woman guest who is more attractive than she. During the party, when a man is talking to another woman, the hostess goes to them, as is customary, and seldom misses the question, "Isn't she pretty?" It is obvious that the other woman is not. The man, trapped, wryly whispers a sad "yes." The hostess triumphantly walks away toward another couple.

Is she triumphant? She only seems to be. All participants in this foul play are fully aware of the whole process and hate it.

"I must admit"

The fact that we use the phrase "I must admit" indicates that we often conceal the truth; otherwise we would say what we have to say. There is much struggle between the tendency to tell the truth and the tendency to lie. This conflict is especially strong in matters of sex and money. In sex, among any other things, one is afraid to admit one's intentions for fear of being rejected; in money matters, one is taught to value other things, like love and spiritual interests, more highly than money. The "must" in the phrase "I must admit" is rather encouraging because it shows the innate need for honesty. In this book, I have repeatedly expressed my conviction that honesty concerning absolute ethical laws is present without the individual's being indoctrinated with the obligation to observe them.

A male patient came to his session with a bandage over a sore finger. He lived in another city and had to drive to the office about two hours in each direction. He began, "The doctor wanted to open it today but, I must admit, I preferred to come here." Asked what he meant when he said that he must admit, he replied, "I am too tight to lose the dollars I have to pay for the session." (He referred to our agreement to pay for appointments not kept through his fault.)

This man needed help for his tormenting social anxiety which disturbed even his work. In his profession he had to meet many people. He was often close to leaving and giving up his work. More than usual, for him, money meant security. On the other hand, he was ashamed to reveal to himself the importance of money. To his analyst, he could admit this more easily.

"Did you hear the joke about . . . ?"

Is there a reader who has not been asked whether he "heard the joke about . . ."? Is there a reader who, before telling a joke, did not raise this question or did not feel like doing so? In asking the question, one hopes that the answer will be negative and the joke can be told. There is a sort of pleading tone in the question, almost a demand that the listener will say no, even if the latter has to lie in order not to frustrate the joke teller. One is inclined to grant the request, even lie, because he would expect the same if the tables were turned.

On one level, the joke teller wants to exhibit himself and to be the center of attention. While the listeners laugh, he, with a contented and jubilant expression on his face, reaps the harvest of his victory.

On a deeper level, there is much more meaning behind the whole scene. In his unsurpassed book on wit, Freud (1905a) has given us the deep meaning of jokes and the process going on between the joke teller and the listener. According to Freud, whose theory I have supplemented, the technique of the joke serves the purpose of concealing, while at the same time bringing into the open, a hidden (repressed), usually sexual or aggressive drive and intention which is opposed by the inner censorship and would be offensive if expressed directly. The technique of (a good) joke serves the purpose of covering up the true tendency and allows us to make believe that we laughed because the joke was funny and not because a concealed drive was released. The technique of the joke saves us from the feeling of guilt for having such tendencies. The joke teller needs to share his guilt with others. The more people participate in the listening and the more people enjoy the joke, the less guilty he becomes. His guilt is still there, though the technique of the joke tried to eliminate it (Feldman, 1932a, 1941a).

"Don't worry"

All people would like to be safe and secure for the rest of their lives. They all know that this is impossible; but only a few accept with resignation this inevitable fact. Most people do worry; and many things about which they worry are not groundless or senseless. Judd Marmor has recently devoted a paper to "realistic worry" (1958). On the other hand, people do not worry about the same thing though their apprehension would be justified. Moreover, those who worry about something at one time experience the fact that the same concern is absent at another time. The knowledge and memory of this does not help them not to worry the next time.

For example, if one's child is gravely sick, and he worries about the outcome, the worry is justified. The question is only *how one worries*. Does he worry optimistically or pessimistically. The average, healthy person does everything he can for the sick child, visualizes the worst as a *possibility or probability*, but still has hopes and hopes to the last moment. Such a person worries optimistically. The others will *mainly* or *only* anticipate the worst. The rational person will accept the possibility of the worst. To the irrational, possibility is a certainty.

A businessman received a note on *Saturday* from the police to come to headquarters the following Monday. The reason for the summons was not indicated on the notice. He had no idea why "they" called him. He started to worry; he worried and worried. Gradually, the worry became unbearable. He could not sleep. He was in a panic. He aroused his lawyer in the dead of night and extracted from him the promise to find out *Sunday* the cause for being called. It turned out that the police had notified him to call for a thing he had lost which had been found.

Flatly telling a mother who has a very sick child not to worry has no effect. The best one can do is *to worry with her* and to comfort her by saying that everything is not yet lost, that there is still hope—in case one believes in what he says.

In the case of the businessman, where the irrationality of the worry is obvious, one should say that there is a slight possibility of something unpleasant but things may turn out well. This will not help much, but at least the one who offers comfort is honest.

Most of the time, the "don't worry" is applied by persons who do not care how anyone else feels. They say lightly, "don't worry" in order not to be bothered by the worrier. They will use this phrase even when there is a good reason to worry.

In this book, I do not want to discuss those cases in which the worry is the main symptom, like the *obsessive thought* of some prospective mothers who fear that the child will be born defective or a monster. One does not do any good telling such a mother that she should not worry *because* there is no justification for the worry. She knows this herself. To tell a person whose worry has assumed delusional proportions that his fears are "only" in his imagination will be of absolutely no help because he is convinced that he is right.

Insincere self-accusations

Insincere self-accusations occur when a person, in order to invalidate the accusations made against him by another, himself makes insincere additions to the content of the accusation.

For example, A. asks B. to put in a few good words for him in order to obtain a job. As the efforts of B. are fruitless, A. accuses B. of not doing his best to achieve the objective. B. becomes upset and, instead of declaring that A.'s accusations are not true, goes into a lengthy, false tirade against himself: "Sure, I didn't do anything. Moreover, I told bad things about you and went to many people telling them what an impossible person you are and saying they should give the job to anybody but you."

This phenomenon has several possible explanations:

First: the accuser is right.
Second: the self-accusation is true; the accused knows more than the accuser.

Third: the accusation is groundless: the accused did everything he could.

Fourth (and this is what interests us most): the accused, true, *did* everything. On the other hand, the accuser may be right in so far as he suspects that the accused, who for several reasons does not like the accuser, does not *wish* the latter to succeed. It is exactly for the latter reason that the accused outdoes the accuser. His intention is to make the accusations appear absurd. On the other hand, he discharges and betrays his repressed wish.

"I am proud of you"

Pride is one of the strongest human emotions. It is the inflation of the self with libido, with importance. Being imbued with pride, the body itself expands, becomes erect; the chest is filled with air; the head is lifted; one occupies more room in space than he did. Children very quickly learn to express pride in this way.

The child is the extension of the parents who *want* to be proud of their children, expect the children to satisfy this desire and to provide them with this kind of gratification. Teachers and institutions want to be proud of their students and staff members. One is proud of one's country, of any animate or inanimate object which serves the purpose of self-inflation.

If pride for others, for example, the pride of parents for their children, is accompanied by love and genuine appreciation, it does not produce any ill effects; but it may cause great trouble in children when they feel that they are loved only on condition that they satisfy their parents' pride. Love offered on this basis may cause grave conflicts because the child needs unconditional love and resents having any strings attached to it. Love offered with a proviso might give rise to a resentment which could persist and often causes serious intellectual as well as other difficulties in later life.

The kind of pride that says, "I am proud of you," without love can be called false pride for both parties. One belongs to a certain circle. He accomplishes something which gives him publicity and makes his "friends" proud of him. The pride of others means close to nothing. He is accorded a transient glory which might even make him uneasy because he now has to live up to the pride-needs of his associates. If he fails, he is dropped. Satisfaction with oneself is not the same as pride in oneself. Satisfaction with oneself means that one has accomplished something that he is capable of doing. It is an inner duty to do that which is satisfactory to oneself; and the fulfillment of this duty does not make one superior to others. One can be superior without the feeling of superiority. Superiority essentially separates one from the group and gives him the feeling of being alone. One has to be a genius to accept this separateness from others.

"Do you know him?"

It is legitimate to pose the question, "Do you know him?" to a listener if one needs information about a third person or, for some reason, it is necessary to know the listener's relation to the third person.

It is not legitimate, though psychologically explainable, to ask when other motives are involved in the question.

Frequently, the analyst hears, "I was examined by Dr. X. Do you know him?" The questioner is interested in knowing whether Dr. X. is known. He also wants to know about the status and reliability of the doctor. Furthermore, he wants information about the doctor and support, from the analyst, for his lack of confidence in his own judgment about the man. The questioner should ask directly what he wants to know.

In another case, the questioner has other motives in posing the same question. When he asks whether one knows Dr. X., he considers the listener socially prominent. He wants to impress the latter. The questioner wants it known that he, too, is becoming socially important enough to be in the company of a socially prominent person. It is remarkable to see how much disappointment appears on the face of the questioner when he is told that Dr. X. is not known.

"Did I tell you?"

We are eager to show off, to be important, to be the center of attention. One of the many ways through which we attain this goal is to tell certain interesting events of our lives. This eagerness is often responsible for the fact that we forget or are uncertain whether we told something or not. We would like not to have told it because then we can tell it again. On the other hand, we are in doubt; and we do not want to be boring.

It often happens that a person practically forgets whether or not he has said something before. He forgets it when he said it; and he forgets that he did not say it. The forgetting is due, not so much to repression, as we would assume, but to a serious disturbance in object relations: he has no interest in the other person but only in himself. It is very rewarding to analyze this phenomenon and trace it to its beginnings, because it leads to important complexes specific to the person, and frequently to earlier traumatic experiences.

"Indeed"

The original meaning of "indeed" indicates truth, fact. When used with these meanings, it is used legitimately. In everyday life, the word is often used to conceal the truth. We are forced to be polite in order to please people. Though they know that the politeness is meant as flattery, they like it. If, in the sentence, "I was happy to meet you—indeed," it were true that the person was happy, it would not be necessary to add "indeed." Usually, before the "indeed," there is a pause as if the speaker needed time to decide what to say. If he is not happy, he lies. In order not to appear a liar, he adds the "indeed" to the sentence after the pause. But he fails because the "indeed" is not true either. One is, therefore, a double liar. At the same time, he reveals his wish to be honest. This is an intricate intercommunication between two persons, both struggling to be truthful.

"Thank you"

Like many others, the two beautiful words, "thank you," are often misused. The following examples of the misuse of the words are from three patients, two males and one female. Whenever I tried to bring home to them an important interpretation which they accepted (with great reluctance), they said, "Thank you," at the end of the session. I knew that they were *not* convinced; therefore there was no need for a "thank you." In my opinion, the "thank you" applied to my interest in helping but not to the content of the interpretation which they only seemingly accepted.

It is wrong to teach children to say "thank you" when we give them a present. Parents are likely to prod their children to say (nicely) "thank you," because the person who brought the gift expects this. The child wants to be loved for itself and will feel hurt noticing that love was given for the "thank you." If thanks are not expected of him, he will love the giver; otherwise, he will either refuse to thank the giver or he will thank him and hate him. A child refuses to say "thank you" because he wants to be loved and wants to love the *giver* for his kindness. Most of the time, the child's stubbornness in refusing to give thanks is misunderstood, misinterpreted. He may even be punished for the refusal. If the child does not get a gift for the thanks, he will later pick up the habit of saying "thank you" through imitation and then it will become part of his behavior and will be genuine.

I once gave a two-year-old girl an outfit for Christmas. I

was invited to the Christmas supper, and the little girl wore the outfit. She was charming as she sat with us at the table. The mother turned to her, asking, "Who gave you the beautiful dress?" No answer. The child was mum. The mother repeated her question. Still no answer. Again, her mother urged her, "Say, Uncle Sandor."

In her desperation, the child said to her mother, "*You* say it." The child had gone through a serious sickness during which she received many shots with needles. She was afraid and clung to her mother all the time. I believe the child felt that the mother intended to make her independent, a state for which the girl was not yet prepared. Later, I told the mother what I felt to be the child's motivation. She understood the explanation and thanked me.

It is my personal conviction that the ideal situation would be one in which nobody should need either to expect thanks from or to express thanks to anybody. The stronger person should give help to the weaker for the reason that he is in a position to give help.

"Don't mention it"

One does something good and nice for another person who thanks his benefactor. The latter's reply is accompanied by a characteristic gesture of defense, "Don't mention it."

Like so many other phenomena of mental life, the "don't mention it" is "overdetermined"; that is, it has different, often contradictory meanings. One possibility is that the benefactor was insincere. The truth is that he was pleased when he was thanked for the good deed; but social amenities imposed on him by the group in which he lived prevented him from an expression of pleasure and made him pretend a humility which he did not feel. He had to pretend that he did not do the good deed in order to be thanked and to be superior to the person who needed his help.

Another possibility is that one is shy and is inhibited in displaying emotions.

Or, one is too emotional, sentimental, and afraid that he will be overly moved and go too far in his response.

Possibly, one may have done the good deed as an atonement for guilt which exists in him for one reason or other. In this case, thanks nullifies the credit due him. There is also the probability that the benefactor meant what he said.

"Believe me"

On one occasion, I was holding my two-and-a-half-year-old grandson in my arm—the boy's mother was standing to the left—when a young fox terrier entered the corridor. It was a strange dog. The boy had seen dogs before but not this one. The dog was not sure of the kind of reception he would get in this strange place. Both he and the boy were puzzled; neither knew how to respond. The child looked at his mother to obtain information about the situation. She smiled, whereupon the child looked down, turned toward the dog and smiled happily. The boy believed his mother.

The process through which one comes to a belief in God, in a cause, in a principle, or in a person is a very intricate one. Honesty paves the way to belief. In my opinion, one of the roots of honesty originates in the mother-child relationship. A mother feels that she must not mislead the child; but she may still do so either through the influence of environment, through wrong conceptions, or through her own complexes. For example, for the sake of attaching the child to her, a mother can make the child anxious about life, can make him insecure and dependent on her.

When we talk about the "believe me" as a mannerism, we mean the usage of these two words in everyday life when a person either finds it an insurmountable obstacle to bring home his point or is made weak in debate by insufficient evidence. "Believe me" is a personal appeal, clamoring in helplessness. It fails. The listener will not yield to the appeal even if he nods affirmatively. It would be better for the speaker to say, "I wished to convince you, but I don't know whether I did or not." When he forces the listener to show an "as-if belief," he drives himself into a doubt, which he probably had in the first place about his project.

"I know"

There are situations in which the "I know" is used legitimately. One can also hear innumerable examples of its illegitimate use.

A female patient suffers, among other things, from a feeling that she is stupid. She thinks that others will notice this and reject her. As a matter of fact, she is a well-educated, intelligent and bright woman. It is extremely difficult to converse with her. In any conversation, it is impossible not to say something which is common knowledge. For example, if one were referring to Lincoln not as Lincoln but as President Lincoln, she might interrupt to say that she knew that Lincoln was a president.

I seldom have time to listen to the radio. When I do, I am subjected to insults like the following: "*I know* that God will bless you." How on earth can anyone possibly know what God will do? What could be said is something like this: "I wish (or pray) that God may bless you."

A greatly esteemed American statesman, in a New Year's message to the Jewish people, spoke highly about the contribution of Jews and Judaism to the spiritual and ethical values of humanity. "I know," he said, "that all Americans agree with me and join me in my good wishes."

The statement was made with the best intentions. The speaker conveyed the impression of sincerity. On the other hand, it was a wish, not a fact, that the speaker *knew all* Americans agreed with him. On the contrary, he knew that *all* Americans did *not* agree with him. From a psychological point of view, he could, for example, have said, "I know that all Americans do not agree with me, but I appeal to them to reconsider their opposing feelings."

One may compare the stateman's well-intentioned remarks to an excellent and abundant dinner in which one finds a sliver of glass. Although the meal is otherwise perfect, it has, nevertheless, been spoiled by a tiny, irritating, indigestible particle.

Mannerisms over the telephone

Some people use their natural voice over the telephone only after they have recognized the identity of the caller. Many use their affected voices even after establishing the identity of the caller who turns out not to be a close friend or a cherished caller. The affected voice they use sounds as if it had come from a remote distance, as if the possessor preferred that ordinary people did not touch them or hear their natural voices. They sound as if they were apprehensive and careful. Only when the caller turns out to be a close friend or someone else who knows them well do they take off the voice-mask and come out of hiding.

Then there are callers who believe that they must immediately get what they want. They cannot imagine the possibility that they have called the wrong number and omit to make sure that they did not do so. I usually get up early in the morning to get ready for work. One morning, the 'phone rang and I answered it. On the other end of the line was a lady who, without even saying hello, realized that the receiver was lifted and said with an enthusiastic, charming voice, "Bill, I had a wonderful night." It was obvious that she had spent the night with her lover, left him, and, as soon as she got home, felt the need to express her gratification over the exciting night. I told her that I fully understood her enthusiasm, but felt that she should be more careful in the future and make sure that it was her lover who answered the call before saying anything. She uttered an embarrassed "thanks."

The "marathon" talks over the 'phone belong to the chapter on loquatiousness.

Does the reader need an explanation of the phenomenon of the person on the other end of the line who disregards the length of the time he talks when he is not paying for the call and is very concise and short when he is paying the toll?

Many people get panicky over a telephone call, whether they make or answer it. This behavior is a sort of examination fear, stage fright, or the result of a need to see the person with whom they are talking. It is an infantile trend. Small children do not want their mother to talk to or to answer them from the side. They want her to look at them, see her face; otherwise, they feel separated and cannot cling (Hermann). (See also Harris's paper on "Telephone Anxiety," 1957.)

A very bright professional man often had ideas which thrilled him, so that he felt the need to communicate them to others. He happened to know an important political figure. At a time when the country needed a wise decision in an important international matter, he thought that he had a good contribution to make. After long deliberations with himself, he decided to call the man on the 'phone. He was anxious about the kind of reception he would get. To his relief and disappointment, the secretary answered the call. Our bright man used a great variety of mannerisms in his two-minute telephone conversation. "It is not terribly important . . . it is not my business . . . you see . . . it is entirely out of my line . . . I don't want to appear arrogant . . . he needn't call me back . . . to be humble." This call occurred in the early stages of his therapeutic analysis. Toward the end of his treatment, he was free either not to call or to call and to say, in a straightforward way, what he wanted, omitting all mannerisms. He made the call. Result—no answer.

"Mildly speaking"

One of the many cheap ways to be witty at the expense of the other fellow is to say something derogatory about him to a third person. The insult may be reinforced by starting with an oblique introduction like, "To put it mildly, he is an idiot," or "to be mild about it," or "to say it mildly, he is very sick."

"Etc."

It is legitimate to use the famous three letters, "etc.," when they serve the purpose of omitting the use of other unnecessary words, or of saving time. Sometimes, "etc." is used because of laziness or because of the inability of the speaker to find proper words to express his ideas.

Very often, the "etc." is used to omit important content. This omission stimulates the listener to supply from his own imagination the omitted part, which is usually a hostile idea. The activity gives the listener pleasure because he expresses the insult not in words but only in imagination. There is a mutual agreement between speaker and listener to enjoy aggression without being guilty because it was only suggested but not expressed.

The following is an example of the vicious use of the "etc." The incident happened long ago during the fascist regime in Hungary when many innocent people were arrested and sent to concentration camps. The police received instructions from the ministry of internal affairs in which there were about eighty items indicating the offenses for which one could be arrested. I heard about an incident from a reliable lawyer who had gone to police headquarters to protest against the arrest of a client and who tried to set free this man who had been innocently arrested. The lawyer took with him a list of the offenses to prove to the police officer that none of the charges listed could be applied to the client for whose release he was asking. The officer replied that it was true that the charge on which the prisoner had been apprehended was not listed but advised the lawyer to see the end of the list. There stood the word, "etc."

A legitimate use of the "etc." is the title of an international quarterly, concerned with the role of language in human behavior and human affairs: *ETC. A Review of General Semantics*. The title indicates that one should not fall victim to easy or dogmatic statements even if they are valid but to think that the phenomena in such statements might have "etc." (other implications).

Listeners who play deaf

There are persons who, because they are so indifferent to the needs and feelings of others or who have a legitimate right to be bored, have acquired the ability to play deaf in such a way that the speaker is unaware that they are not listening.

The reader has probably encountered the kind of person who, in the course of conversation, makes a statement that can be refuted with evidences of its falsity. The speaker, instead of taking into account or consideration what the other has said, plays deaf and continues the story as if nothing had been said. The speaker uses the listener only as a receiver. In one of my patients, a woman, I could ascertain the cause of such behavior. She had lost most of her material possessions. This misfortune, in her case, meant the loss of her social standing. This she could not stand. As she could not tolerate having anything more taken away from her, she *insisted* on holding on to what she had left—including her verbal pronouncements.

"It"

"It," an otherwise very useful word, is often employed by many persons to cover up their unwillingness or inability to see and to express facts. It is an everyday experience in the office of the psychoanalyst to witness a patient's resistance to knowing, seeing and facing the hidden meaning of his trouble. As a result of this resistance, the patient's conflict is expressed through symptoms.

A male patient said, "When I eat only light things like milk or eggs, I can handle *it*."

For the sake of treatment, it is of paramount importance to know what the patient means by saying "it." Even though he knows that his stomach and all the other parts of his digestive system are healthy, he is still unable to venture to eat a good steak though he would like very much to do so. At home or in a restaurant, he envies others who dare to eat a hearty meal without worry. He orders milk and eggs—he, the wealthy man. Whenever he tries to eat a good steak, he has to stop because his whole body "churns up." This man, from his early youth, had always been afraid to enjoy anything, to make decisions about matters through which he would benefit in material gains or sensual pleasure. He always expected the worst in order to avoid the worst, which is death. This is his "complex." It is this "complex" with its content that he means when he says the "it." To pursue the meaning of the "it" is an important and helpful technique in the "working-through process" of the analytic treatment.

"What's new?"
and
"How is everything?"

People address each other with the phrases, "What's new?" and "How is everything?" in order to make a bridge to conversation. It does not matter what they say; it matters only that they should talk to each other. The phrases do not mean the same to all people. To some these are serious questions which bring them into confusion so that they do not know what to say. They wonder what the other person wants.

Does the questioner want to know what they read in the newspaper? Should they say everything when asked, "How is everything?" The cause of such anxious confusion in the case of a professional man was his mother who had completely dominated him. He never knew what would please his mother. In another case, also of a professional man, the patient was an only child who had become aware how much his parents wanted a girl in addition to him. In order to make his parents happy, he often played the role of a girl and tried to be both a girl and a boy. The end result of his pretense was a long series of paralyzing symptoms. He never knew exactly what to say or how to behave.

The same confusion might be caused in certain persons by the question, "How are you?" as was shown by Berne (1953).

"Well"

When forced to answer a question, we pause and start with a nice "well." We all do it. We cannot stand silence. We need to cling to something (originally the mother, as proved by Hermann). The "well" is used to give us time to collect ourselves and to overcome a separation from the person who asked the question and left us alone.

"So what?"

"So what?" We use these two words as a magical device to help us resign ourselves to the inevitable. One might say it to himself, to others, or have others say it to him. Often it is meant earnestly. At other times, it is said in a superficial attempt to get rid of the problems presented to one person by another.

A very poor man went to a wise man with his big problem. He had nothing left in the world but a rooster and a hen. He had to slaughter one; otherwise he would starve. He did not know which one to kill and asked the wise man to help him with his decision. The wise man told the poor fellow that the decision was quite simple and that all he had to do was to kill the rooster. Our man said that this was impossible because the two birds loved each other very much and the female would be most unhappy being separated from the rooster. The wise man then said that if this were so, the hen should be killed. "This would be impossible, too," said the man, "because the rooster loves the hen very much and he would be very sad being separated from her." To this, the wise man replied that he would have to think about the problem and that the poor man should return the next day for advice. When the poor man returned, the wise man presented his decision, the rooster should be killed. The poor man exclaimed desperately, "I told you that if we do this, the hen will be very sad."

The wise man replied, "So what? She will be sad."

Dangers one meets when talking of his children

We completely lose our objectivity and *believe* that the person to whom we present our child will be just as crazy about him as we are. A parent is completely blind when he is showing the picture of his week-old child or grandchild, who is mainly a nondescript mass, and expects an enthusiastic response. He demands that the other should look and be as blind with admiration as he. The other has no choice. He must agree and lie.

There *is* genuine interest. There are some babies who are beautiful at birth, but these are the exceptions. Later on, after a few months, the great majority of babies are the embodiment of charm, loveliness and wonder of life. Most close relatives will find the baby beautiful whether he is or not.

An anecdote has it that while two men were walking along, one of them called the other's attention to a little boy coming from the opposite direction. The boy had an enormous, distorted head. He was hydrocephalic. The first man said, "Look. Isn't that terrible, the head. . . ?"

The other commented, "It is my son."

The first, trying to save the situation, hastily added, "It suits him well."

A man meets some parents who kindly ask about his children. Misled by his pride and vanity, he steps into the trap and begins to talk about the children. Hardly does he say a word before he is interrupted by a barrage of stories about *their* children. Sometimes, they listen with patience, but this patience is calculated to place another trap under the speaker's feet.

Whenever I am asked about my grandson, I am delighted to tell that it is an undiluted joy to observe him and that the baby learns something new every minute; whereupon I am informed that all children learn rapidly at this age. I was annihilated by this comment. If *all* children do this, there is nothing special about my grandson. It was *exactly* the grandfather's intention to make it known that *only his* grandson learns something new every minute and that, compared with him, all others are just ordinary children.

"We like it this way"

A man is invited to dinner. Everything is delicious. The guest praises the hostess, especially emphasizing his appreciation of the skill with which she has prepared the meat. She answers, "We like it this way." Why does she say this? Is she hurt? After all, she was praised. Does she think that the praise was insincere so that she has to defend herself by expressing apologies indicating that she was not in a position to prepare the food in a different way because she is accustomed to doing it "this way"? Or did she want to add to the praise, implying that nothing is unusual because it is a *rule* in her house that everything be delicious? The praise, though understandable, cannot be appreciated but can be considered rather as naïveté on the part of the guest who is graciously forgiven.

The use of corrupted and foolish words in affectionate relationships

In the exuberance of affection, language leaves many people in the lurch. We *must* create our own language. The sillier it is, the better it is, and the more satisfied we are. The newly created language makes us happier because it is something beyond anything that exists. It can be understood only by a man and his mate or by a parent and his baby. It is not exactly baby talk except in tone. Such language is a regression to infancy during which there was only happy blabbering, snuggling, and blissful senselessness as when nothing existed but love.

I cannot present an illustration of some thoroughly "deciphered" corrupted and foolish words, because the presentation may reveal the identity of a patient. Often such words can be traced far back into the past, to relations and to other important persons and situations.

Anything that the beloved person does is wonderful. There is a need to describe his actions by a word or words. These words often refer to the most intimate love-activities, mainly those in which the genitals or bodily functions are involved. They have some resemblance to the neologisms of schizophrenics and especially to the comical and bizarre word formations in dreams and wit formations (Freud, 1900, 1905a).

Greenacre, in *Swift and Carrol* (1955), presents relevant examples. She writes:

[1] artificially manufactured words like "Glubbdubrib," "Luggnagg," "Traldragdubh," "Clumdalditch," "Clumegnig" suggest an onomatopoetic derivation from the sound of drippings and droppings, possibly originating in the

overly intense preoccupation with toilet functions . . .
[p. 102].

[2] [In "Notes on Nonsense" (pp. 265-277):]
Nonsense is not only the loss of reason or loss of expected
order, but it is the defiance of reason which men value
most, and it is achieved by apparent isolation, inconse-
quence and generally heedless disconnection. There is a
quality (generally quiet) of explosive destructiveness about
sheer nonsense—an unannounced nihilism—which is never
absolutely achieved to be sure, but is felt in its subtle
implications [p. 271].

Parents and relatives, in their exuberant enthusiasm about
the baby or young child, burst out saying, even to beautiful
children, "You stinker, you ugly duck," and the like. In my
opinion, such expressions mean that love transcends or removes the boundaries of taste. The exuberant ones would like
to do "ugly things" like touching any part, even the ugly
ones, of the child's body.

Exclamations in joy and anger

In joy

On receiving good news, especially when it comes unexpectedly, we hear certain words of exclamation like *"Oh,
boy," "Oh, brother,"* and *"Oh, mama."* In my opinion, the
"oh boy" comes from the frequently observable fact that on
the announcement of the delivery of a boy baby the mother
and other relatives use these words in their joy and delight.
The words show a preference for the male sex. We never
hear "Oh, girl."

The "Oh, brother" probably originates from the same
source. It is good to have a brother (though this feeling
might later change, and, in certain cases, a coming brother is
not welcome at all).

The "mama" was the first source of pleasure in the matter
of feeding (mouth, breast). The memory of this pleasure is

so indelibly engraved in our minds that whenever something good happens, we come back to it in the exclamation, "Mama."

The same can be said about the noise made with the lips and tongue, the "tch . . . tch . . . tch," when we are delighted by a physical or spiritual pleasure such as food, the sight of a good-looking female, a picture, an enjoyable speech, and similar things. The "tch . . . tch . . . tch" is the sound of the suckling baby. We are eternal babies.

Snapping of the fingers is done in many similar situations. It will be discussed in a later chapter.

We hear the phrase, "I almost died (of joy or pleasure)" or "I am dying to see her (or whatever it is)" uttered in an ecstasy of delight and in delightful expectation. We all know that the person did not almost die and that he would have avoided the experience had he known that it might lead to death. The phrase cannot be related to the fact that some (sick) persons die even in joyful excitement. The most intense pleasure is sexual orgasm. Women, especially, refer to it with the expression, "I almost died." Because the sexual pleasure cannot be mentioned publicly, its opposite is used. While living in Europe, I often heard boys, at a joyful, pleasant occasion such as an exciting sports event, say, "I almost went off," hinting at orgastic seminal discharge.

Expression through the opposite appears in several other situational exclamations. I happened to mention to a mother that my grandson cut his first teeth; whereupon she chimed in saying, "This *snotty* X. (her son, whom she adores) got his first teeth, too, when he was about that age. He refused to eat unless he was put on the breast and this stinker bit me so often." It is possible that, besides the previous interpretation, there is a fear in her that the listener may be more interested in her son if she pretends to disapprove of him instead of praising him. Furthermore, she could have been angry that the baby hurt her and took this opportunity to discharge the anger.

At a professional dinner, doctors are placed at different tables. At one of the tables, there are six prominent doctors. Up comes another doctor, walking toward the table. His face expresses delight that he can consider himself as belonging to this group. When he reaches the table, he greets the others with, "Hi, bastards."

The mother of a few-months-old baby relates that her husband who idolizes the infant often talks to the child, saying, *"You stinker, you ugly swine, I hate you."*

I have witnessed some strange scenes among children between the ages of six and ten. They meet; they move toward each other so close that their faces almost touch; they giggle, laugh, roar and make the most impossible, idiotic faces. In one case (two girls), I think, with good reason, that the behavior was a displacement of the tendency to exhibit their genitals to each other.

In anger

The degradation of the excretory organs and their functions (as being "dirty") and the subsequent degradation of the sexual organs and their functions to the level of the degraded excretory functions is *one* of the causes for the use of certain "obscene" words in certain situations. One such situation is the state of anger. The same reasoning can be applied to the use of these words in curses, or in blasphemies in which they are mainly thought.

Instead of paying due respect to the excretory organs which are indispensable to life, instead of bearing in mind that we were all born between two excretory organs, instead of realizing that the functions of the excretory organs are gratifying and pleasurable, instead of giving the drives subserving these organs and functions a chance to become sublimated in the form of ambition and genorosity, instead of teaching our children that all these functions are present in respectable persons—instead of all this, most of us besmirch the excretory organs and functions with deceptions, hypocritical negation, which force the drives inherent in those organs to be pent up and to explode in affective situations to which they do not belong.

A profound source of the use of obscene words was discovered by Hermann (1949). This source refers to the mother who allows herself to be touched anywhere by the baby. The infant, being very small, perceives the mother as big and fat. This feeling of bigness and fatness appears in the juicy, sensual and lush, obscene words used by adults.

The use of "obscene" words as such, or in blasphemy, or in cursing appears in different forms: such as an accepted group characteristic, or as an obsessive impulse, or as an expression of anger. The main force in the words is aggression (Montagu, 1942; Eliasberg, 1942; Bose, Law and Ganguly, 1951; Devereux, 1951; Ferenczi, 1911; Stone, 1954).

When the absentee is always wrong

Certain sayings are applicable in all circumstances. Most of them are used only to serve the purpose of the speaker. For example, the saying, "Where there is smoke, there is fire," is always true when taken literally, but not when taken figuratively. Some people can create smoke from nothing, without a fire, especially through rumor and gossip. When one is able to follow the chain reaction in this process, he can discover the underlying complexes in all the people involved.

For example, an old, frustrated lady, A., tells a younger man, B., that another old lady, C., confessed to her that B. made passes at her. It was possible to establish the truth. The younger man did make passes at young, attractive females (and this was known to both ladies). The man, who was present at a public gathering, was noticed by lady C., who came from the far side of the assembly room to ask him for some professional advice. Some days later, when ladies A. and C. met, lady C. told lady A. that B. made passes at her. Both ladies would have liked to have such an experience.

Lady A. should have known that Lady C. was indulging in wishful fantasies, but she needed to believe that C. was right because she desired the same kind of experience, and therefore reproached B. for his alleged improper conduct. Had the man made passes at C., she would either have not mentioned it to A. (attractive women usually do not mention their husbands when other attractive males make flattering passes at them) or have made a federal case of the matter (because of her conscience) as a reaction to the pleasant stimulation.

In general, he who is absent is wrong because the persons who were informed do not have the courage to convey their disbelief. They want to please the speaker and attack the accused to convince themselves that they are not cowards because they believed the accusation.

One might ask what they gain. After all, they are assuming the unpleasant task of telling the third party something which is painful. They do it, first, because the pain comes a little later, and, second, because they enjoy both situations, hearing and telling. Mature persons would not make any judgment from one bit of information, especially not when such information concerns a friend about whom they know different.

Appropriating the child when he is praiseworthy and disowning him to the mate if not

One often hears and probably himself often says to his mate when a child misbehaves and causes worry, "Your son (or your daughter)." But when the child is good and arouses pride, the parent claims the youngster. Then the child is "my son" (or daughter). A parent wants only good things and would like to withdraw from anything unpleasant.

A classical example of such denial is recorded in the Bible, Exodus, Chapter 32. Moses was with the Lord on Mount Sinai, receiving the commandments. He was delayed. The people became impatient and urged Aaron, the chief priest, to make them a god. And Aaron made them the golden calf. "And the Lord spoke unto Moses: 'Go, get thee down; for thy people, that thou broughtest up out of the land of Egypt, have dealt corruptly.' " As the reader can see, the Lord said "*thy people*." The commentators on the Bible wondered why the Lord said "*thy people*" when he often talked about them as "*my people*." The Chief Rabbi of Great Britain, Dr. J. H. Hertz (1938), supported by traditional sources, comments, "God disowns the sinful Israelites. He refuses to acknowledge them as His people."

"I don't know"

If someone is asked for information which he does not have, he legitimately uses the phrase, "I don't know." The use of the phrase is also legitimate when he knows the answer but he wants, for his own reasons, not to tell it. In the latter case, he does not tell the truth; but the "I don't know" is still legitimate.

On the other hand, we meet many persons who use the "I don't know" when they do know the answer or they do know what to say. In my paper, "Mannerisms of Speech" (1948), I have presented two examples of the latter.

A law student sought treatment for anxiety about his examinations for the bar. He had passed all his previous examinations and claimed to be well prepared for the last one also, saying that he knew all the material but that the idea of the examination made him feel that he would get stuck, that nothing would come to his mind, and that he would therefore fail. He was a shy and timid man, twenty-eight years old. Because of his timidity he had only superficial social relationships. He had very few sexual experiences; it took a long time for him to take a definite step in this direction, and when he did so the sexual act was unsatisfactory and he suffered from ejaculatio praecox. Although he was, in general, on good terms with his parents, he felt uneasy in talking with them, especially with his father.

During the course of treatment it was noted that the patient interlarded his sentences with the phrase, "I don't know," and this always before he said something about which he was intellectually absolutely sure. The writer tried an experiment with him. In coming for treatment, the patient had to use several streetcars, transferring twice. He was asked to tell what steps he took in getting home from the office. He replied: "I don't know. I'll leave this office; then, I don't know, I'll go to the corner, and I don't know, take streetcar number so and so; then, I don't know . . ." Thus he continued with every step until he reached home, or "passed the examination." He passed this miniature examination because of his feeling of safety with the writer and because he could use his crutches. But the idea of the real examination was more fearful, and because he might not be able to use crutches he did not dare take it. It was obvious that the patient was afraid to betray his knowledge of something unrelated to the actual questions he was called upon to answer. As far as he could recall he started using "I don't know" at about the age of fourteen. At that time because of his growing sexual urges, he was afraid of his father, and although he craved the support of his mother, he could not reveal himself to her in this matter as he had previously done in others. Having lost his mother's support he replaced her with an oral regressive defense, a "clinging to," as a defense against the threatening father [Hermann, 1936]. In the face of the examinations for the bar he felt that the mother's support was no longer available or effective. His anxiety came to the fore in any personal relationship, and especially when he was speaking. The use of the "I don't know" meant: "Mother, please, protect me against father. I don't know anything about sexuality." This was not true, but although he knew it, he was afraid to take responsibility for it.

A young violinist came into treatment because his arm trembled the moment he took his bow to play in the orchestra at public performances. This occurred after he was promoted to sitting closer to the conductor. He was the only son of a domineering and aggressive mother, who from early childhood had impressed upon him that he was frail and weak, that he could not take responsibility, and needed always to be taken care of by her.

Previous to this neurosis he had had a similar spell of anxiety when, at the conclusion of his studies, he had first had to play in public. After the concert he did not go out with the other boys, as was the custom, but because of his anxiety he went straight home, and (at the age of twenty-four) got into bed with his mother "to be under her wing." He married against his mother's will, and preferred to visit his mother without his wife. Whenever his wife asked him what he had done at his mother's, or his mother asked him about events in his own family, he prefaced his reply with, "I don't know." This underlying conflict was extended into his speech no matter with whom he talked: "I have to say that I do not know what I actually do know, namely, that I have not yet sufficiently matured as to be able to make a definite choice between my mother and my wife."

"Curiously enough"

The word "curious" has several meanings. Referring to "curiously enough," we mean that something gives the feeling that a certain phenomenon is odd. The word "odd" also has many meanings. What we want to discuss in this book is how people, in everyday communication, use "curiously enough."

Somebody says that a certain person whom he has not seen for a long time has arrived in town. He adds, "Curiously enough, I thought of him yesterday." He means that the connection between the two events is an unusual one.

In a recently published book, a certain author offers new ideas. "Curiously enough," comments a reader, "the Bible and the Talmud expressed similar ideas long, long ago." Here the "curious" means that something unexpected happened, though there is a great distance in time between the two events which are, nevertheless, still close. This thought is connected with a pleasant feeling. One can feel that there are no distances in time and space; there is no separation; one is immortal. In the case of the appearance of a person whom one had mentioned the day before, the pleasant feeling comes from a wish, present in all of us, to prophesy, to foresee, to be omnipotent, and to have secret powers.

Conventional comments on parting from somebody

It is painful to separate from those we love and blissful from those we dislike.

The phrases "See you again," "Take it easy," "Was glad to see you," "Come again," "Don't work too hard" can contain warmth or can mean nothing, but nothing, whatsoever. They may be used to maintain a bridge in the form of a hope, a promise to stay alive, to stay in contact with the other person, not to separate from him; and they can mean that one person does not care if the other drops dead.

These meanings were admitted by patients in analysis. One is expected to use these phrases because he lends himself to illusions rather than facing unpleasant reality. In my opinion, one should not expect love when there is no reason or cause to get it. Everyone should do his best to create good relationships in which, at departure, these words have genuine meaning.

There is a distance of about two yards between my waiting room and office. As a rule, when one patient leaves, I open the door of the waiting room which had been closed by the coming patient, and invite the other into the office. One patient was greeted by a "How do you do?" He answered, "Fine" (as is expected by society). The moment he entered the office, he said, "Lousy."

It was a relief for both of us.

"Why? . . . Why?"

The thoughts expressed in this chapter are based on the analysis of two cases in which the exclamation, "why . . . why?" was outstanding. It is suggested that conclusions reached in these analyzed cases may be applied, at least in principle, to similar or identical observations made in everyday life.

The two patients, both females, were always tense, and always spoke in a very lively and excited manner. Their voices were characteristically shrieking. As E. Shapiro (1927) points out, the voice-dynamics, including the intonation, speed, continuity, rhythm, pronunciation, vocabulary and style, have always to be taken into consideration in the analysis of speech. I agree with Shapiro that "the voice is a social as well as an individual phenomenon."

S. Neuman (1939) made some interesting observations on personal symbolism used by a patient.

A girl, in treatment, often complained that her mother was always "nagging her to go out with boys." "Why," she said in a loud voice, "why doesn't she leave me alone? What business is it of hers whether I get married?" The girl wanted to get married, but her neurotic symptoms made it impossible for her to do so. Her mother had no idea about the exact nature of the girl's neurosis. The latter could not confide in her mother. Furthermore, as an important factor in her neurosis, there was a strong "father complex" present, manifesting itself in frequent affectionate teasing between her and the neurotic father. In this triangle, as often happens, all three persons involved, daughter, father, and mother, unconsciously perceived what was going on. The mother, like all mothers, wanted her daughter to get married for the girl's happiness. In addition to this, she wanted to eliminate a dangerous rival from the house. The girl wanted to get married; but because she was attached to her father, she delayed doing so by means of her symptoms. The father was ambivalent too. He wanted the daughter to get married because that was the way it should be. On the other hand, he begrudged the loss of his daughter. The girl knew all this very well. She knew why the mother was urging her to get married. By shrieking the "why . . . why?" she denied this knowledge.

The other case was a woman who claimed that she was the most loyal and humble of friends. She was loyal, but she was humble only in appearance. She wanted to be acknowledged as socially superior to her female friends. They did not like this and gradually dropped her. She became very indignant; and whenever anyone dropped her, she became very upset and exclaimed, "Why? . . . why?" She knew why, but she did not want to admit that she knew.

"I want to ask you something"

When there is a meeting or gathering where it is understood that one may ask questions, it is legitimate to stand up and ask; but there is no need to say that one wants to ask a question simply because it is agreed that the objective of the gathering is to encourage the asking of questions.

The same is true in private conversations. Many people, however, being skittish, timid or hesitant, introduce their remarks, after a pause, with the "I want to say something" or "I want to ask you something," instead of immediately telling or asking what they want. One could say that this is done out of politeness. It seems so, although one can be polite without using such an introduction. The analysis of persons who frequently use this mannerism disclosed that they are either afraid of being considered aggressive or they *are* aggressive and are afraid of being so. The reaction is a repetition of a childhood situation. Often children are not permitted to ask questions or to assert themselves. They are taught too much to be silent, "polite."

When the listener, after hearing "may I ask (or say) something," remains noncommittal, the speaker will be embarrassed. He needs and begs for permission and encouragement.

The situation is clearer in the case where a speaker asks, "May I *tell* you something?" In this case, the speaker will tell the listener unpleasant things about the latter. Then the expression is similar to the "I don't want to hurt you, but . . ."

"Isn't this terrible?"

A case which has already been mentioned in a previous chapter is here repeated for the sake of presenting another aspect of the phenomenon.

In an advanced stage of her analysis, a married patient related that her neighbor, another married woman, stopped the patient and whispered, "I heard that Mrs. X. (a third neighbor and also a married woman) has a lover. Isn't this terrible?"

The patient did not show much interest and said, "That's her business."

The other woman replied somewhat angrily, "What do you mean that this is her business? Would you associate with such a woman?"

The patient answered, "If she is otherwise a good human being, I would."

"I would not," said the other indignantly.

From other such experiences, I feel justified in assuming that the patient was not interested and did not become upset because she did *not* entertain desires to have a lover, but the other *did* and did not want to be aware of it. The neighbor needed to confess this in a negative way. She needed strong disapproval of such conduct in order to strengthen her defenses against the wish to have a lover like the condemned neighbor. It seems to me that this is similar to what Mazzanti and Bessell (1956) called "Communication through the latent language."

Perhaps, the following event belongs in this chapter. A patient said, "My girl friend who knows that I am coming to you for treatment, and who intends to come to you too asked me whether you were married or not."

The reader, already indoctrinated, knows by now that it is *she*, the patient, who is interested in this also; and it is important that *she* is interested. The other's curiosity is, in the present situation, irrelevant. The patient *was* interested before her girl friend and was afraid to investigate by asking the question directly. The patient who was, to be sure, a beginner in her analysis, did not admit that she wanted an answer for herself. No, she "pretended" that she would like an answer for her girl friend. I leave it to the reader to decide whether the patient was pretending or whether she repressed her curiosity.

In everyday life, women would have much less resistance to asking such a question. Social relations are different from that of the analytic situation. In the latter, the patient comes for *treatment,* and the *professional distance* easily activates repressed important events with identical or similar content which in the *anayltic situation* seek to come to the surface through *transference.* It is characteristic of psychoanalytic treatment that such questions are *not* answered. Frustration stimulates further material.

"Oh, it is wonderful; you shouldn't have done it"

It never fails. Is there a grown-up man who has not had the experience of surprising his lady with a beautiful present? Her face beams, and she makes the famous, rapturous exclamation, "It is beautiful. It is wonderful. You shouldn't have done it."

The man knows and feels that she means that he should have done it. Why, then, does she say, "You should *not* have done it"? Why does she say the opposite of what she feels, means, desires, and wants from the man?

The expression must have a meaning. It has a very good and important meaning. Wives with a conscience are ambivalent about receiving gifts from their husbands. On the one hand, they feel that they should get attention and admiration for whatever they represent and give to their husbands; but, on the other hand, they do feel guilty, not for what they have done (if they did not) but for what they thought of doing; and the wish is father to the thought. They have sometimes hated their men. They have thought about possible second mates in the event that the present one died. They have entertained disloyal ideas. After years of marriage, it is unavoidable to have such ideas and wishes.

Now, the man comes home with a wonderful gift. What to do with the latent guilt feelings? She says, "You shouldn't have done it" (but she does not say why not). She wants the husband to *convince* her that it is imperative to bring her gifts because he loves her beyond everything and that what she wished, thought, did or wanted to do are as nothing compared with what she means to him. Nothing is costly to a woman when it expresses that she is wonderful, attractive, divine. She needs to know that the husband does not give the gift for social reasons or obligations but from strong love.

"It struck me funny"
"It was funny"

A patient was discussing at one time with her (virgin) daughter the latter's feelings and responses to the boy who was courting her. The girl said that when she was with the boy she had a *"funny feeling in my stomach; like butterflies."* Such a reaction is obviously a sensual-genital response. It is not only symbolic but in addition it is a conversion symptom, a displacement from below above.

A young married woman who was sensually very much interested in another married man, and who was frigid in her marriage, mentioned in an analytic session that "it would be funny" to be married to a man of the same age as her father, who was a friend of her father, and who was for many years her father's business partner.

> Analyst: "What do you mean by funny?"
> Patient: "It would be thought-provoking."
> Analyst: "What thoughts could it provoke?"
> Patient: "I don't know."

At the time of this conversation her analysis had not yet progressed to the stage at which this could be interpreted. This was done later; the father's friend represented father; the "it would be funny" meant that something repressed was stimulated. To have "fun" often means that one will permit oneself to gratify a suppressed and repressed drive.

A male patient related a dream in which (among other things) he saw a composite picture of two male friends. In the course of the dream, he put on a hat and became aware that it was not his hat but that of somebody else. When he awakened, he felt that the second part of the dream (with the hat) was "funny." In real life, one of the friends in the dream used to have a good time by putting on his head the hats of different people, both male and female. Lately, the friend's habit had annoyed the patient. He worked together with the two men in the dream, and he was often in conflict and confusion as to how far he should yield to their opinions and how far he should stick to his own. Should he use his head (hat) or their heads (hats)? Should he be active or passive?

I have discussed the symbolic meaning of "hat" (and other men's furnishings) several years ago (1932b).

Another source of fun is misrepresentation, which means putting across something that is not true; like "taking somebody for a ride" or "pulling someone's leg." The fun, in this case, lies in the speaker's knowledge that the listener is unaware of the true facts. For example, a man telephones another who is not available. The latter's secretary answers the call, and the speaker assumes the identity of an important personage. The secretary is sufficiently fooled to accord the impostor the respect due the man whom the caller is impersonating. The reader may fill in the details as I set the scene.

Caller: "Hello. Is Dr. H. there?"

Secretary: "I am sorry. Dr. H. is in conference. Is there a message?"

Caller (realizing that the secretary cannot identify him): "This is Dr. S. (a prominent man)."

A happily married young man took his wife and visiting sister out to a restaurant for dinner. During the course of the meal, he said to his sister, "Honey, will you please pass the butter?" Usually, the only person whom he habitually addressed as "honey" is his wife. Later, his wife told him that it struck her "funny" when he called his sister "honey." The wife knew that the man was fond of his sister. In my opinion, the husband's "honey" was understood by his wife as an incestuous feeling and this was labeled as "funny."

You bad man. You brought this miserable weather with you. Why? Why?

A man leaves his home town in beautiful weather. He arrives in another city in which the weather is nasty. He visits friends who tease him, "You bad man. You brought the bad weather with you." He wants to be a "good sport" and even finds some kind of pleasure in entering into the game. He smiles, shrugs his shoulders, as if to say, "Sorry. It is true this nastiness is in me. I just cannot help it. The devil is working in me." The visitor is not subjected to this teasing if the weather is fine. He does not get the credit for it.

We can do nothing for or against the weather. We are helpless and at the mercy of nature. This makes us uneasy and insecure. We regress to a primitive stage of mind, to a magic-animistic way of thinking, when we, in our helplessness, attributed adverse happenings to evil spirits whom we believed to influence through different rituals and ceremonies (Ferenczi, 1913). Those evil spirits are also deeply buried in our minds and reappear under certain circumstances. The man who enters into the game enjoys being the powerful evil.

The "wet blankets"

People who spoil the fun of others are called "wet blankets." They ruin the pleasant excitement of planned entertainment. They are too sober.

There are excusable and inexcusable "wet blankets." My mother was a classical example of the first type.

We lived in a small town, Galanta, at that time, in Hungary (it was ceded to Slovakia after the Second World War). I was about seven years old. I had a friend who was at that time my ideal, about three years my senior, Desiderius Ruhig. It was he who disclosed to me where children came from and *how* they came. It was agreed between us that, with the exception of our parents, all our friends were born through the sexual union of their parents. We parted undecided about the origin of *our* birth. Our discussion was kept a great secret. When we met the parents of other children, we looked at them askance.

The same friend taught me to smoke, a thing we were not supposed to do. Therefore, we did it secretly. We went to the peripheries of the town where we loved to go anyhow, and there we "suffered" the first cigarettes. After all, we were grownups; we knew where children came from. At that time, I already had several siblings; and it was hard, very hard, on my father to provide us with clothing. We had to be very careful. Twice a year, each boy got a new suit.

Walking with my friend, I wore my new suit. Between my two fingers, I held a cigarette. We were smoking. Then, suddenly, we saw our school teacher coming toward us. The cigarette was too costly to throw away. I do not remember what my friend did; but I turned my cigarette into the hollow of my palm and put my hand into my pocket. I needed only half a minute or so until we passed the teacher. I thought that we had escaped. We did; but to my horror, I noticed that my cigarette had burned a hole through the pocket of my suit, my new suit, and was peeping out of the hole. It was horrible. I felt the world had come to an end for me. I threw away the cigarette, left my friend and went home. My mother was a genius at mending things. I went to her with tears in my eyes, and I showed her what had happened. Without saying one word (fortunately nobody else was home at that time), she mended and ironed the damaged suit. It was perfect, and I was happy. From that time on, I never gave up hope in my life. I hoped when things were at their worst that a good turn would come. I accomplished everything the hard way, but I accomplished what I wanted.

And such a mother was a wet blanket? She was. When I was ten or eleven, we moved to the capital of Hungary, beautiful Budapest. When I started to work, I bought my own suits, neckties, socks. Whenever I visited my mother and whenever she noticed that I was wearing something new, her first reaction of joy showed plainly on her face; but then she would say, "This necktie is very nice but raindrops might stay as spots," or, "This suit is beautiful, but the pants will shine quickly."

She wanted the best for all her children, the best all the time. She wanted her children not to be deprived of anything and not to suffer any disappointment. She wanted to prepare them for any eventuality.

On the other hand, there are many persons who though they do the same thing and act in the same way do not have a lofty aim. They are "real" wet blankets. They cannot tolerate anyone's being optimistic or enjoying anything without throwing a fly into the soup.

I feel I have to protect persons who are unjustly tagged as

"wet blankets." For example, there are husbands who work hard all day long and need a good night's rest if they are to get up early in the morning to go to their jobs. When a man like this goes to a party with his wife, they agree not to stay long. But she has a good time and the other guests beg her to stay. She would like to do so, but her husband wants to go home. Although he, too, would like to stay, he knows from experience that if he does, he will be tired the next day. Everyone gangs up on him and calls him a "wet blanket." He feels miserable whether he stays or whether he goes. He can't win, and probably neither can the author.

Appropriating another's views and then turning them against him

I have one classical case of the mannerism of appropriating another's views and then turning them against him. Perhaps, the reader can supply other examples from his observations of this phenomenon being used in similar or more subtle ways in everyday life.

One talks to a lady about a play that both have seen. She offers sharp criticism. She did not like the play. Then the other chimes in and tells her all about the excellencies of the play. He liked it. She, forthwith, astounds him with a remarkable mental calisthenic. *She* will tell *him* what she has just heard from him. *She* will behave as if it were the other who said what she said and goes on convincing him how wrong he is. She must always be right, and she takes her rightousness from anywhere and in any way she can get it.

"They"

One learns by experience that it is wise to secure sleeping car tickets well in advance of a trip. Accordingly, he has the tickets already in his possession a month before the date of his departure. He has weighty reasons for traveling overnight, in a bedroom, if possible. This time, he got bedrooms round-trip. In due time, he gets into his bedroom, has a comfortable trip, and arrives refreshed at his destination. After days of tiresome business, he returns punctually to the station and falls into reveries, visualizing that he will soon be in his bedroom, will relax and have a good sleep. The next morning, he will be in his office in good condition.

The ticket is checked by some man in uniform. It is remarkable that such men all look alike. The traveler presents his tickets; and there it comes. The uniformed one says that the bedroom has been taken away from the prospective passenger and exchanged for a roomette. The difference in cost will be refunded. He reaches into his pocket, takes out the proper sum, and for him the matter is settled. But not so for the traveler. He is annoyed. "That's not fair," he feels. He tries to protest, in vain. He feels like the hero of a Kafka story, who is thrown and pushed around without having the slightest idea who could be the master and the instrument of his sad plight. The uniformed one says that "*they*" made the change. " 'They?' Who are these 'they?' " asks our hero. "They in . . ." he is told. He can do nothing. The uniformed one is only a tiny little cog in the big machinery.

The train is late. The traveler has time. He goes to the station master and tells his story, asking whether the latter is interested in finding out exactly who those "they" are. He is. He and two more officials are mobilized. Much telephoning goes on; and finally, they find out exactly who those "they" are, what company they represent, in what city and at what address.

Shands (1958) discussed a patient who referred to other persons as "they" without mentioning their names.

One should not accept the "they" without knowing exactly what it means. It is used as an effective, influencing tool and device to make a person feel that he does not *need* to think. If "THEY" say or do it, then it must be so. "They" takes advantage of the images of authorities which, during childhood, were deposited or placed in the mind and sank into the unconscious where they remain, in adults, in a latent state. When a "they" comes along, these images of authority are revived, take over the individual, maim and kill his self. He is not thinking for himself. Others have taken over his thinking. He does not know when and how "they" will deprive him of his own thinking.

Excessive laughter during speaking

It is the intention of this chapter to discuss excessive laughter when, for the listener, there is no reason to laugh. Only the speaker finds good cause to laugh. In other words, we are not considering the matter of excessive laughing when a joke is related and everybody laughs. We are concerned only with the matter of the communicant's laughter.

I know two ladies, one of whom laughs whether her story is a sad one or a neutral one; the other laughs only when the story is neutral. The excessive laughter is not usually present when they laugh for reasons that would cause anybody to laugh.

The first lady has a most unhappy family life from which she cannot escape. When she talks about her troubles, she laughs so loud that one can hear her a block away. It is transparent that finding fun in her misfortune is her most effective weapon.

The other woman is a narcissistic person who is always acting. When she tells what happened, whether she is good or bad, whether she loves or hates, the only thing that matters is that she must be in the picture. She finds whatever she does so entertaining that she bursts into laughter, while the listener has no response; or, if he does, has one of annoyance and irritation.

Crying at the Happy Ending*

The brevity of this communication does not do justice to the importance of the widespread, psychological and social phenomenon of crying at the happy ending. I am aware of this fact and expect that the readers will be overwhelmed by reactions stimulated by their own experiences. Some may find my interpretations and suggestions difficult to accept, insufficient, and incomprehensive. However, the conclusions are based on careful, long and painstaking analyses of patients who, in the course of their treatment for other purposes, presented this phenomenon. Encouraged by these findings, I took the liberty of applying this knowledge to events and cases I did not have the chance to investigate through personal interviews.

In our culture, tears are usually shed as a result of physical and mental pain, grief, sentimental experiences, exalted scenes, and at the happy ending of a tense or perilous situation. Tears caused by violent laughter or coughing have no psychological origin. According to Darwin (1873), they are the result of muscular and vascular processes caused by those actions.

A man who by cruel fate had been stricken since childhood by several different physical infirmities, who, in addition to these traumatic events, lost his mother when he was very young, and who was harshly terrorized by a threatening and dictatorial father, developed a painful and paralyzing neurosis. At the end of his long analysis, which he felt helped him a great deal and opened to him the possibility of a happy life, he said, "Thank you. You were so good to me." He then burst out with crying which he could hardly suppress and, in embarrassment, left hastily. Right or wrong, crying in men is considered a weakness.

Why did this man cry when he expressed his gratitude at

* Reprinted from *Journal of the American Psychoanalytic Association*, Vol. IV, No. 3, pp. 477-485, July, 1956.

the happy ending of a long and painful journey of his life? Was he happy? Was he full of joy? He was. The question is whether he cried *because* he was happy or for some other reason which was stirred up *at the occasion* of the happy ending. In my opinion, the latter interpretation is the correct one. This man had suppressed tears for more than two decades. Now that things took a turn for the better, the suppressed tears were released. True, he was helped a great deal, but would everything from now on in his life be without pain and trouble? Hardly! Life is tough even when one has become well. Furthermore, the separation from one who "was good" to him reminded him of the only other person who had loved him and taken care of him after his mother's death. This person also died at an early age. He was sad and in pain, because he was again to be separated from a kind and loving person, his therapist.

A tough and aggressive businessman burst into sudden, loud crying and sobbing when he observed in a motion picture that an unhappy misunderstanding between two good friends, followed by a period of long and bitter hatred, was happily clarified. As a result of this, they fell into each other's arms. This man was ruthless and more than unfair in his business life. He did not permit himself to have feelings of kindness toward anybody except the few members of his close family. This hard exterior was but a front, for deep down in his heart, like everybody else, he craved to love and to be loved. When the motion picture showed that hatred, hostility and cruelty gave way to love and brotherhood, he still felt that he was the loser despite his happiness that things turned out well. This, and not the joy of the happy ending, made him cry. It should be emphasized that he was happy and joyous but that he cried for the abovementioned reasons and not because an unhappy situation was happily resolved. Furthermore, the story with the happy ending also made him feel guilty for being so cruel in his professional life.

A male patient related in his analysis that his eyes became watery when he looked at a commercial advertisement presenting a lovely and smiling mother bending over a healthy, happy and smiling baby. This man had serious emotional difficulties in his marital life. He could not tolerate any justifiable criticism. He wanted, like a child, unconditional love. The picture which moved him so deeply did not portray a sad event but a happy one. Did he not like the picture? Was he not happy to see the happy scene? Why then did he cry? It was disclosed in his analysis that the lovely and sentimental picture made him sad because he realized that in reality the happy child-mother relationship was no longer attainable. He had to realize the sad fact that he was a grown-up man and had to face all the consequences of reality, including the fact that his wife was entitled to expect certain nonsexual and sexual gratifications from him in order for her to consider him a normal husband. He found the picture lovely and charming. On the other hand, the picture stirred up feelings of frustration which made him sad. The joy was there, but the tears were caused by associations which led to sad events.

Suppose that a heroic captain orders all men to abandon a badly damaged ship for the saving of which all hope had been abandoned. He remains on it to the last moment, and he is saved only after several trying days. His wife, who has followed his plight by radio announcements, learns of his rescue and cries with joy. She is full of joy and happiness; but is it true that her joy and happiness over her beloved husband's rescue made her cry? For this case, we can readily accept the interpretation which Weiss (1952) offered in a fascinating, brief paper. He states that in such a case we encounter the phenomenon of the "delay of affect." As long as one worries about the fate of the beloved, as long as the wished-for happy solution does not yet take place, one suppresses the sadness. When everything turns out well, one permits oneself the discharge of the repressed sadness. Weiss also thinks that it is not the joy that makes one cry under the above-mentioned circumstances but that, in the last analysis, the tears are due to sadness. Furthermore, Weiss realizes that the "delay of affect" is not the only explanation and that there are other possible causes for crying at the happy ending. I have already presented two theories: one, that the happy ending reminds us of the lost happy past; the other, that the happy ending makes us realize that there is a kindness, love and goodness that we could exercise but do not. The latter instance can be seen in the case of the "tough businessman."

Parents go through many emotional tribulations until their child grows up, goes through school and reaches the happy day of graduation. When they see their child marching solemnly toward the platform, they burst into tears. They say that they cry from joy and happiness. They say this because they feel happy and, therefore, in my opinion, it appears to them that the tears are tears of joy and happiness. The graduate usually does not cry. The only ones who do are the parents, relatives, friends, and perhaps some emotional and sentimental strangers. But is it true that those tears are tears of joy just because they appear *when* one feels happy and joyous? Is it not justifiable to apply Weiss's explanation, at least as one possibility, that for long years the parents, relatives and friends suppressed a great deal of worry about the future of their child and, now, at the happy ending, they release their accumulated apprehensions through tears which they call "tears of joy" and "tears of happiness?"

The beautiful bride stands at the altar with the handsome bridegroom. She is happy; it is the happiest day of her life. This is the moment she dreamed of for so long. The dream comes true. The bride may or may not smile, but she does not cry. (A middle-aged woman told me that she cried at her wedding because she was not sure whether she loved her husband and was afraid that she would not be happy in her marriage.) The bride's parents, relatives and friends may cry, and usually do. When asked why they cry, the answer is always that they cry because they are happy, that they are overwhelmed with joy. They feel that they are happy for her and are shedding tears of joy. Some say that they cry because they lose their child through marriage. I believe that they cry because they feel that, up to this time, the child was safe in their protection but that, from now on, the bride, especially, faces a difficult and uncertain future. Behind the present happy and joyful event, looms the sadness over the uncertain future of the beloved child.

A male patient had a brilliant brother who excelled in studies, in sports and in social relationships. The patient, on the other hand, was timid, shy and anxious. His brother once praised him and the patient burst into tears. During the course of his analysis, it was realized that he cried because he was sad that the praise came so late. Although he was happy when the brother praised him, the tears came not for what he had received but for what he had not received in the past.

When this man was five years old, his mother gave him an old tennis racquet. He burst into tears, which puzzled his mother who could not understand. He was happy, but still he had to cry. The tears were tears of sadness. He had had very little contact with his mother and for long years he had been taken care of by a nurse. Mother's kindness reminded him of the dormant, painful and sad fact that she had not given him attention. The tears were not tears of happiness but tears of unhappiness. This bright, essentially strong man could not use his excellent capabilities because he had to withdraw to his fantasies in which he compensated for his inner loneliness.

A female patient cried when she observed a little boy who was overwhelmed with joy when his parents presented him with a pair of new shoes. The patient knew that the boy's parents were poor and that the shoes were made of cheap fabric. She knew that the boy was unaware of the fact that there were much better shoes available for those who could afford them. The little boy was happy because he thought that the shoes were wonderful, the best shoes in the world. The patient understood and appreciated the happiness of the child; nevertheless, she was sad because of what the child was missing. Her tears, again, were not tears of joy.

The Bible offers the most moving and wonderful example of our problem, with the story of the meeting and reconciliation of Jacob and Esau. After a long period of bitter rivalry and hatred which separated the two brothers, they met. The Bible (Genesis 33:4) says, "And Esau ran to meet him, and embraced him, and fell on his neck, and kissed him; and they wept." The hatred gave way to love. Why then, did they cry? There is a very unusual kind of printing in the original Hebrew text. Above all the letters of "kissed him," (*vajishokaehu*), there are dots. Already in my early childhood I loved to read and study the Bible, and once my father, who was a profound scholar in this field, told me what the dots could mean. I was told that, despite the reconciliation, Esau still hated Jacob. When Esau kissed his bother, the impulse to bite Jacob flashed through his mind, but he checked it. The dots above the letters are symbolic marks of teeth. In his commentary on the Bible, the Chief Rabbi of England, J. H. Hertz (1938), remarks that "The Rabbis doubted whether the kiss of Esau was genuine or not." There are two possible explanations for the weeping at the joyous and happy ending. The brothers cried either because, at the moment of the reconciliation, they were reminded of the bitter hatred in the past, or because they felt that the reconciliation was not a genuine one. Possibly both feelings were present.

After long and strenuous preparations in competing for the title of Miss or Mrs. America, a few girls stand on the platform waiting for the final decision of the "judges." The name of the winner is announced and, often, the winner faints or cries. Engel (1950) explains one of his patients' fainting as a hysterical conversion symptom. This takes care of the fainting, but what is the cause of crying? After all, Miss or Mrs. America wanted to win, and she was happy to be the winner.

If asked about her reaction, she would say that she was crying because she was happy. I have never had the pleasure of analyzing a Miss or Mrs. America. I can only guess, on the basis of analytic investigations of other similar cases, what the hidden motive of the crying might be. We can assume that she cries because she knows that this is a passing glory. Time passes and age will destroy the glorious features of youth. But probably there are other additional and individual reasons for the crying. Since this paper was read, I was informed by two reliable persons that, when they watched the television presentation of one of the beauty contests, they distinctly heard the sniveling winner whispering to herself, "Daddy knows." Her father had died a year before the event. Is it far-fetched to assume that the tears were caused by the sadness that the father could not witness the glory of his daughter?

According to Darwin (1873), children cry out loud when they are hungry or suffering from some other distress. They cry out for aid and protection. Through a chain of physiological connections, the crying affects the lachrymal glands which secrete tears. Therefore, "suffering readily causes the secretion of tears, without necessarily being accompanied by any other action."

Shedding tears is a protective reflex action when the eyes are endangered by irritating, foreign bodies. The protection of the eyes for the purpose of self-preservation and libidinous gratification (looking and being looked at) seems to have become the model of protection for any kind of insecurity. This could be pain, hunger or any kind of distress like mourning, sadness, grief, or the sudden increase of any psychic-emotional energy thrusting itself on the mental apparatus. It is possible that even a sudden eruption of a happy emotion becomes so painful that it has to be removed. The mental apparatus cannot tolerate such a great tension (Freud) and attempts to get rid of it by a primary reflex-defense mechanism, shedding tears. The alternate crying and laughing in an intense and sudden happy or unhappy situation might become understandable. Even happiness can be painful if it is too intense.

Some people cry at the pleasurable gratification of orgasm in sexual union. Some people experience great embarrassment when they confuse the words "funeral" and "wedding." Others cannot help smiling when they express their sympathy to mourning persons. Probably the attraction of opposing poles in thoughts and feelings is a fundamental characteristic of our mental behavior. Masserman (1954) would call this the "inner dialectic of human behavior." A close relative of mine apparently felt the need of telling her experience to another human being. After experiencing the greatest suffering and blow that could be inflicted on a human being, she said that, when she and her husband returned home from the funeral, they felt a strong urge to conceive another child, which was born to them nine months after the date of the funeral. The same urges were reported by many persons who attended funerals. The idea of life stirs up the idea of death and vice versa.*

In summary: analytic observation encouraged me to assume that crying at the happy ending is due to a "delay of affect" (Weiss, 1952); to sad events the memories of which are stirred up by the happy ending; to guilt, "how sad it is that we are bad, though life shows that one could be good." I offer another possibility as an explanation for the crying at the happy ending. As children, we are happy; we are loved and protected. Despite our pains and frustrations, we believe that life is essentially joyful. As children, we do not

---

* The most striking example is the crying after hearing the news of unexpected recovery of gravely hurt, or sick, close relatives. The good news is received with profound joy and happiness and is followed by crying. In many cases, one can observe a "composite" facial expression: crying and smiling. The painful concern about the fate of the injured or sick person was checked and controlled for a long period of time. The hope for a happy ending kept the tears at bay. Now that the unexpected but hoped-for recovery has taken place, the undischarged tears are permitted to come to the fore.

know that the time will come when death will put an end to our happy object relationships. As children, we think that the world consists of children, young people and old people. We believe that we shall stay young forever. Gradually, we realize the bitter truth, but we still cling through hopes, illusions and temporary happy events to the idea that life is a happy proposition and we shall always be together with our beloved ones. Even those who believe strongly in a life hereafter cry (with some exceptions) when they have to separate from earthly forms of those whom they dearly loved. When something makes us happy, especially when a sad and painful situation turns out well, the fundamental knowledge and feeling that this is only temporary and not lasting breaks into our mind and makes us cry.

Small children do not cry at the happy ending. They smile because they do not yet accept the fact of death. Crying at the happy ending probably starts when death is accepted as an inevitable fact.

We do not cry only for the past unhappy events which are over anyhow, nor for happy events which we cherish, but we do cry that the happy childhood with its illusions is gone and we cry for the inevitable, the separation from the beloved ones.

There are no tears of joy, only tears of sorrow.

The avoidance of details in presentation

Psychoanalysts realized that conclusions reached through the analysis of patients could be justifiably generalized and applied to everybody. There are only quantitative and not qualitative differences between individuals. To cite only one example, when we sleep and dream, we regress to a level on which the psychotic mind works and operates in the waking state. In healthy persons, when awake, this regression is checked. The "primary process" is replaced by the "secondary process," as Freud (1900) has shown. Briefly, in the "primary process," we are completely under the influence of the "pleasure principle"; in the "secondary process," we yield to the "reality principle," to reason and logic (pp. 588-609).

When a patient enters into analysis, he is called upon to tell everything that is in his mind *now* when he talks aloud. He is warned that he should leave out nothing, but nothing, and that he should resist any stimulus which would suggest to him that what is in his mind is irrelevant or unimportant. I recall two male patients who accepted these conditions and *thought* that they adhered to them; but they did not because, most of the time, they talked in generalities, abstractions, and not in details (Ferenczi, 1919).

If either talked about a party which he attended, he talked about it something like this, "I had to go to a party. It was a bore. There was a character who annoyed me. I got a head-ache; I still have it . . .," and so forth in this manner. We could get nowhere until, without calling the patient's atten-tion to this mannerism, I urged him to talk in detail, i.e., to tell where the party was, who was the hostess, whether he went alone or with his wife, whether his wife wanted to go or not, the nature of his relation with the host and hostess, whether he knew them before the party, who the guests were, what character annoyed him and caused him the headache, what annoyed him, whether he talked or not and if not, why not, and, if so, what was the nature of his talk and that of others.

Neither of the two men, both wealthy, when talking about money, ever mentioned figures. This information is withheld in social life by many persons for good and bad reasons; but in analysis, one *has* to talk about the sum *if* it comes into his mind. And it is impossible that if someone mentions getting "a nice check" from so and so that the exact amount should not be in his mind. If there was a feeling of reluctance to mention the sum, the patient should still say the sum *and* tell about his feelings of reluctance.

While in Europe, I heard the following joke. A man meets

his friend who just came back from a business trip to a big city in another country. The conversation goes as follows:

Questioner: "What's new in C."

Friend: "Nothing. No, nothing."

Questioner: "How is it possible that in three days you spent in C. nothing happened?"

Friend: "Oh, well, a dog barked."

Questioner: "A dog barked. Why did he bark?"

Friend: "Somebody stepped on his tail."

Questioner: "How come?"

Friend: "There was a big crowd."

Questioner: "Why was there a big crowd?"

Friend: "Somebody was publicly hanged."

Questioner: "Publicly hanged! Who was he?"

Friend: "Your brother."

In the two patients, the reason for using this mannerism went back into the past and was one of the deep sources of their neuroses.

In his childhood, one of the patients was rebuked by his mother when he asked her a question related to her breasts. This, and similar other scenes, made him feel that he should not ask about details; otherwise, he would be rejected.

The other, in his early youth, was strongly admonished by his mother never to meet and never to mention the father who divorced her. This was a very hard task because the boy loved his father dearly. He became very cautious in talking about any matter. It is in the nature of defense that it is drawn not too close to the danger line but far away from it.

Innuendoes

Tension, fear, conflict, hate and pleading for love may all be involved in such innuendoes as, "Darling, you didn't invite me to the party I heard you gave"; or (sister writes to brother), "My dear, you haven't written me for such a long time"; or "I didn't know that your daughter got engaged. My congratulations, dear."

Behind the innuendo, lies the thinly veiled anger and aggression of hurt people. Because they are hurt, they look for a remedy which, unfortunately, the innuendo does not provide. The proper remedy would be either to remain silent and bear the pain or to say one is hurt, ask for an explanation, and be ready to accept the consequence. Instead, these people create confusion by being both pleading and aggressive, thus subjecting themselves to what will probably be an unsatisfactory reaction. In spite of sincere and insincere apologies, they will get neither a frank explanation nor an acceptable settlement of the problem. Even though they may receive an invitation, a reply, or an announcement, they can never be sure whether the courtesy extended them is genuine or not.

Begging the question

Begging the question is one of the most pernicious of mannerisms. It presents to the listener as an established and proved fact something which is not, or at least has not yet been, so established and leaves him only one alternative, to believe what the speaker says.

A demagogue does not let the other person think or have a choice in forming an opinion. He puts his idea in the mind of the listener as a fact.

Some examples will illustrate how this phenomenon is used in everyday, personal communications.

A lady who is not willing to consider her character trends as neurotic likes to pin on others the label, irrational. She likes to make it appear that in her curiosity there is only good will, sympathy, social and scientific interest. She says, in the course of a conversation with another, "What kind of neurosis is this in your daughter that she wants to become an actress?" Her intention is to make the other go further with such a premise as if it were true that the desire to become an actress is scientifically proved to be a neurosis. She is interested only in making the other accept the idea that the daughter is neurotic when the latter is not. The listener is inclined to yield because he is saved from thinking or because he is under the influence of some complex.

Another example: "I told you about his morbid insistence on always telling the truth." She wants to accept as an established, scientific fact that always to tell the truth is morbid. It is possible that one can be morbid in telling a truth unnecessarily; but her aim is not to discuss *this* morbidity. She has ulterior motives.

The importance of the first name

When we meet a stranger, we immediately want to know whether the individual is a male or female (especially in the case of children where the clothing does not make this distinction clear), his name, and the names of his parents. In certain places, the child is not considered to be socially existent before being named. The name is identical with the person as a being. It belongs to his "self." The most beautiful examples of the emotional importance of names were presented in a profound and extensive study by N. Fodor (1956).

C. P. Oberndorf (1918) speaks about persons who do not like their names and should like to change them. He mentions Abraham's paper (1911), in which Abraham calls attention to the fact that a person's name often causes that person to have definite psychic reactions to his name, such as scorn, pride or shame.

In "Reaction to Personal Names," Oberndorf (1918) presents examples of cases in which individuals had unpleasant emotional reactions to their names. These reactions were caused by the idea that their names concealed weaknesses in personality which the individual wanted to hide. He further says that these names supplied an unconscious outlet for

remedying the deficiencies that they implied. Oberndorf
thinks that what a person believes is somehow reflected in his
name either positively or negatively. He also cites Silberer
who said that the name of a person was his shadow.

Karl Abraham (1911) agrees with Stekel who, in a paper
on "The Obligation of Names" (1911) wrote about the
hidden relation between names and professions and also
between name and neurosis. Stekel has shown with many
examples that the name obliges the person or calls to the fore
psychic reactions, like pride, defiance or shame. Abraham says
that a boy who is named after a hero will feel that he must
copy him. Abraham also mentions Goethe (*Wahlverwand-
schaften*, Part 1, Chapter 2), who writes about a man whose
name was *Mittler* (mediator). Because of this name, the man
who had at first been a minister was forced to become a lawyer so that he could mediate between people.

In our present culture, we have one or more first names
and, usually, one last name. In addition, most persons have a
pet name or a nickname. To call a person by his first name
means either that the person is a child to whom one may
therefore be close or superior, or a grown-up to whom one
may be close and socially equal. In places where it is customary to say "thee" (*"du"*) to a person, the use of "thee"
means an additional privilege. To use the pet name of a person or to call him by it is also a privilege that people like to
grant to each other.

Now, there is an interesting mannerism observable with
some people. In the course of a conversation, they refer to a
socially prominent person as though they are very close to
him by using his pet name. This name is used very casually
to make the listener feel that nothing unusual is indicated. In
most cases, the speaker expects the listener to ask about the
identity of the person who was mentioned by his pet name.
If the latter does so, the speaker will assume an indignant
expression which says that the other must be either stupid or
socially inferior not to know this or that he should have

known that the speaker is sufficiently prominent socially to participate in parties or gatherings of prominent people all of whom he addresses by the first name. The speaker, usually, is not prominent, and the listener could *not* assume the closeness of the two persons involved.

In our social life, many people, especially women, take the privilege of using this mannerism very quickly. The victim has to be a good sport about it. In certain circles, it is a habit to establish this kind of communication quickly; and it is either liked by everybody or so much abused that it means nothing.

The listener may or may not be close to the third person. If he is and the speaker knows this, then the latter desires to indicate that he is on the same (high) social level as the listener. If the speaker knows that the listener is not close to the person in question, then the speaker wants to show off and emphasize his superiority over the other.

The reader will observe many variations of this mannerism in his own social circle.

The speed of speech

Slow and halting speech

Slow and halting talk is used legitimately on some occasions because of the gravity of the total situation. This chapter is restricted to specific cases in which this mannerism is one of the most prominent characteristics of a person and is close to being a symptom and a problem for the speaker himself. Women use this particular kind of speech mainly when they are depressed.

In the case of a male patient, it was disclosed that the slow and halting speech was due to compulsive and obsessive thoughts which had to be checked during the course of conversation.

In another case, also a male patient, the mannerism was

caused by grave *doubts* and concerns about whether or not he would say the right thing.

In a third case, again a male patient, the slow talk was the result of a series of severe traumatic experiences, to mention only two: a suicide in the family and his mother's hospitalization because of her depression. Those in whose family such things have occurred should talk softly and should not call attention to themselves. Sometimes such talk aims at making the listener crane his neck. Persons who talk in this way abuse the scientific and social inclination of others to listen.

In many other cases, the slow and halting talk is a *group mannerism,* which, in certain places, gives the air of dignity, prominence, and an aura of aristocratic origin.

Shouting speech

It is customary for children and adolescents to shout because they want to be heard and noticed.

In an adult patient, shouting originated from the desire to be noticed not on the basis of achievement expected from an adult but on the basis of being recognized and considered as a *child.*

Behind the shouting speech of a female patient was the feeling that, at home, she was neglected and her wish was that *only* she should be heard. This characteristic attempted to prevent the listener from chiming in. *Only* she knows everything.

In many instances, the shouting voice is caused by a feeling of inferiority for which some persons want to (over)compensate by shouting or speaking loudly, especially at public places. It is a transitory, characteristic mannerism of youth.

One of the primary fears of mankind is the fear of the shouting voice (Hermann). It is most frightening in childhood but remains dormant through life, even in maturity, in most people. The fear of this shouting is exploited by the demagogues. He who tells the truth and has good intentions does not need to shout, rave, rant, or hit the table.

Fast speech

Some people have the remarkable ability to talk very fast and still clearly. Nevertheless, such speech might become burdensome to the listener, at times to the point of being unbearable. The fast speaker seldom gets tired.

The use of similes and metaphors

From the very beginning of time, communicating human beings have inserted, into their speech and writing, similes, metaphors, comparisons, examples, and analogies.

As children, we begin to learn about the world through our perceptions. It is a long way from such learning to the ability to form abstractions. When we explain something, we like to consider the listener a child. Therefore, besides using gestures, we like to illustrate our presentations with forms which are closer to our senses than to our thinking.

Even scientific writers trained to use and to understand abstractions, when talking or writing to highly educated persons, like to use similes and metaphors for the sake of vivid elucidation, especially when the subject to be presented is difficult, new, or both. This tendency was studied by Geraldine Pederson-Krag (1956) in an interesting paper in which she shows how extensively Freud used metaphors. I agree with her that the use of metaphors has advantages and disadvantages. The disadvantage lies in the fact that "on many occasions, they insidiously confuse us and impair our understanding . . . by too faithful adherence to the implications . . ."; on the other hand—and this is an advantage—"whatever obscurities arise from metaphorical associations and implications, they are more than compensated by adequacies of description imparted by these figures of speech."

The Old and New Testaments as well as the Talmud are full of the most beautiful similes, metaphors and parables.

Certain patients, and many persons not in analysis, make extensive use of these figures of speech in their presentations.

Ferenczi (1915b, 1919) devoted two illuminating papers to this phenomenon.

A female patient, talking about having become upset in a group, said that she felt insecure and "as though the bottom of a tightly closed box had dropped." Now, this patient had many symptoms, one of which was frequent urination. She had grave difficulties in falling asleep because she felt that there was still some urine in her bladder, "the bottom of a tightly closed box."

It was noticed that one of the men in a group always used metaphors. When asked why he did so, he said, "Because I am not educated enough and I cannot express myself well."

Another very bright, though uneducated woman patient could not talk at all without making extensive use of similes and metaphors. She was aware of her abilities and made extensive use of them. She considered herself superior to others in general and to her husband in particular. Everybody was a child to her.

Ella Freeman Sharpe, in a profound study of this subject (1940), avers that "crystallized metaphors . . . reveal past ages of history. Individual metaphors reveal also the experiences of forgotten years." Sharpe offers excellent clinical examples for her theory that "metaphor can only evolve in language or in arts when the bodily orifices become controlled. Then only can the angers, pleasure, desires of the infantile life find metaphorical expression. . ." She presents several clinical examples, two of which are herewith quoted. A patient says, "I see your point of view, but I don't take it in"; or "she is always giving me the cold shoulder." The first, according to Sharpe, refers to suckling experiences; the second, to psychic reaction to weaning. On the basis of my own experiences, I agree with Sharpe's view that "crystallized metaphors reveal past ages of history." This view is also supported by Cassirer (1946) who speaks of "metaphorical thinking."

Annihilation of professional integrity

There is a seemingly innocent mannerism through which a person intends to destroy someone's professional integrity by emphasizing his profession. If a lawyer, physician or man of no matter what profession should make a statement or act in a manner characteristic of his profession, which statement or action is unsatisfactory to another, the latter might say, "And you, a lawyer (doctor or whatever), could make such a statement?" The speaker is acknowledging the professional man as an expert, but a lousy one. He does not say that his target is a "lousy expert." He mentions only that the person is an expert, but in a way that destroys the latter's expertness.

"If you don't mind"

Perhaps, the reader can—I cannot—find a legitimate use for the "if you don't mind."

If one wants to get to his seat and in order to do so has to inconvenience another person, it would suffice to say so pleasantly, to give a hint, without words, of such intention, or to apologize for the inconvenience. Everyone knows through experience that nobody likes to stand up and let the legitimate seat owner pass, but there is no choice. In the course of time, people might even become indifferent to being disturbed. But, if the holder of the ticket says, "If you don't mind, I would like to get to my seat," then he has expressed something he did not dare to say or did not want to say directly. He wants both to attack and to be safe against a counterattack.

A wife (according to her husband) has been nagging her husband for two days to dispose of the garbage. He did not do it. His wife, after working hard, is resting in a room near the kitchen and notices some noise coming from that direction. "What are you doing there?" hollers the wife.

"I'm taking out the garbage, if you don't mind."

Is it possible that she minds? She is pleased; but she *did* mind his having postponed the job for two days. Now, at last, when he does the job, she does not mind. *It is he who minds doing the job even now.* With this, he expresses his anger with his wife for expecting him to dispose of the garbage.

Another example: A man is called to the police station where an officer questions him without telling him openly why he was called. The man answers but gradually becomes indignant and impatient and interrupts the officer, saying, "Would you tell me why I was called here, if you don't mind?"

Our vexed man minds that he is not told right away the reason for being summoned. He notices that the officer "minds," at least for a while, telling him. Both have definite reasons for what they are doing.

What the man wants to say, is "I mind that you are beating around the bush. I am fed up with your comments and don't care what reasons you have for questioning me." He is innocent. This is his strength; therefore, he is able to be self-assertive and challenging to authority.

"Where do you hide the matches?"

When one is invited to a party, he wants to be pampered, flattered, indulged and generally treated like an infant. If his feelings and wishes are not immediately gratified, he wants to hurt. Therefore, he uses the most impossible excuse to do so. "Where do you hide the matches?" he demands, instead of asking for them.

A guest expects the hostess to act like the mother offering her breast.

Many people feel that others do not care for them and, furthermore, want to frustrate them. They are ashamed to reveal these ideas but wait for the opportunity to express them in a seemingly facetious manner. The anger and aggression will come out.

PART TWO

Gestures and Other Nonverbal Expressions

GESTURES

The "mannerisms of speech" should include gestures and all kinds of bodily movements which accompany, augment or substitute for speech. Gestures are conveyed by one person to another in visual, tactile, and (rarely) olfactory ways. Their principal medium of communication is the visual one. After Ruesch and Kees, we can call them *nonverbal communication*, which is the title of their book (1956). The study of this area belongs to "kinesics," which, according to Birdwhistell (1956), is "a systematic study of how human beings communicate through body movement and gesture."

There is the great *field of drawn symbols* which often convey more than long speeches (Koch, 1930), and the ideographic writings as shown in the classical book by Diringer (1948), in which, for example, a girl relates her sad love plight only through drawings, without a single word. Pittenger and Smith have also contributed pertinent data in their paper on pauses (1957).

For thousands of years, scientists have been interested in the exciting subject of gestures. The bibliography is tremendous. This study is analytic and medical, because it draws mainly on experiences of analytic practice. Observations made of children in the prespeech period and after, observations of patients in the office during analytic treatment, and observation of people in our everyday social activities can yield a rich harvest of material for the study of nonverbal communication.

The most painstaking studies and research work on babies was done in recent years by R. Spitz (1945, 1946, 1949).

His findings and conclusions have become classical treasures in this field.

Whenever possible, we shall attempt to trace the origin of a movement back, genetically, to its very beginning. Investigations convince us, even though we could have assumed as much, that bodily movements were effective communicative tools in the struggle for life in which aggressive or defensive action had to be taken. The movement expressed a need that had to be communicated to another. The great scientist who initiated the genetic approach to the subject of bodily movement was Darwin, whose book (1873) has already been mentioned. Most of the gestures and other bodily movements express the same drive at the present time as they did at the time of their origin, though some went through certain modifications, became "culturalized." Be that as it may, we shall focus on what these bodily movements mean *today*, both to the maker and to the observer, the "communicant and the receiver" (Berne, 1953). Critchley (1939), too, recognizes gesture as "a primitive component of speech" and as a "forerunner of speech."

To keep some order in this vast territory, I have decided to start with the motions of the head and end with the motions of the feet. In between, I will discuss the manneristic and expressive movements of the whole body.

Expressive movements of the head

The erect head expresses self-esteem, self-confidence, courage, looking ahead, health, stamina, pride, and strength. The bowed head expresses humility, resignation, guilt, and admission. Characteristic is the head position of priests and other clergymen who consider the parishioner a child in trouble who needs and will be offered care like a lost lamb. It indicates satisfaction that the parishioner has, at last, found the right source of charity and forgiveness. The ducking head position indicates that one admits having been caught but is still a good boy to whom others should not be harsh. Looking aside is an admission of embarrassment and reveals a wish to hide, not to be seen. Lifting the head and bending it forward with chin up indicates defiance. The characteristic movements of the head to express confirmation and negation are well known (Kulovesi, 1939; Sugar, 1941).* We are impressed by the position of the heads of athletes who dash ahead, and by that of predatory animals when they dart at their prey.

The head is lifted upwards when a person is thinking, as if he would ascend to his brain or seek heavenly advice. Freud, in his paper "The Moses of Michelangelo" (1914), presents a great variety of impressions which several connoisseurs of art gained from the head and figure of the statue of Moses.

A professional man whom I could observe several times while discussing a subject in a group pushed his head and upper part of his body forward like a swimmer who has to overcome resistance to proceed. The resistance, in this case, was probably anxiety. Perhaps, at this point, we should mention the interesting phenomenon in which a *negative head motion is made at a positive exclamation*. For example, when a person relates that he has seen something spectacularly beautiful or terrible, he will shake his head in such a way as to indicate denial. In my opinion, this mannerism intends to express the fact that the sight was "unbelievable," that it was so extraordinary that one would not believe it if he saw it.

Mannerisms of dressing the hair

We shall confine ourselves to certain manneristic phenomena in wearing and dressing the hair as can be observed in our *present culture* in both sexes.

* During the time when the manuscript of this book was being corrected, René A. Spitz's admirable study, *No and Yes: On the Genesis of Human Communication*, was published (1957).

First of all, there are many and diverse group patterns which indicate belonging to a certain specific nationality and age group. The coiffure is different in different places. Babies have a characteristic hair-do. So have boys and girls of different ages. Be that as it may, to have hair and to have an individualistic hair-do is of great importance to everybody.

Many persons, on the other hand, insist on having a hair-do which is at sharp variance from that of their group. They stick to this difference by all means. From this group, I would exclude certain immigrants who are reluctant to change their external characteristics. The latter have a certain image of themselves without which they feel very uncomfortable. They need time, if they plan to do so at all, to change and to "become adjusted." It is different with their children who grow up in a new environment and do not differ from other children unless the parents force them to adhere to the old patterns. If the children are thus forced, they suffer greatly. Conflicts arise between children and parents. The children may even be ashamed of the parents and develop guilt feelings as a result of their shame.

Any long-standing, stubborn *individual difference* has unconscious roots. These differences reveal exhibitionism and other different libidinous drives as shown with convincing clinical examples by Berg (1951).

Manneristic activities with hair and face

Many people like to play with their own hair and with the hair of another, usually beloved person. Among lovers, this is one of the cherished occupations. Interesting contributions to the symbolism of hair were made by Melitta Sperling (1954) and by S. Lorand (1929). One likes to play with the hair of children.

Similarly, people like to touch or rub different parts of the face, to play with pimples, warts, moles, and to squeeze blackheads. Some persons derive great pleasure from doing the same for others. It is a striking phenomenon to observe that some persons' mouths water while performing or observing such activities. As a matter of fact, particles removed from one's own skin or from that of others may be taken into the mouth or even swallowed as in nose-picking and nail-biting. There are a great number of people who beg someone else, like a mate, child, or friend, to rub their scalps. To many people, this is a cherished expectation when they go to the barber for a scalp treatment. They have a feeling of frustration if the barber overlooks even a small area and have to make up for the missing gratification. In some persons, such skin care may invade the sensual territory, even causing genital excitation so that the activity becomes libidinized (Hermann, 1936).

The driving force behind this kind of activity was discovered, after intensive studies, by Imre Hermann. Applying the results of his observations of subhuman mammals, especially anthropoid apes, to human beings, he found two primary instincts in operation, "to cling" and "to go" (originally to cling to mother and to go away from her to search for a new object). Hermann's theory can be applied to the vast phenomena of normal and pathological human behavior.*

I accept Hermann's explanation that the above-mentioned activities, practiced in a state of restlessness, tension, are regressions to the instinct pair of clinging and going and express a situation in which after having clung to the mother, one is forced to leave her. The classical example is the "grooming" activity of certain apes. It is not lousing but a form of skin care, love and care in general, which they extend to each other with astoundingly deep intensity and devotion. The primary unit of mother-child relationship is dis-

---

* It is a pity that Hermann's masterwork (1934a), published in Hungarian, has not yet been translated into English. Some information about his theories can be found in his German papers (1936, 1941), and in his book, also in German, *Die Psychoanalyse als Methode* (1934b). A good, though short, informative report is contained in a paper by Géza Róheim (1942).

cussed from the psychosomatic point of view by Therese Benedek (1949).

Some people, in meditation or in a state of embarrassment or anxiety, touch their own noses. One clinical example of this was given in my paper on "Mannerisms of Speech" (1948):

> Touching the nose is a common habit. Symptoms involving the nose are especially overdetermined. The sense of smell and thinking are closely correlated. Many people put some part of the hand to the nose while speaking, in lieu of the undesirable gesture of covering the whole face. They feel "covered" if the nose is touched even by a single finger. In many persons this gesture indicates anxiety, a kind of stage fright requiring a magic touch through which they feel unseen.
>
> A masochistic patient, a scholarly man, had, with an elderly woman beneath his social standing, a relationship in which she spanked him on the naked buttocks until he developed an erection culminating in a "most gratifying" ejaculation. He presented two interesting characteristics: when he walked or stood he kept the upper part of his body erect, so that his buttocks protruded; he had a mannerism of tapping his nose while speaking. He touched his nose with the right index finger, moved the finger away and brought it back with a jerk, which certainly looked like spanking. He had been spanked by his mother, but in such a way that his genitals were against hers—by holding him between her legs. When spanked, he used to feel "as if a tack were being driven by hammering into a board." His outstanding clinical symptom was his anxiety, which caused a complete social paralysis. The anxiety permeated all his activities, especially walking and speaking. By the magic gesture of "spanking" his nose, the anxiety was allayed and the wish gratified [pp. 364-365].

Looking back at this case after about seventeen years I realize that at that time I was not yet aware that behind the patient's mother attachment, manifesting itself in the perversion, the instinct pair, "to cling—to go," was in operation.

Facial expressions

After searching in libraries for references on facial expressions, gestures, habits, patterns, and the like, one gets dizzy and discouraged after a while. The more one searches, the more references he finds; and when he reads them, he finds still more references. It is an impossible task. I did the best I could do and apologize for any omissions.

For the layman, there is no trouble whatsoever. He is an expert like everybody else, both in *reacting to and understanding facial* (and other) expressions, and in *acting them himself*. To *know* what they mean, to *know* how they originated, to know how they developed and why—these are different matters.

The origin of expressive movements are the same in all human beings; but there are tremendous differences between individuals. The same expressive movements are individually different in different persons. I therefore agree with Allport and Vernon (1953) that "most movements have other non-expressive and expressive features," and that, for example, while blinking is common to all men, there are individual *manners* of blinking.

On the other hand, one is forced, on the basis of observations, to assume that facial expressions and other expressive movements were handed down to us by our progenitors who acquired them in the struggle for survival. It is fitting at this point to quote from the classical book of Darwin (1873). At the conclusion of his book, he writes,

We have seen that the study of the theory of expression confirms to a certain limited extent the conclusion that man is derived from some lower animal form, and supports the belief of the specific or sub-specific unity of the several races; but as far as my judgment serves, such confirmation was hardly needed. We have also seen that expression in itself, or the language of the emotions, as it has sometimes been called, is certainly of importance for the welfare of mankind. To understand, as far as is possible, the source or origin of the various expressions which may be hourly seen on the faces of the men around us, not to mention our domesticated animals, ought to possess much interest for us. From these several cases, we may conclude that the philosophy of our subject has well deserved the attention which it has already received from several excellent observers, and that it deserves still further attention, especially from any able physiologist [p. 367].

Time has shown that to put *that* much emphasis on physiology, one had to be imbued with the scientific orientation of the period in which Darwin lived. Since then, psychology, of which Freud was the greatest exponent, has made great contributions. In understanding human phenomena, biology and physiology are indispensable, but they cannot furnish us complete comprehension without the aid of psychology. Therefore I shall continue, as I have done in the previous pages, to emphasize the strong psychological and emotional factors in human beings which use the *physiologically given paths and bodily instruments to express their past and present struggle for existence, and to achieve gratification.*

Noncommittal facial expression

The noncommittal facial expression *is* an expression on the face; but, *seemingly,* it betrays only that the person does not want anyone to know anything about his feelings. There is no expression on the face; *the lack of expression is the expression.* It is a "poker face."

Two male patients both had expressionless faces. As a matter of fact, those with whom they were in contact, wife, friends, and colleagues, considered the nonexpressive face the main characteristic.

The first man (briefly discussed on page 15) was forced into treatment by his wife who declared that unless he could change, she would have to divorce him because it was impossible to live with him.

The prognosis is unfavorable if a patient does not come voluntarily, under the pressure of his suffering and need for help. Nevertheless, a so-called trial-month analysis was initiated, giving both patient and therapist a chance to explore the possibilities. Whether it was a month or not, I do not remember. The fact is that shortly after the beginning of the treatment, the patient admitted that he was a sick person and that he wanted help. The treatment went on. The beginning itself was characteristic. *He did not care what happened to him* or, at least, so he pretended. This attitude was a defense against any possible dangers which might develop in case he showed his feelings or revealed what he wanted. It was this defense that was expressed on his face.

This man did not show any emotions. He even wore glasses which reinforced his intention to hide. He loved his children; but, if they, for example, came home and enthusiastically dashed toward the father, hugging and kissing him, he remained unresponsive. He was the same with his wife and with everybody else. He reacted the same way to bad news. He did not cry and he did not laugh. It appeared as though nothing moved him. The reader must know by now that his love life was a poor and miserable one, whether sex was in prospect or whether there was an affectionate togetherness with his wife. When his wife became amorous, the slightest sign exhibited by her killed any prospect for sexual intercourse. He could not function; he was impotent. On the other hand, when it appeared that nothing was expected, he could function; but even then, the whole process was a mechanical one. There were no emotions, no affectionate motions, no words, in short, none of the common features of this act.

At the time he was in treatment, many pictures of Chaplin were being presented. The audience roared with laughter, but not our man. His face and attitude did not change. He even looked around with astonishment as if scolding the audience for their foolish reaction.

He had a cherished fantasy. He pictured himself reaching the age of eighty. He would be sitting in his chair, resting, engulfed in his thoughts, oblivious of the world, when a sudden knock on the door would bring him back to reality. When he said, "Come in," a strange character would enter. It would be Death.

"How do you do?" Death would ask.

"Fine," would come the answer.

"Well," Death would say, "you have reached a ripe old age and have had a wife and children and a profitable profession. You were and are wealthy. It was nice, wasn't it? Now, all this will end. Let's go."

"What are you talking about?" the patient would ask. "I will go with you but you seem to gloat over me. You sound as if you think I am losing something. No. I lose nothing. Did I have fun? Did I enjoy my money? my wife? my children? Did I cry or laugh? Did I get anything? No. I got nothing, nothing whatsoever, and you do not take anything away from me. Let's go."

This fantasy became the pivotal part of our work. We needed to know what happened to this man's life. The following story was revealed and pieced together in the course of the analysis. As a youngster, the man was like any other child, full of joy, expectations, desires and need for love. He loved to live. But there was something that killed life for him: his father. The mother played no role. She was subdued by her husband, a well-to-do man, who was a loveless tyrant. The patient was not deprived of earthly, material presents. His father gave him many things that all other boys used to get. But how? The father bought the boy, for example, a bicycle which he loved, but when the child misbehaved, his father would deprive him of it for days as a punishment. The boy grew sad and frustrated. The same thing happened with everything that the child got from his father. Gradually, he developed a defensive attitude. Whenever his father would ask him if he wanted to skate, the boy would not display any desire, though he joyfully anticipated the fun. He pretended that so far as *he* was concerned, it was immaterial whether he skated or not. *If his father* wanted him to skate, he would. This attitude, a habit at first, later became a condition. Feelings were gone. The meaning of the fantasy is now obvious to the reader. *The patient would rather be frustrated than deprived of what he had.* The figure of Death (in the fantasy) represented his father. This is what we psychoanalysts call male "castration fear." It is a misnomer because castration would mean the removal of the generative organs, the testicles, and not the executive organ, the penis. Every boy goes through a phase in which he is concerned that something bad may happen to his genital organs. In most cases, this fear becomes the representative of all previous fears and concerns that we all encounter in our very early years of life and appears in hundreds of direct and disguised forms (Freud, 1905b).*

The other "poker-faced" man was a younger unmarried, well-educated businessman of about twenty-five. His main complaint was complete sexual impotency. He knew this from practice. He had fallen in love, but he had no sensual feelings the moment sexual activity was expected. He told his girl about his trouble. With his knowledge and permission, she came to see me twice, inquiring about the possible outcome of the treatment. The prognosis seemed to be good. The girl loved the young man and let him do with her what he wanted. He had his own apartment; and she often spent the night with him. The strange thing for him was that when the

---

* About eighteen months after the birth of her brother, a two-and-a-half-year-old girl went up to her mother and said, "Mama, I lost my leg and now I am a girl-woman." This observation belongs to the "castration complex" of women. The girl observed that her brother had something that she lacked. We can observe here a symbol formation at its inception. The leg and the male genital appeared to the girl to be identical in form.

girl was asleep in bed near him, he felt virile, active and full of strong desire; but when he wanted to go into action and had to awaken his partner, his desire and executive virility disappeared. The solution of his problem was accomplished mainly through the understanding of his expressionless face. He, too, had a poker face. It was rigid; it looked like a mask. There was rarely a motion on his face. The man was not co-operative. Like the man previously described, he could not muster up enough interest. He often missed the sessions. The lack of interest was considered a symptom, a resistance whose source we sought. We achieved the solution through the analysis of his lack of emotions in general, and specifically on his face. As a schoolboy, he was already known as a poker face. The boys liked one of his performances for which they considered him a great actor. He could change the expression on his face from one thing to its opposite, from smile to mask-face, in no time. After the analysis of his poker face, the whole situation changed. The man became normal, attained potency, and married the girl.

This patient lost his mother during his adolescence. It was a great blow. His father was remarried after about a year to a lovely young, attractive woman. The stepmother affectionately loved the young man, who, at that time, became sexually sensitive and needed great powers of control not to be aroused by the affectionate behavior of his stepmother. She was childless and needed to consider the young man as a child. For these reasons, the patient avoided any physical contact with his stepmother as much as he could. He succeeded through the help of a very attractive maid who had been in the house for many years and to whom our patient became attracted. Whenever there was an opportunity, he managed to be in the room where the maid was working so that he could kiss and hug her. He became excited. He would have liked to do more, but there was no opportunity for this because his stepmother was almost always around. After having been with the girl for a short time, he quickly left lest his stepmother discover him. After leaving the girl, he was afraid that the excitement would show on his face. In order to avoid this danger, he forced himself to assume a face without expression because he dreaded having his stepmother become aware that he was a *"man"*! After a while, as in the previous case, the forced lack of expression became first a habit and later a condition. The trouble was caused by the fact that at the same time that he feared tell-tale evidences of sexual excitement on his face, he was having powerful erections which could have been quite revealing. These, too, he had to suppress; and he succeeded! Necessity created a condition in which there was no excitement below or above. This history explains the loss of virility when the girl was awake to perceive his excitement, and his potency when she was asleep.

It is necessary to mention that the situation in his adolescence, as described, revitalized an earlier, identical infantile conflict in which his mother was the main object. In both cases, the real threatening figure was the father.

Expression of disbelief

Usually, disbelief is connected to and accompanied by the reactive affects such as anger, suspicion, ridicule, derision and the like.

In this chapter, I shall report and analyze a specific, expressive facial reaction caused by disbelief that I have often observed in social life and that I could more closely study in a female patient.

The latter often mentioned a woman friend who, according to the patient's conviction, was very unhappy, but "fooled" herself and tried to deny her feeling. On one occasion, in talking about the same friend, the patient mentioned a characteristic experience and illustrated her disbelief. While talking, she protruded her two lips, forming them into a cup, accompanying the gesture by a particular guttural and nasal sound. She looked as if she had something hot in her mouth which she did not want to swallow until it had cooled off.

In *contempt*, too, one protrudes the lips, usually the lower more than the upper. Again, this leads us back to the taking of food or refusing it. It is the first important activity and experience.

Disgust

In observing emotional expressions, the analyst has a unique advantage. He can notice the phenomenon the moment it is "born" (*in statu nascendi*) on a person about whom he knows a great deal. He has many data for a correct interpretation. About the expression of disgust, Darwin has filled his book with penetrating observations.

I will report about a form of disgust which can be observed in our everyday life. I was in the position to make a safe analysis in one case, that of a young, attractive girl with serious neurotic symptoms. On the merit side, as has already been mentioned, she was very attractive; but because of certain complexes, she had grave difficulties in choosing the "right" man for herself from her great number of suitors.

Once she was talking about a man who, in the opinion of everyone including her mother, would be an excellent choice. She enumerated many of his advantages, but the man did not attract her physically. She paused for a while. One could see and feel that she was visualizing sexual union with him. In her silence, her whole body shuddered as if to shake off somebody who touched her. Her face was distorted with disgust. She made a rejecting movement with her lips and uttered an emphatic, "uh."

Grimaces

A grimace is a distortion of the face, an autoplastic caricature of an emotion.* The meaning of the grimace is close to a person's consciousness and is capable of being controlled. Not so the tic, which can appear on the face or on any other part or parts of the body. The person can do nothing about the latter. He cannot suppress it and has no idea about its meaning. The source and meaning of the tic can be disclosed through analysis. A grimace is always facial. Both grimace and tic are jerking movements (Feldman, 1926).

Annie Reich (1949) mentions an interesting case concerning the art of caricaturing, mimicking or impersonating others. It has to do with a young woman's comparing herself with her mother and sisters.

In most instances, when a person makes a negative decision, he will express his rejection not only by words but by accompanying his adverse feeling with facial distortion, facial expressions, and grimaces. The differentiation among the three is vague (Critchley, 1939).

A person, in a mood of rejecting something offered to him, may close his eyes spasmodically, turn his head away, turn his nose and nostrils to one side, draw the lips aside and, to some extent, turn his whole body aside.

One can easily realize that all the primary reflex-like movements which can already be observed in a baby a few days old, or at any time during infancy, are put into operation later. In the beginning, these movements refer mainly to food. Offer a child food, or, later, anything else, and he will turn away, close his eyes, turn aside his head, close and draw aside his lips and his nose if he dislikes the offer. If we do not like somebody, we say "I cannot look at him." "I cannot stomach him." "I cannot smell him." "I cannot touch him."

* The interested reader is referred to the psychoanalytic study of caricature by Ernst Kris and Ernst Gombrich (1938).

"I don't want to listen to him." Eyes, nose, mouth, ears and fingers are turned away, closed, opposed. Any contact is rejected or made difficult.

All later situations, though they are different from the original, will be reacted to as they were in the beginning, in the most primitive and most important period of our life.

An attractive grown-up girl was obsessed by a fear of rejection. Once when she was walking down the street, she became aware that a man to whom she had been introduced was approaching her from the opposite direction. When she saw him coming, she distorted her face the moment she thought that the man would be able to recognize her. When asked why she did this, she said that she wanted to avoid the possible danger that the man would not remember or recognize her. Such behavior on his part would mean that she could not impress men. She distorted her face, thinking that the distortion made her unrecognizable and unidentifiable. It also allowed her to deceive herself by pretending to believe that the man (this was in Budapest, where men greet women first) did not greet her because he did not recognize her.

For information about the clownish, grotesque and queer mannerisms of schizophrenics, see R. Bak's profound comments (1943).

In the course of years, several patients and nonpatients have asked me about the reason for their smiling when expressing sympathy to the bereaved. They try to suppress the smile in vain. It is embarrassing. The struggle between expression and suppression ends in a smiling grimace.

Kris (1939) calls this phenomenon *"pathognomic parapraxis,"* in which an "awkward and embarrassed smile or faint laugh appears on the condoling person's face." In Kris's opinion, "a repressed, condemned—and usually aggressive—thought has presented itself. . . There has been a failure to integrate contradictory impulses, the intended impulse and the one which breaks through. But," says Kris, "that failure to integrate emotional expressions—may be brought about by fatigue."

Already, in 1909, Freud, in his famous paper, "A Case of Obsessional Neurosis," mentions a classical case of this kind. He wrote:

> The conflict between love and hatred showed itself in our patient by other signs as well. At the time of the revival of his piety, he used to make up prayers for himself, which took up more and more time and eventually lasted for an hour and a half. The reason for this was that he found, like an inverted Balaam,* that something always inserted itself into his pious phrases and turned them into their opposite. For instance, if he said, "May God protect him," an evil spirit would insinuate a "not" [pp. 330-331].

In several patients, the smile was an expression of protest against any imposition. Therefore, when a person attends a funeral and offers his condolences, an involuntary smile breaks through. This may happen not only to the outsider who offers sympathy but to the one who is mourning yet who protests showing grief at the time when it is expected of him. He wants to mourn when he feels sad.

I suspect that the same reasoning may be applicable to the slips of the tongue through which people confound the word, "wedding" with "funeral" and vice versa.† I am not unmindful of the facetious explanation that a wedding is the funeral of one's freedom; and a funeral can be likened to a joyous wedding if the deceased is hated by the survivors.

On tickling and ticklishness

The study of tickling and ticklishness—a special form of communication between persons—can be considered as an

---

* Balaam (Numbers 22:23), a sort of magician, was hired by the Moabites to curse the Children of Israel, who came out of Egypt; but the Lord turned his curses into blessings.
† See "Crying at the Happy Ending," pp. 175-183.

attempt to shed some light on the interplay between sexuality and aggression.

The rhythmic character of a stimulus necessary to produce tickling was recognized by the great physiologist, Johannes Müller. According to Müller, (1840), the sensation of tickling and of sensual pleasure can be elicited on any part of the body; most strongly on the genitals, less on the breasts, lips, skin and muscles. I. Hermann (1934b) agrees with Müller and adds his observations that in children during thumbsucking, there is a specific rhythmic motion. Phylogenetically, according to Hermann, this is identical with the "chattering" of apes. This "chattering" (a tongue-lips motion) is seen in all their friendly and sexual activities. Ferenczi (1924), when writing on "economy of expenditure," thought that such an economy of cathectic energy might produce the "sensuous feeling of tickling" and believed that the majority of the ticklish parts of the body, especially the axilla, might be genitalized. Sadger (1921), whose work on skin and muscle erotism is outstanding, quotes Stier, who noticed that children are very ticklish. When one stimulates by light touch the inner side of the thighs, one can elicit a laugh of a sexual character and often it may lead to a sudden erection. M. Buch (1909b) notes the interest of Spinoza and of Plutarch in tickling. J. C. Gregory (1924) devotes a whole chapter in his profound study to the problem of laughter and ticklishness. He maintains that tickling can be a mixture of pleasure and pain.

Darwin observed that anthropoid apes are ticklish, especially under the armpits, and utter a sound which is like human laughter. With a small piece of paper, he touched the sole of his child's foot when the baby was only seven days old. The foot was suddenly jerked away and the toes curled up, as in an older child. Such movements, according to Darwin (1873), as well as laughter from being tickled, are manifestly reflex actions. This is likewise shown by the minute unstriped muscles, which serve to erect the separate hairs of the body, contracting near a tickled surface. Ticklishness has been noticed in cats, horses, and young pigs. Chimpanzees and orangutans, when tickled, rolled on the ground.

This "rolling" can be observed in children, and often in adult human beings as well. This is in accordance with Hermann's "whirl-theory of instincts." Instincts, according to Hermann (1934a) produce a whirl-like condition (physiologically referred to the vestibular apparatus), and it is the orgasm that straightens out this whirl in the ego.

Darwin considers ticklishness a "reflex action." In my opinion, this suggests that ticklishness is a useful action, or at least that at one time it was useful for the survival of the species.

In order that tickling should produce laughing, the object of the tickling has to be in a receptive mood; and even if he is, he will go into a defense reaction, usually by withdrawal. Besides withdrawal, a hostile or disliked person's tickling will cause pain, anger and even bring about a violent counter-attack, especially when the tickled person did not expect the stimulation. One of my female patients, when tickled suddenly and unexpectedly from the back by her husband, turned angrily and violently, and slapped him on the face. Her response was different when she anticipated and expected his tickling. At such times, she responded with laughter while defending herself. This patient had, since childhood, been very resentful and easily hurt by others. She had the feeling that others were always taking advantage of her. Though she was sure of her husband's love, she reacted as if he were taking advantage of her when he tickled her unexpectedly. This is an exception, however. In most cases even unexpected tickling will produce the usual response if the recipient feels secure and sure that the intentions of the active party are not hostile. When tickling has erotic aims, it is necessary that the person in the passive role be pleased by the erotic intention of the other. If these conditions obtain, it does not matter whether the tickling is expected or not.

One may tickle a person in order to create a comic situation. The active party may use a blade of grass or similar object to tickle the passive party and deceive him into thinking that an insect or some inanimate object is the cause. "Economy in comparison expenditure" (Freud) will render pleasure to the active party. The reaction of the passive party will depend on the latter's mood and his relationship to the first person.

M. Buch (1909) writes about a mass hysteria in the Protestant congregations in Cevennes, in 1760, during a religious persecution of the people. It was a kind of chorea major. The main manifestations were trembling and convulsions. These were called the "Trembleurs de Cevennes." According to Buch, investigators of that time found that these people had analgesia and anesthesia which made the usual corporal punishment ineffective. For this reason, apparently, tickling was used for torturing and punishment. It was said that some people were even tickled to death.

Many writers have recognized the essential difference between itching and tickling. Alrutz (1908) mentions that, according to Richet, the difference is that tickling is elicited by the touch of another person while itching has an internal cause.

Some investigators believe that one cannot tickle oneself, that the tickling has to be done by another person in order to bring about the tickling effect. According to Sternberg (1909), the tongue is the only organ that can be tickled by the person himself. This is not in accord with my experiences and observations. One can tickle the palms and the soles (and sometimes even other parts of the body) by oneself.

The importance of the general mood (feeling at rest and comfortable) is emphasized by G. Stanley Hall and A. Allin (1897).

Even though not intended as such, tickling may at times be unconsciously accepted as a libidinous gratification. In the episode of mass hysteria and religious persecution described by Buch, the victims apparently responded in this way though it was meant as punishment by hostile persons. Also, along this line, I remember a Charlie Chaplin movie in which Chaplin overpowers his big, strong adversary by tickling his soles. It appears that if genuine danger is not present, a stronger person can be successfully held down and tickled by a weaker one.

One must always consider the total situation, with special attention to the nature of the relationship between the tickler and the tickled. Buch (1909a) noticed this, "in a way," when he wrote that in children it is not so much the tickling itself but the comic situation which makes the child laugh when tickled. He refers to two cases. One was the case of Kasanovski, a seventeen-year-old girl, who was resistant to tickling when in a hysterical, sad and religious mood, but responsive with laughter when tickled in the armpit or on her soles when in a mood of delirious elation, even though she was almost analgesic to needle pricks. The other reference was an observation related to Havelock Ellis by a physician who found that grown-up girls in a manic state are strongly ticklish.

The role of expectation and imagination is shown by the fact that one can experience a tickling feeling or feeling of itching merely by having the idea that insects are crawling on the skin.

The response of laughter in the tickled person does not always occur. It is present only when one is tickled by another person; otherwise, not. A depressed person does not respond to tickling and will not laugh (Basler, 1912). As mentioned before, a hostile relationship, or a bad mood, will also eliminate laughter in the response.

Observations of everyday life and analytic case material support the views that in tickling and ticklishness, there are three outstanding characteristics: aggression, defense response to the aggression, and sexuality.

The majority of the authors, however, are somewhat at a loss to integrate aggression defense with this aggression and sexuality. In my opinion, some deficiencies exist: (1) there is insufficient consideration of the interrelationship between the tickler and the tickled person; (2) they do not offer analytic material in a psychoanalytic sense; and (3) little or no attention is paid to tickling when it takes place between persons of the same sex.

In our Western culture, among males, especially at puberty, when in a playful mood, masculinity is tested on the ground of whether the boy (or the man) is ticklish or not. If he is ticklish, then this would prove that he is not yet quite a man, that he is a "sissy," girlish, feminine. A man may tickle girls, but he himself should be resistant to tickling. During puberty, I and other boys often tested each other with the so-called "Hussar-grip." This consisted of grasping the thigh of the other person, starting at the knee with the thumb on one side, and the other fingers on the other side. The grip then progressed further above, pressing delicately upwards toward the loin in the direction of the genitals. If the person could stand this stimulation without any reaction, it was considered a "sure" sign that he had the power to control himself, that he was a man and not a woman. Exactly the identical play was described by M. Buch (1909a).

Women consider men's tickling approach as one of sexual interest. Again, it depends on the nature of the relationship how women will react. If they favor the man, they will laugh, giggle, scream or run away, even though they like it. If not, they will show anger and scold the man for his aggressive-sexual action. This sham fight, or mock fight, was recognized by M. Buch and other authors. But Buch advocates much caution in assuming a fundamental relationship between tickling and sex. According to Buch, the sexual part of the reaction is secondary. In this respect, Buch is at variance with several other authors to whom ticklishness means primarily a sexual action, aggressiveness being secondary, the means to achieve the sexual goal. To Havelock Ellis, sexual intercourse is closely analogous with tickling. Sternberg criticizes Buch's intention to minimize the role of sexuality in tickling. According to Sternberg (1911-1912), the desire for sexual activity aims to do away with the ticklish feeling. "Frictions in sexual intercourse," he writes, "are identical to scratching and rubbing away the tickling feeling." The same is true of hunger and food intake.

Are women more ticklish than men? The consensus of opinion among writers is in the affirmative; but I believe that men are just as ticklish as women, the only difference being that men control ticklishness in order not to appear feminine. Women do not control it; they use it for their own purpose in courtship.

Men, usually, do not tickle each other. This is a tacit agreement between them. It is not advisable for a man to tickle another because there is a great likelihood that the tickler will meet with a strong aggressive-defensive action. The tickling might stir up a dormant atavastic tendency to fight the other man, to eliminate him, to destroy him. Furthermore, the tickling might stimulate latent homosexual feelings.

In German and in Hungarian, the clitoris is called "*Kitzler*." In German, *kitzeln* means tickling; and in Hungarian, *csiklo* and *csiklandozni*. Now, the question arises whether in those two languages, the clitoris is considered as originally and fundamentally ticklish or whether, in a different sense, the clitoris is considered a "ticklish" organ in that one must know just how to touch it in order to create a sensual stimulus. According to I. Hermann and G. Roheim, calling (in Hungarian) the clitoris an organ which is very ticklish is secondary, and it is an onomatopoetic word (Hermann).* The same question can be raised regarding the Latin word for tickling, *titillare*. Some authors mention that, in different countries, tickling means sexual intercourse. In the vulgar slang of Hungary, the word itching is preferred for this purpose. In a personal communication, the late A. Kinsey

* Personal communication. The writer is indebted to Prof. Thomas A. Seboek, Indiana University, for data on this word in Hungarian.

affirmed that there was no word in the English vernacular for the word clitoris. In his interviews, he heard that women refer to the clitoris as "the little man in the boat," or "the spot."

During the last two decades, tickling play and sensitiveness to tickling seem to have been on the decline. The personal relationship between the two sexes has changed form somewhat in that the courtship has become more direct. Blushing and a strong response to tickling used to be considered as indications of virtue and innocence. Girls were more sensitive; and with their defense against tickling, they expressed both their understanding and their (mock) protest.

Some women may gradually lose their ticklishness with persons with whom they have sex relations; but they may continue to have and show it toward men with whom they do not have sexual relations. Ticklishness often declines with age, but this cannot be stated as a general rule.

Tickling has a great deal to do with teasing in which aggressive, defensive and sexual tendencies also play an important role. This was shown in two profound papers by Brenman (1952) and S. Sperling (1953).

The father of a three-and-a-half-year-old girl related to me that his daughter said to him, "Tickle me"; and she lifted and spread apart her legs. The little girl must have witnessed or experienced tickling in her environment and understood that she could use it for her own seductive purposes without revealing in words whether she had conscious knowledge of the sexual implications of tickling or whether she had an instinctual understanding "only." Children are very keen in such matters. Parents often tickle their children. It is a sexually tinged play between them, and the parents do not want to be aware of this. It would be better if they avoided it.

A patient often saw his father tickling his mother. The mother would laugh, protest and shout, "Stop it." On such occasions, the patient kicked his father to make him stop tickling the mother; but the father teased him by continuing despite the boy's protest. As a child, he had overheard what went on in the parents' bedroom. He thought that father was tickling mother. He heard mother laughing and protesting, and the bed squeaking. When the boy reached puberty, the father often tickled him. The patient responded with convulsive laughter. His analysis disclosed that he had enjoyed it. His enjoyment of the tickling was an expression of his passive, feminine, latent homosexual attitude by which he attempted to settle his castration fear. (This patient also mentioned that, during puberty, he and his boy friends often tested each other's masculinity through tolerance of tickling.)

Another male patient related that when he was five years old the nurse bathed him and his brother. While the nurse was busy with his brother, he knelt down and looked under her skirt. She noticed this and told his parents. They punished him by making him stay in bed the whole day. The father told him that he was punished because he had tickled the nurse. This was not true. Either the father or the nurse made up the tickling story because of their embarrassment and their wish to avoid recognizing the sexual aspects of the matter directly. These and other cases prove, in my opinion, that there is a conscious or unconscious tendency or understanding between the two parties, the tickler and the tickled. Aggression is necessary to arouse, to stimulate, and to take possession of the object in case the goal is a sexual one. Aggression is necessary to achieve dominance for the sake of eliminating the object or rendering it helpless and powerless in a competitive game or serious fight. There is a conspicuous defense from both sides against being tickled. If the tickler has sexual intentions, then there is a playful, stimulating defense reaction. If the tickler has aggressive intentions, the ticklishness is either absent in case the aggression is hostile or present in a defensive response in case the aggression is playful and nonsexual. If a person is not interested in another person, in any sense, he will not be inclined to tickle that person even if he knows that the latter would be interested in being tickled.

I had the opportunity of analyzing a woman in whose case tickling was the center of the whole neurotic condition. This sexually very sensitive woman was frigid in sexual intercourse but could reach orgasm either by thinking of tickling or masturbating while having a fantasy about tickling. She responded with tremendous anxiety, trembling and profuse weeping, when tickled or when somebody else was tickled in her presence. The word, tickling, uttered by others in her presence had the same grave effect. She phobically avoided using the word herself for the same reason. But if she heard of someone being tickled or heard the word being used while she was not present in the same room, she felt tremendous sexual excitement without any anxiety. She would then masturbate with "satisfactory" orgasm.

Since early childhood, anxiety or sexual excitement resulted from tickling in this patient. She often witnessed her father tickling her mother who laughed, giggled, defended herself and told him to stop. She also saw other male relatives tickling women. For this patient, tickling represented *the* sexual intercourse. She identified herself with her mother or mother substitutes when tickling was in the picture. Her anxiety was caused by the danger that she and others might become aware of the incestuous desire in being stimulated by tickling. When she was alone, the danger was not that close. The word, tickle, is very extensively used in a metaphorical way, e.g., "The idea tickles me"; "I was tickled to death"; a "ticklish" problem (a problem which must be dealt with delicately. One has to be cautious because if one does not handle it well, the effect might even be the opposite of the one expected).

It appears that the laughter in tickling originates from the economy of energy expenditure. A certain amount of energy is necessary for the constant alertness needed for the sake of controlling aggression and sexuality. In the play of tickling, this alertness is reduced, and the saved energy (Freud) is discharged in joyous laughter. *Aggression and sexuality are fused in tickling.*

There is some identity and some difference between touch and tickling. Under certain circumstances, the reaction to touch creates the same defense reaction as tickling; but, on the other hand, there is a definite difference in sensation. Touch is not rhythmic. Tickling needs a quite different touch. There is a transition between the two; either the same end organ can react differently according to the nature of the stimulus, or Alrutz (1908) may be right in assuming that there is a specific end organ in the skin for tickling.

The slightest touch to the body of an infant (I have observed this in a six-weeks-old infant) will be answered by a defense reaction. Sudden loud or unusual noise will have the same effect. In 1918, E. Moro described a phenomenon which since has been called the "Moro reflex." He writes, "If one places a *young* infant on a bassinet and hits the pillow on both sides with the hand, the action will be followed by a particular *movement reflex* of the baby in which both arms are symmetrically abducted with slight tonic movement, like an arch, and closed again. Simultaneously, a similar motor action is shown by the legs" (my translation). According to Moro's brilliant observations, the reflex is most conspicuous in the first few weeks and then weakens gradually. It is not present after the third month except in premature children. "In order to elicit the reflex," writes Moro, "it is not always necessary to use the above-described manipulation. The same movements sometimes appear when one puts the infant in swaddling clothes or when the infant awakens" (p. 1150). Moro considers these movements as a sign of "natural clasping-reflex" (*Umklammerung-reflex*) and an atavistic phenomenon (p. 1950). Hermann (1936) was strongly supported by Moro in developing his theory of the primordial instinct pairs of humanity: "to cling—to go." I observed that the

Moro reflex can be produced, not only by hitting the pillow on which the infant's head is resting, but also by touching any part of a *sleeping* (or unaware) infant's body. This touching will produce the same defense reaction—clasping or clinging to (the mother) for protection against anticipated danger aroused by the feeling of being touched. From here, there is the transition to tickling which is a special (rhythmic) kind of touch. The same touch, which under certain circumstances produces the Moro reflex, i.e., defense, is reduced to a pleasant tickling or sensual response when danger is absent and in its place love and safety are offered. Adults while asleep or inattentive will show defense movements (but no longer the total Moro reflex) when touched by insects or similar irritating stimuli. Horses can make their skin tremble in the spot which is irritated by flies or other pests. Like Darwin, Buch (1909) comes to the conclusion that ticklishness of the skin is a phylogenetic inheritance of the animal and human species. Stanley (1898) has come to the same conclusions: ticklishness "is a survival of long past ancestral experience" (p. 235). It appears to him that "ticklishness implies tentacular experience. By temporary self-extension, even low amoeboid organisms have slight but suggestive touch experiences that stimulate very general and violent reactions, and in higher organisms extended touch organs,—tentacles, antennae, hair, etc. . . ." (p. 235). Stanley believes that "the pleasurableness of tickling . . . is in its playfulness and in reviving the vast mass of ancestral play experience" (p. 236).

At the end of her (experimental-physiological) paper, Elsie Murray (1908) gives a summary of the views of Darwin, Grocs, Kroner and Sully, who believe that, in ticklishness, the psychic attitude and disposition are essential. She reports the views of Allin, Bronson, Hall, Sully, Sherrington, who believe that the tickle-reflex-response is the *"survival from some ancestral instinct."* Gregory (1924), too, believes that sneeze, cough and ticklishness are defense actions. According to Gregory's "relief theory," what was once a struggle and

protection against real danger was, in the course of time, reduced, through tickling, to play.

In my observation, the palms and the soles of the feet are the
most ticklish parts of the body. The next most ticklish parts
are the armpits, sides of the chest, inner sides of the thigh
and the lips. The palms of the hands and the soles of the feet
probably derive their sensitivity from the fact that our ancestors walked on all fours and used these sensory areas to
test the environment for possible dangers. The "universal
distribution" of ticklishness indicates to Robinson (1894)
that "the most ticklish regions correspond to the most *vulnerable* spots in fight."

It depends entirely on the circumstances and the relationship of two persons, whether the tickling is intended and
perceived as an aggressive or as a sexual action. Human beings
and other members of the animal kingdom come into physical
contact with each other for purposes of self-preservation,
mating and play. If an individual of the animal kingdom
comes into physical contact with another in order to devour
it, to destroy it, then aggression and counteraggression (as a
defense) will not produce ticklishness at all. If the aim is
mating (sexual), and the aggression is used lovingly, the response may or may not be ticklishness. In play, whether for
sexual purposes or mock fighting, it can easily turn into
ticklishness. This demonstrates that in human beings, tickling,
which is an aggressive action, is used for sexual purposes just
as well (Alexander, 1950; Freud, 1905b).

The life instinct (Freud) represents the interest of the
maintenance of the individual and the species; it comprises
aggression, sexuality, and defense aggression. The individual's
premium for maintaining the species is the orgasm with its all-
pervading psychic effects. When in normal and neurotic
manifestations, therefore, tickling is used as a representative
or disguise of sexual and aggressive tendencies, it only follows
an already given phylogenetic path.

To silence by 'sh'

In no time, anyone can most certainly be aroused to hatred, to a desire to liquidate, kill or destroy a person who silences him with a "sh." The one thus silenced has these reactions even though the "sh"-er is an otherwise beloved person like a wife, husband, child or best friend. The reader probably knows this full well since he himself has, in all likelihood, had the same reaction to being hushed by a "sh." While I do not know whether or not this dangerous action is ubiquitous, I have observed it in both Europe and in America.

When one is either at a party where there is a group who are listening to radio, television or whatever, or at a concert and he whispers something to his neighbor, he may be attacked by a "sh." The "sh" hits him like a bullet right in the middle of his heart. Somebody orders *him, him,* to be silent, to keep his mouth shut. The face of the attacker shows annoyance, irritation, and anger. His eyes are fiery, piercing. His mouth is like a megaphone; teeth, somewhat closed. He hisses, "sh." The silenced one is killed, paralyzed. He remembers that he himself has done the same thing to others, and he may feel that the other person is right. But this feeling vanishes quickly and he remains hurt, angry, furious, and out of countenance. He will never forgive the silencer.

The same lip-mouth position and the "sh" sound are displayed and employed in a benevolent form, with warm and loving feelings, when one has a baby resting in the arms and wants to put him to sleep. On such an occasion, the face is not angry; there are no hostile feelings. "Sh" is like a lullaby. The intention is the same, to silence the child, but for the best and most kindly purpose. The listener, the baby, loves it. This silencing is, then, emphasized in other situations and turned into an angry, hostile action, into an aggressive "sh."*

* Perhaps, it was about thirty years ago that a very talented school teacher gave a lecture on the origin of the letters of the alphabet. I regret

Chronic criers

From Darwin to analytic observers, there is agreement of opinion as to the genesis of crying, which serves the purpose of eliminating pain, be it physical or psychic. Analytic studies, as that by Greenacre, found interesting differences in crying between boys and girls, extending to later years, as proved by the analysis of patients. Greenacre (1945) found a connection between urination and weeping. The boy's genital organ is visible earlier than the girl's. The genital organ of the male is more inclined to aggression; and the boy is more capable of discharging tension through urination than is the girl, who, by displacement, discharges tensions through weeping. As a matter of fact, even our society encourages boys to abstain from weeping as a device to relieve tension. It is not considered manly. I agree with Greenacre, who distinguishes between *shower* weeping and *stream* weeping: "In the shower type, there are copious tears with very little provocation and without much sobbing or crying. Sometimes, these floods of tears appear indiscriminately with any emotion. In the stream type, little obvious emotion is evident but a stream or trickle of tears rolls down the cheek when certain sensitive, deeply repressed subjects are touched in the analytic work" (pp. 62-64). An interesting analysis of pathological weeping was recently published by Lacombe (1958). He equated the tears with the mother's breast.

Being hurt forces one to a state of regression in which love, security and warmth were given to him. Heilbrunn (1955) states: "Tears are wet and warm. Perhaps, these qualities suggest the warm and wet prenatal surroundings, and thus simu-

---

that I cannot recall his name; it was probably *Gabel*. What remained in my memory, though, was his explanation about the letter "s," not in printed but in written form. The letter "s" in Hungarian is pronounced "ash" or "sh." If one turns the letter "s" on its back, then, according to Gabel, it looks like a baby resting in the arms of the mother, lovingly "sh"-ing the baby.

late intrauterine life, which is the goal of regression. (It is an interesting fact that amniotic fluid and tears are strikingly similar: in content of sugar, protein, and sodium chloride, they are almost identical.) It seems plausible to suppose that the feeling of tears on the skin is reminiscent of existence in the amniotic fluid" (p. 252).

Peto (1946) looks at weeping and laughing from the standpoint of race- and self-preservation and considers both as a tendency to get rid of pain. There are persons whom I would call "chronic weepers" or, rather, "chronic criers," because, being extremely sensitive, they always find a cause for crying. I am thinking, specifically, about two female patients who both belonged to Greenacre's "shower type."

The first was a young girl who, whenever she was accused of the slightest offense, wept right away. Tears came out like a bombshell. She never could admit that she was wrong. When she thought that she was "innocent," in addition to crying, she shouted and made counteraccusations.

She had wet the bed from childhood on throughout adolescence. It was about the time of transition that the crying habit began. There was reason to assume that the bed-wetting was connected with masturbatory activities and with their suppression.

A male patient who occasionally wet the bed late into his forties reported that he often awakened in the course of the urination in bed; and before he came to his senses and realized what was going on, he had a cozy feeling as if he were in a tent, nicely protected, while outside it was raining heavily. This reminded him that, as a small child, when it was raining he liked to be home alone with his mother, looking out the window and eating something that his mother had given him. For years, he was permitted to be in bed with his mother before going to sleep and after his father had left for work in the morning. When it was raining, he stayed inside the house. He loved to hear the patter of the rain drops on the windows. He recognized that the same sound was relived at the end of the wetting. This man's case looks very much like a confirmation of Heilbrunn's proposition (1955). In addition to all these things, this man—something rare in men—could cry very easily.

The other case was that of a married woman in treatment because of a grave neurosis which had paralyzed her life for more than ten years. She was a great crier. It was always the same cause which provoked the crying: she felt that people were not considerate of her. Whether her husband, her children or her friends were among the inconsiderate did not matter. She cried and cried. She always carried tissues with her at first. Later, she used the tissues I put near her. Often she forgot to use them. In such a case, tears rolled down her face and onto her clothing until she realized what was happening and wiped them off. Whenever she talked about her main complaint in the office, she cried copiously.

The analysis disclosed that this woman's complaints were well-founded. She *was* a neglected child. She had been neglected by her mother and by her siblings. In the course of time, she came to expect that people would not consider her, that people would misuse and abuse her. *But she herself also created situations* in which she would be mistreated.

From early childhood on, she noticed that there was only one thing through which she could get attention, even though negative, namely, crying. Even then, she was not "considered." The members of her environment were disturbed, puzzled and unable to understand her. She became a problem child, but she received attention. The price was high.

I know several persons who can cry whenever they want. They might be known for this ability and called upon to demonstrate it. They do. When asked how they do it, they reply that they think of something sad; or, most of the time, they think only how sad it is to cry. And then they "just" cry. "Just."

Pride

Besides the face, all parts of the body can take part in expressing pride. The whole body becomes erect; the head is lifted; the face is either radiantly smiling or showing contempt for others; the chest is expanded; the nose is lifted and turned aside as if to avoid the smell of common mortals; the arms are often folded over the chest; the gait is like that of a peacock; the walk is firm. In certain places, at least some time ago when men wore vests, they inserted their thumbs inside to make the vest protrude. Besides the desire to express, "Look how big I am," these gestures often are a displacement from below upwards: the penis exhibited. It is amazing how proud men are of their male organs, and especially of the erection of the membrum. There is hardly anything more depressing and ruinous to a man's self-esteem than to have that organ be considered small, to feel that the erection is not strong, or to know that it does not function properly. A man can be acknowledged as the greatest, he can have everything that only few have; but if the penis and its functions are faulty, the man considers himself as nothing, nothing. It takes a tremendous shifting of psychic energies to enable a man to resign himself to the slightest damage to this organ or to its faulty and deficient functioning.

It is the same with the beauty of a woman. It may not be enough to be beautiful; but if a woman is beautiful, she has something, at least, of which to be proud and to give her self-esteem. This attitude is a dangerous condition because beauty does not last forever. Nevertheless, when it is there, the woman tries to her last breath to maintain her attractiveness. Since, especially in the present time, society has permitted a fetish to be made of the breasts, women exhibit them as much as they can and are proud of them. They walk erect and expand their chests.

To illustrate the "nose in the air" pose indicative of pride, there is the anecdote about little Morrie. One day, little Morrie walked down the street with his nose pointed toward heaven. Puzzled by the unusual stance of the boy, one of his friends decided to ask him about it. "Are you so proud, Morrie, that you have to keep your nose up so high?" asked the friend.

"No," replied Morrie, "I am not proud. I am wearing a jacket made from my father's trousers."

On a deep psychological level, the joke indicates that pride is often a reaction formation against drives which are otherwise distasteful. This refers to false pride.

Many men, for fear of exhibiting a small membrum, avoid activities and places like locker rooms where they may be in danger of being seen nude by other *men*. Some patients told me that whenever they go swimming at a public beach, before getting back on dry land, they lift their trunks in order to permit air to get between the trunk and the body. This action will cover up the part where the genitals are located and prevent the contours of the small genitals from being seen by other men or women. In most cases, they do this in order to prevent other men from making comparisons. Men who thus attempt to conceal themselves are not so much afraid of women; they assume that women will not look or will not have sufficient basis for comparison. (These men probably do not know that *some* women, either for fun or because of a very disturbing compulsion, *do* look. A woman once told me that a few of her girl friends "organized" a secret "group" whose main objective was to take cognizance of and keep "records" of men, rating them according to a certain code.)

On the other hand, there are men who are extremely inhibited and take irrational precautions to avoid having the penis be noticed, just as some women take precautions to avoid having their breasts be noticed.

There is some similarity in the emotion of pride to that of smugness, about which Arlow wrote an interesting paper (1957).

Hiding the breasts

All "nonverbal communications" previously discussed and those which are to follow belong to "mannerisms of speech" because they replace speech or vice versa. People do not get together to be silent. If they do not use words, they communicate with signs, gestures or other nonverbal expressions. Many patterns, habits, and expressive movements under discussion are absent in privacy. They emerge when individuals meet, because, for various reasons, people do not put everything into words, their communication takes recourse to nonverbal forms and expressions.

Many adolescent girls, noticing the development of their breasts, feel the need to conceal them. This need may be due to a general inhibition of sexual drives, but it may have more specific causes. Some married women who have children also may hide their breasts.

A sixteen-year-old girl was brought to me by her mother, who said only that the girl was too shy and blushed too much. Treatment was not necessary because the girl was unusually communicative and her problem was not deep-seated.

The girl said that she blushed only when she was in company or on the street. She was in the habit of carrying her body bent and she blushed when she held it erect. When, in the course of the interview, she was asked what caused her to keep her body bent, she replied that if she did not, her breasts would show and she was ashamed of them. After some explanatory and encouraging comments, the girl left. I was informed that the trouble was "cured."

The other case was that of an adult, unmarried woman with sexual experiences. In the course of the analysis, she related that as an adolescent girl, she noticed when walking with her (beautiful) mother that the latter was very much looked at. She knew that her mother was very proud of her own beauty and very much concerned about losing it in her later years. The patient felt sorry for her mother, particularly when the girl, because of her youth and attractiveness, was becoming the mother's rival. To do as much as she could to help the situation, among other devices, the patient, both in public and at home, kept her body bent in order that her breasts would not attract men. This tendency was strongest when she was in the presence or company of her mother (Feldman, 1922).

Mannerisms with the eyes and looking

When we meet and converse with a person, we *look* at and *see* each other. If we do not, there is some trouble. *Looking* and *seeing* are *two* different features of *one* process, as Devereux (1956) has very rightly pointed out. Looking, according to him, is a psychologically active step; it is spying; while seeing is psychologically passive, "taking it in."

One can look and not see. One can look and see only the part one wants to see. One can see and look in such a way that he can see what he is not supposed to see. One can even see without looking. Many people have troubles with the use of their eyes.

One talks to a lady wearing a low-cut dress or shorts displaying charming features of the body. He will hurt the lady if he does not see what she wants him to see; but he must not look. If he looks, then he is spying; and she *has* to object, remove herself from his presence, and consider him something less than a gentleman.

A man looks differently when he is a doctor, examining an undressed woman. She is nude, not naked. She will know exactly how the examiner looks; and very few women will tolerate his looking in such a way as to *see* that she is nude, though both know that she is.

One may see his mother, sister, or other female relative in negligée, but one does not look in such a way as to make them feel that they are in negligée.

If we dislike a person, we may look at him but not see him; we may even turn away from him because we hate to see him, and we do not want to be seen by him.

The meeting of two pairs of eyes is one of the closest possible relations, whether this meeting expresses love, hatred, or the hundreds of variations between these two emotions.

The eyes are cast down when one does not want another to see what he could betray; nobody wants to reveal himself in this way. On the other hand, one looks into the eyes of the other when there is nothing to conceal, but rather wants the other to see everything.

We are touched by the "innocent look" of children, by the look of lovers who unite through their eyes. We are frightened by the angry, piercing, and fiery eyes of a threatening person. We look askance when we are suspicious. We can look pleadingly, reproachfully. We can have a guilty and a forgiving look. Our eyes can smile; and our eyes can hurt, punish, beat, spank, kill, love, and adore. Our eyes can show desperation, firmness, confidence, elation, and depression. The eyes can be seductive, inviting, and forbidding. The eyes can give and receive orders. One can read from the eyes and from the way a person uses them.

There are great numbers of neurotic disturbances involving looking and seeing, but it is beyond the scope of this book to deal with them.

There is the *habit* of rubbing one's eyes, not because they hurt or itch, but because of a reason unknown to the person who does so. Ferenczi has written an interesting paper on this habit (1914a).

Eyes and looking play a great role in superstition. We hear about the dangers of the "evil eye." The reader, if interested, can find extensive information on this subject in Seligmann's book (n.d.).

There is an interesting habit or compulsion in some people which can hardly be noticed because they do it very surreptitiously. I was in a position to discover the cause of this habit in a patient who used it extensively. I have reported it in the paper on "Mannerisms of Speech" (1948) in the section subtitled: "Connecting one point of the body with several points in space":

I have often wondered how I could have overlooked this action in so many patients, remembering how often I have seen it. One can better observe it when the patient is seated in a chair rather than lying on the couch. Then often one can clearly see that while the patient is absorbed in choosing one part of his body, the tip of a finger, the tip of the knee, or the tip of his shoe, and is trying to bring it in line with several points in the room or even beyond it through the window.

Patients in analysis are often under pressure of anxiety, transferred onto the analyst, when facing him or when facing the unconscious. To relieve this anxiety the patient removes himself by this action from the whole situation. With the clarification of such actions a great deal of resistance is removed. It is possible that in neglecting them we might fail in our therapeutic goal no matter how well the analysis is progressing in other respects. We well know that often the analysis of a seemingly innocent symptom can contribute a great deal to the overcoming of resistance, aside from the fact that the patient may become interested in it, and the solution might be impressive [pp. 366-367].

When we want to have a talk with somebody, we ask, "When can I *see* you?" as if seeing him were more essential than talking with him, or as if one without the other would not have any meaning. It can also happen that when somebody is given an appointment to "see" the doctor, he comes but does not look at the latter. He might look but does so turning half away so that he sees only from the side.

A woman could carry on a lengthy conversation with her friend without once looking at the latter. As she talked, she looked first in one direction and then in the other rather than looking at her friend.

A male patient, on entering the office, looked first, quickly, to one side and then just as rapidly turned to the person with whom he will be talking. It was later revealed that the first glance was toward a supportive, though invisible, mother.

People attend a meeting where they sit around a table. They are aware of each other's presence. They see each other, but they do not look at each other. If one glances up and notices that another is staring at him, he looks too but quickly averts his gaze. A tremendous amount of self-control is necessary not to look again to see if the other is still staring. The first wonders whether the latter has been looking at him continuously and, if so, why. It takes effort not to take a second glance. If the meeting lasts long enough, the one stared at will succumb to the urge to look. He will be satisfied when he has assured himself that the other is no longer staring.

If this staring takes place between members of the opposite sex, it is understood that some erotic intention exists and the struggle involves the matter of making or not making the intentions obvious. If they are two persons of the same sex, the struggle involves competition for power and, often, latent homosexual tendencies.

If two people of the opposite sex look at each other while passing on the street, there is an emotional reaction. If the man looks at the woman a second time, she will avert or drop her gaze. Her thought, in noticing the man's way of looking, is that his intention is rape. She drops her gaze because she does not want the man to know that she understands his thoughts or that she has similar thoughts of her own.

When two people of the same sex pass each other in the street, there is ordinarily neither emotional reaction nor second glance.

Blinking as a mannerism

Blinking is an eye-protecting reflex. It distributes the necessary moisture over the surface of the cornea and removes irritants from the eyes. Blinking becomes a mannerism or symptom when it is done for purposes other than these. Ponder and Kennedy (1927) observed that normal frequency of blinking was present in completely blind or almost blind persons, that the rate of blinking increases in states of anger and sudden excitement. They consider blinking as a "relief mechanism."

Blinking as a symptom can be observed in "nervous" children in states of tension, anxiety, and the like. Unlike the normal frequency of blinking where the action is not striking, the mannerism of blinking is striking and calls attention to itself. The latter is rapid, frequent, and uncalled for. In grownups, it is similar to a tic. The difference is that, in the mannerism, the blinking is chronic; while in the tic, it is infrequent and appears suddenly as a jerk and may not appear for a certain length of time after which it reappears. I found that, in youngsters, in whom the blinking can be considered a symptom, besides being a simple "relief mechanism," it is an escape from being looked at by other persons. For a short period of time, the eyes, through the blinking, are covered. The person is in the dark, is not seen and does not see the observer. The causes for not wanting to be seen may be different; but they usually stem from guilt and fear that the subject will betray himself. Children may resort to blinking to conceal masturbation; in adults it may stem from the same cause or from a desire to conceal something else. The proof for this is the fact that many persons blink intentionally, in a sheepish way, to indicate that they did something which they reveal by pretending that they want to hide it.

It is well known how skillfully women use blinking. Here, the sexual meaning is obvious. The eyes can symbolize both male and female genitals. That they can represent the testicles is shown in Sophocles' play in which Oedipus blinds himself for having committed incest. Blinking is, again, a displacement from below upwards. In the above-mentioned paper, Devereux (1956) presents evidences of the fact that eyes can be a feminine symbol. In a play that I saw long ago, a man, after a whirlwind courtship, proposes marriage to an attractive girl. She is pleased but tells the man that she will need more time to decide because she has known him for only a few hours. The man wants an immediate answer and asserts that she can find out quickly whether she is physically attracted to him. He proposes that he will kiss the nape of her neck. The girl turns her back toward the man who then kisses her neck three or four times. She reports (to the audience) the result (a positive one, "of course") by blinking, as if tasting something to find out whether she will take it or reject it. The sexual symbolism and the displacement from below upwards was made obvious by her.

Blinking is also used for testing other things. It can be a sort of lie-detecting test. If one can stand looking into the eyes of another without blinking, either he has told the truth or he is an inveterate liar. At least, one should blink when he lies to indicate that there is some honesty in him, that he is not a liar, and that he could not help lying.

Blinking is also used to test the courage of a friend. In my early adolescent years, I was often subjected to a test (which I also have used on others) in which another boy met me, stopped me, assumed a serious face, and asked, "Do you have courage or not?"

I: "I have courage."
Friend: "Let's see. Look into my eyes." (I did.)
"Were you in the woods?"
I: "Yes."
Friend: "Did you see a wolf?"
I: "Yes."
Friend: "Were you afraid of him?"
I (emphatically): "No!"

In the meantime, I stood there at attention, looking into the eyes of the testing friend who stretched out his arm and made rapid movements very close to my eyes. If the eyes blinked, I was a liar; and the blinking was proof that I was a coward. If I did not blink, it was fine, and I was happy.

Blinking with only one eye is used by women, usually of ill repute, for seduction and invitation to further sexual action. If this is the purpose, it must be done with only one eye. The same meaning may be conveyed by another phenomenon, a feminine hair-do that covers one eye. Such a hair-do intends to create the desire in man to uncover and to see the eye, again a displacement from below upwards.

For the same reason women like to wear dark glasses. It is true that the glasses may protect the eyes from the sun (but not always); but wearing them provides a secondary gain. The dark glasses tempt man to uncover the eyes and create in him a desire to get closer to their wearer.

A man and his daughter attend a meeting at which the daughter reads a scientific paper. The father, who does not want his relationship to the girl to be obvious, winks proudly and broadly at the end of her presentation, indicating that she did a good job. This one-eyed blinking is a private matter; it shuts out other people. The privacy is communicated through the sexual significance of the blink, again a displacement from below upwards, indicating that one first covers the genitals in order to disclose them.

Clearing one's throat

It is legitimate to clear one's throat to remove mucus. When clearing the throat serves different purposes which have nothing to do with the throat, we call it a "mannerism." It can happen that, in a state of tension, mucus may be deposited so that the throat must be cleared of mucus deposited for emotional reasons.

An artificial cough often represents criticism, doubt or surprise. For example, if someone talks of himself with a superabundance of self-confidence, the listener may give a little chortling cough. Sometimes, the communicant does this himself for fear his statements will be too much for the listener. Thus the communicant vaccinates himself against his own hostility.

One enters a room and wants to call attention to his presence. He coughs, in such a way as to clear his throat, in order to be noticed by someone either in the same room or in another room in which the visitor assumes the other to be and from which position the latter cannot possibly be aware of the presence of the visitor. This, then, is a signal. Instead of shouting, "I am here," or going to the other person and performing some action which may turn out to be disconcerting, one coughs.

When speakers appears on the platform, before beginning to talk, they do different things like fussing around with their notes, drinking a glass of water provided for them. They may also cough and clear their throats. In this case, the latter action indicates anxiety, a feeling of being cornered, a feeling of being restricted. One coughs as if to liberate himself, encourage himself to begin to talk.

Some people cough when, in the course of a conversation, they do not speak the truth. The cough may be a spontaneous one. But if it is artificial, we consider it a "mannerism." A lie makes a person feel uncomfortable. To solve the conflict, at least partially, a compromise takes place. One tells a lie; but, at the same time, he admits it with a "noise," the cough.

It often happens that when I greet a patient in the waiting room, the latter answers with the customary, "How do you do?" or something similar, and coughs. This may be a symptom and a mannerism. As has been said before, sometimes one cannot draw a definite line between the two. I have always paid special attention to this mannerism, and have never failed to find that such a cough signals a complex. For this reason, I consider the analysis of mannerisms therapeutically important. One "works through" and makes deeper the patient's and the therapist's findings.

The loosening of the collar

A person may not be aware of having loosened his collar, or he may do it intentionally in order to communicate something to another.

The gesture is legitimate when the air is stuffy and hot; but, all too frequently, it is not made for this reason. A person may grow warm in the "heat" of excitement. In this case, loosening the collar is partially legitimate and partially not.

Our main interest is the intentional loosening of the collar of the shirt or jacket, in which case the gesture is artificial and, therefore, a mannerism.

In my opinion, a classical case would be the following: a person involved in a heated debate makes some statements which are refuted through valid evidences by a listener. Because of the refutation, the communicant would be compelled to admit that he erred, that he was wrong, or that he prevaricated. But he is the kind of character who does not become anxious if cornered. Then, as in blinking, he *pretends* that he is in trouble in order to have some good point on his side.

The person employing a mannerism often does not achieve his practical goal, because, as Berne (1953) says, the receiver can understand more than the communicant intends to convey. Berne realized that this is especially important in the *transference and countertransference* situation. He also says, "The receiver is not interested in the information the communicant intends but in the psychological reality behind it."

Spitting out

Spitting from a digestive point of view and in order to eliminate unpleasant matters from the mouth is important; but it is amazing how much bigger a role spitting has in the emotional, psychological, social, and ritualistic life of mankind.

"Spitting," writes Darwin (1873), "seems an almost universal sign of contempt or disgust; and spitting obviously represents the rejection of anything offensive from the mouth. Shakespeare makes the Duke of Norfolk say, 'I spit at him— call him a slanderous coward and a villain.' So, again, Falstaff says, 'Tell thee what, Hal,—if I tell thee a lie, spit in my face.' Leichhardt remarks that the Australians 'interrupted their speeches by spitting, and uttering a noise like pooh! pooh! apparently expressive of their disgust.' And Captain Burton speaks of certain Negroes 'spitting with disgust upon the ground.' Captain Speedy informs me that this is likewise the case with the Abyssinians. Mr. Geach says that with the Malays of Malacca the expressions of disgust 'answers to spitting from the mouth;' and with the Fuegians, according to Mr. Bridges, to spit at one is the highest mark of contempt" (pp. 260-261).

We all know that it is the same with these things in our present time. To spit at somebody, or to spit into the face of another shows terrible contempt; but the contempt is greater when one says, "I don't *even* spit in your face," as if the saliva which belongs to the self, though it is used for spitting out and for showing contempt, is much too valuable to be used in this fashion. On the other hand, the greatest sign of acceptance is the toleration, in any kind of love relation, of another's saliva on the lips, the mouth, or any other part of the body. Such acceptance is a sign of perfect union, sometimes greater than the sexual one.

Spitting is often used for magical purposes. In Hungary, when somebody made his first money in business, he put the money in his palm and made quick spitting movements, while at the same time uttering the words, "Your father and mother should have many sons." These actions meant that through spitting a magic generative action was initiated which should result in the multiplication of the money so that one would become rich. One also performs a magic action to get strength for a fight by spitting into one's palm and rubbing the spittle all over. The action is performed not only, as one might think, to make the grip stronger. More anthropological and folkloristic material can be found in Róheim's paper (1921).

In 1928, I witnessed the following scene in Budapest. A mother pushed a carriage in which her baby, a few weeks old, was resting. A woman friend happened to pass by and stopped. It was the first time that she had seen the baby. She looked into the carriage, and profusely expressed her delight in the baby's beauty. Then she made rapid spitting movements. Asked why she was doing this, she replied right away, "I have never had any children. The child is beautiful. I am happy for the joy of my friend who has a baby; but at the same time, I envy her. I am afraid that my envy might harm the baby. In order to protect the baby from my envy, I am spitting out my envy."

As the reader can see, we may consider ourselves civilized; but culture is only a thin veneer on the surface of our minds. If we scratch it, the primitive emerges. Frazer (1922) writes, "In the island of Nias the hunters sometimes dig pits, cover them lightly over with twigs, grass, and leaves, and then drive the game into them. While they are engaged in digging the pits, they have to observe a number of taboos. They may not spit, or the game would turn back in disgust from the pits" (p. 218).

There are champions in the art of spitting. They can spit straight at a target, like a fireplace, many yards away. I once had the honor of spending a week end in the home of a Quaker family in Pennsylvania. We gathered in one room to listen to the reading of the Bible by the head of the family who often sent a spit-bullet off toward the fireplace. He never missed.

People like to spit from a height into a body of water and they enjoy the ripples created in the water by the impact of the spittle.

As a boy, I and my friends had spitting contests. To make the spitting more effective, we hit the back of our heads with our hands at the moment we spat in order to reinforce the power of the spitting.

Adolescent boys like to spit to indicate that they are grown males.

Women seldom spit. It would not appear feminine to spit. Spitting is a masculine trait. It is again a displacement and an indication of masculine aggression and virility.

Sticking out the tongue

Perhaps it was in 1955 that I read a newspaper report about a man in a small town in the United States, who one day telephoned his neighbor to ask him to come out on the porch with his whole family. The neighbor had a wife, a son who was a soldier home on furlough, and an eight-year-old girl. They all came out. The man who had telephoned approached the house and shot them all to death. Asked by the police why he had done it, he replied that he killed them all because the girl stuck her tongue out at him.

The custom of sticking out the tongue, as far as I know, is practiced in Europe and in America. It can probably be seen in many other places.

It is done in different forms. It may appear when a person is self-satisfied because of having been smart; and, often for any other reason, so that he laughs, protrudes his lower lip, and flattens his tongue on the protruded lip. In another form, the mouth is opened wide, while the tongue is dangled in the hollow of the mouth, by which action the person intends to express his gloating over another person, usually uttering, "Ha-ha-ha," as if laughing at him.

The sticking out of the tongue for the purpose of expressing contempt, derision, rejection, or the like, is done differently. The tongue rests either on the lower lip, or is pointed out like a spear; and sometimes the gesture is accompanied by a noisy sound, like "beh," usually when the person does not want something like food or some other inanimate matter.

Or, it may be directed against a person. It is this latter mannerism which can be thought by others to be very hurtful and may make them angry, or, as we have seen, mad.

Children permit themselves to do this more often than do adults; but the latter regress to this performance when in a gay mood or, mainly, when in a state of anger. In grownups, the same tendency to convey contempt is expressed not by sticking out the tongue but by a characteristic movement in which the posterior is turned toward the other person, hinting at an invitation for the other to do that which is ordinarily done with toilet paper, with his tongue. Or, in many places, the same tendency is shown by sticking the thumb out of the closed hand. This gesture will be discussed later.

The tongue is a very important organ. We could not talk without a tongue. We taste with it. It helps us to decide whether something should be incorporated or rejected; and, in itself, it is an incorporating and rejecting instrument. Pointing it at another person means, "I don't want you. I reject you."

The posterior part of the body serves functions which are important to life. In women, it is considered the most cherished part of the body. It conceals the opening of the intestinal tract through which waste is eliminated. This function becomes degraded only in the course of time; but it still maintains its top interest. It remains a source of gratification for needs, curiosity, and secondary stimulation in sexual foreplay. It assumes an outstanding role in perversions. Man's attitude to it is ambivalent. It can denote, at once, something desirable *and* disgusting.

Flugel (1925) cites Jones (1914) who regards the tongue as a phallic symbol. In my opinion, the tongue can symbolize both male and female genitals because it is hidden like the genitals. It is an insult to show the genitals not for pleasure but for the rejection of the pleasure.

Those who have traveled in Europe may have observed that

when the train moves in the open and free country, grown-up girls and women salute (or reject) the travelers by turning (or even baring) their posteriors toward the train. The same motion is observable in certain types of dancing in which the skirt is lifted and the posterior is challengingly exhibited.

By sticking out the tongue, a person exhibits, symbolically, the sexual organs—not for invitation, but for contemptuous rejection, as if to say, "Look what I have. You would like to enjoy it. No! You won't get it. Ha-ha-ha!"

Giggling

Giggling is a particular kind of laughter. It can be elicited by physical stimuli, such as tickling, and by psychological stimuli, such as anxiety-arousing, erotic, and comical situations. In my opinion, giggling in an anxiety situation is forced and make-believe. The person forces himself to deny the danger. Here, giggling is close to the so-called hysterical laughter after a great trauma.

Children of both sexes giggle. As they grow, girls retain the habit, but boys change it to a "snicker," a "chuckle," or a "smirk." Although the best gigglers are adolescent girls, all women do it well. In the course of time, giggling becomes a feminine characteristic. In one of the best papers on laughter, Edith Jacobson (1946) gives an account of such experiences with a child. She also includes interesting information she received from a psychoanalytically trained observer in a nursery school, concerning the giggling and laughter of pre-school children in response to situations of instinctual danger. This report says, among other things, that boys and girls up to four years of age respond to anxiety situations by giggling; but they do not giggle over anatomical differences. They find words having to do with the genitals and toilet functions extremely funny when slightly changed and applied by displacement to other objects. Children have to be three or four before they giggle directly at sex differences.

Exactly the same things make adolescent girls giggle. Many of the situations causing giggling are close to comic, as recognized by Jacobson. A man is comical when he runs after his hat blown off by the wind. He is close to catching it when he fails. If he should run the risk of being hit by a car in the course of frantically running after his hat, the onlooker would be horrified; the comic aspect would be lost. Similarly, when girls notice some slight disorder on the pants of a boy or a teacher, they will giggle; but if either should expose the genitals, they would run away in terror. I once treated an eight-year-old girl who related with great glee and laughter that her father's shirt, which he used to tie around his body while getting washed in the morning, almost slipped down. The father, showing great embarrassment, quickly replaced the shirt.

It is remarkable how little is necessary to make girls giggle. A boy is puzzled and does not understand what girls are giggling about when he approaches them in a corridor or on the street. It may be that his necktie is not straight or a shoelace is loose. It turns out that anything which, through association, hints, in a veiled way, at something sexual, will cause giggling. A girl needs company in order to giggle. If she is alone, she bears the whole responsibility, and she may be considered "bad." When others are with her and a group is created, the strength of the group makes the giggling acceptable. If the guilt is shared, then the action is sanctioned.

A *group* of girls will giggle or a *group* of boys will "snicker" more easily than a girl or boy alone. Giggling is a "social act," according to Ernst Kris (1938, 1939): "Group laughter, as shown in infectious laughter is to be understood as repression in common; what is tolerated in this case need not be some special way of thinking or aggressive thoughts, but the behavior itself, namely, laughter."

A mother relates, "One year ago, a boy friend of my daughter taught my daughter, who was at that time seven, the word, fart. The children were playing 'Jacks.' One feature of the play is to say 'cart.' The boy whispered to my daughter 'fart' (as sounding like 'cart'), whereupon my daughter started to giggle and she giggled for hours at home."

In a lecture, illustrated by motion pictures, Spitz showed many of the stimuli which elicit laughter in infants (see Spitz and Wolf, 1946). As has already been stated, Freud (1905a) must be credited with having laid the fundamental groundwork on wit, comedy and humor.

Yawning

We are interested in yawning from an emotional and social point of view; but we are mainly interested in it as a way of "nonverbal communication." Its physiology is beyond our present interest.

In a group, a woman considers a man's yawning as an insult because it indicates that the man is not interested in her as a woman and that he is bored. Both men and women apologize to each other by saying, "It's not the company, it's the hour." But who believes the apology is not "just" courtesy? Everyone has thus apologized even when, in truth, he was bored. The last part of the statement needs further elucidation. We have all experienced the fatigue that forces us away from company because we are overwhelmed by the need and desire for sleep. If this is obvious, then the yawn causes no hurt. But this is rarely the case. No matter how tired one is (barring emergencies), he can still be alert and attentive *if* he is intensely interested. But one cannot always be that interested even though he is expected to be. Women, especially, want men to make the supreme effort not to yawn in their company. Good manners require that one should, at least, apologize (it's not the company, etc.) if he yawns. Under all circumstances, one should cover his mouth. Many people who comply with this social demand do so gladly; there are things in their mouths which they do not want others to see.

Whistling and humming a tune

When performed melodiously and moderately, whistling and humming can be a kind of art. Children love to be hummed to sleep. Lovers, or friends, like to hum or, sometimes, to whistle together. They may even agree on a special, invented and agreed-upon whistling melody to communicate with or to send messages to each other.

Then, there is the famous "whistling in the dark," meaning, "I am not afraid. I even betray that I am here." The latter indicates genuine or feigned self-confidence, strength, and firmness.

On the other hand, whistling can be used in a defiant and derogatory manner. One does not whistle at a dignified person in order to stop him or to call him. If he is a friend who will accept such a communication, then it is all right to whistle.

One may have an argument with his wife or husband or with a stranger. To show that he does not give a damn or that he ignores the other and what was said, he whistles or hums a tune. This can be very insulting, upsetting, and aggravating to the situation.

Hat mannerisms

A man's personality (his character) depends on the constitutional heritage he receives from his ancestors, on the drives and instincts with which he is endowed at birth, on his prenatal and postnatal environment, including his mother, father, family, race, group, country, education, and on whatever else any school of science can contribute.

As Freud has shown, human beings want gratifications. They want to avoid pain and frustrations. Though our fate rests on our anatomy, we can break our chains and create the most sublime, spiritual treasures. Ferenczi once said that even cathedrals are built of bricks and stones.

Until our personality attains its final form, we go through many complicated periods. It is the aim of analytic therapy to correct the errors in the process of growth.

The personality reveals itself in thousands of ways. Everything that a human being does reflects his history and his make-up. In this book, only a very tiny part of the ways in which the self is revealed has been shown, through analyzing the habits, mannerisms, verbal and nonverbal communications between men.

The analyst's work is very arduous. He needs immense patience to be able to go into all the details of human manifestations and to understand them. Often, therefore, his findings and conclusions may seem to many to be far-fetched, exaggerated, and unjustifiably generalized. We are bound to make errors; but not everything said by analysts is erroneous. Errors may be made, but they may also be corrected. As observations accumulate, the analyst finds himself, from year to year, on ever firmer ground. On the other hand, there always remain open questions in science.

The reader may wonder why it is necessary to say all these things in a chapter concerned with hat mannerisms. Because the conclusions drawn from seemingly unimportant things are weighty, the introduction to this brief chapter could have been used to begin every other one.

Where we live, men and women generally wear hats. Women wear most extravagant hats. Their chief concern is that the hat be new and that it make them attractive.

Men want this too; but many men wear the same hat for long, long years. One may see from a man's hat whether he is a youngster, an oldster, a dignified man, a clergyman, a scientist, or a no-matter-who.

Some pull the hat down to their eyebrows; some almost completely cover their eyes; some carry their hats jauntily on the side of their skulls; some exhibit their forehead, lift their head, and protrude their bellies as if they disdained walking and would rather roll.

In my youth, I was fascinated by a neighbor, a married man, who always wore his hat tipped completely to the right so that it covered his right eye. I wondered how he could move without having the hat fall off his head. This went on for years. I was also astonished that the neighbor did not change the position of his hat even when walking arm in arm with his wife.

Bent on finding out the cause of this mannerism, I once asked the man for an explanation. He answered frankly that everybody could see how ugly his wife was. In wearing his hat tipped to the right, he managed not to see her. Eventually, it became a habit for him to wear his hat tipped to the right no matter with whom he was walking or even when he walked alone.

Even without Freud, everybody knows that sex is an all-pervading drive in every living creature; but nobody would admit it until Freud came to make us realize how pernicious it is to deny the presence and importance of sex. In order that sex should not have an *irrational* dominance, one has to admit and gratify *that* much of it which is *rational*.

Sex is repressed through rational or irrational means; but for whatever reason it is so repressed, it manifests itself in derivatives and symbols. Analysis of the behavior of human beings makes it imperative to recognize this and to accept the fact that sex, like other drives representing the "life instinct" (Freud), is everywhere—even in the fact that human beings invented the hat and continue to wear it. The hat can be a sexual symbol.

The candidate for a political office "throws his hat into the ring." Competition is an honorable, manly trend. Men compete with each other; and by so doing, they want to show all other men and all women that they are admirable. In sports events, the male supporters of the winning team throw their hats into the air with great happiness. This gesture is an extension of the size of the main male pride, the genitals.

Some years ago, I met a man who suffered from a checkroom phobia. He would not go to any public place of amusement where he would have to check his outer garments, including his hat, coat, umbrella and rubbers, because he was afraid that they would be stolen. His effects had been stolen twice. Therefore, he would attend a concert or similar affairs only during the summer when he would not have to check his belongings (the checking was mandatory in Budapest, where he lived). This man's phobia stemmed from a displacement of "castration fear."

Taking off the hat, a European custom, was reduced in America to tipping the hat. This custom has now almost disappeared. The original meaning of removing the hat was the self-abasement (Freud) of its wearer before another. If the hat was taken off or tipped to a woman, the gesture was meant as a token of complete self-abnegation, an insincere and hypocritical invitation for the lady to step on the man, and as a masochistic tendency covering up the truly aggressive motives behind the gesture.

Freud (1916) mentions that taking off the hat in greeting is symbolic of castration. The hat is used in different ways in greeting: it may be tipped to the side, completely removed straight up into the air, or held in a humble position over the chest. Further examples may be found in other writings of Freud (1900, pp. 355-356, 360-362, 652) and Robitsek (1925).

Smoking mannerisms

Though those who smoke do so when they are alone, smoking is one of the features of social relations between people. People like to smoke when they are together, when they converse. It is a sign of hospitality, kindness, and it keeps the conversation rolling. It bridges the initial strangeness between individuals who meet for the first time or between those who are not very close. As with drinking and offering food, smoking is, again, an activity which begins with the hands and, especially, with the mouth. The cigarette (cigar, pipe) burns; it is something warm, something to handle, and something distracting. Ferenczi (1932) went so far as to say that smoking, like (neurotic) counting, chanting, and thinking, aims to hold off death.

Smoking, a very widespread habit, is more than a habit; it is an addiction, opposed by doctors, many of whom are themselves heavy smokers. I believe it was Nothnagel, the great physician, who was asked to give a lecture to his colleagues about the effects of smoking on the human body. This he did, saying frightening things about the possible consequences of smoking. After he had finished his talk, he smiled and said, "Now, gentlemen, it will be a delight to light a cigar." He took a cigar from his vest pocket and lit it. Smoking *is* an addiction. One difference between smoking and drug addiction is mainly that the former is socially sanctioned. A second difference is that even though smoking may be harmful, its harmfulness is not identical with that of drug addiction. For example, many persons, even though heavy smokers, would abstain from tobacco if convinced that the continuation of its use would mean *impending* danger for them. This is not true of a drug addict.

When alarming reports spread over the country about the harmful effects of smoking, many people "cut down" or use different filters—for a few days. Cigarette stocks go down for a while; and the "wise" buy shares, knowing that the panic will soon be over and the stock will go up. (I have no such stocks.) Thomas Szasz (1958) points out that in smoking, some people expose themselves to dangerous consequences such as cancer and other physical troubles in order to prove that, when they are unaffected, they were right in feeling that nothing alarming would happen to them.

Smoking begins, usually, in early boyhood. It is awful. One coughs; his mouth stinks; he becomes nauseous; and he drops it. Then one tries again. As Ferenczi (1912), said, smoking and sexual intercourse are things which are permitted to grownups and prohibited to youngsters. The parents eventually become resigned to it; after all, they themselves *smoke openly*. If they do not, their resistance against the smoking of the children lasts longer. The connection between smoking and sex has been illustrated in a previous chapter.

This does not mean that smoking and genital-sexual gratification are identical. Not at all. Before genital sexuality takes over the leading role in pleasure, there are several other stages of sexual development, as proven by many, indisputable, clinical facts. The strongest source of libidinous drive is the oral one. Though life starts with breathing, the need for food seems to be the primary drive. Oral pleasure is not confined to the time of food intake. The main evidence that it is not so confined is thumb sucking. In the course of reading this book, the reader may have gained information about other libidinous drives, and the great multitude of derivatives of those drives, especially the oral ones.

Smoking is an oral activity; one should bear in mind that it is a regression, especially when it becomes a habit. The regression is caused by frustrations; mankind *is* unhappy. The time when we were at the breast (or bottle) was *the* happy time. For both sexes, those two hemispheres were the "land of milk and honey," the "social security." As we grow older, life becomes more and more difficult. It becomes filled with apprehensions and anxieties. All relations stir up conflicts; and we need, in one way or another, to conjure up the happy time. One way of doing so is to smoke.

In this chapter, we are mainly interested in smoking mannerisms; and there are many. I was able to establish their "meaning" in the analysis of different patients. The majority of patients smoke during the sessions. (And so do most of the analysts. Freud was a heavy smoker.)

Chain smokers are persons who light one cigarette (cigar or pipe) after the other. Some use the burning cigarette, which they intend to discard, for lighting another. Some get up at night to smoke. Smoking is often connected with drinking. One does both. There are smokers who never carry matches. They look for somebody else to provide the light, apparently to make smoking identical with breast feeding by connecting this activity with another (male or female) who represents the mother.

Some persons "must" have a cigarette after sexual intercourse, as if the genital gratification did not release all the libidinous need which also has to be complemented by oral gratification.

There are persons who do not smoke but who carry matches to help out smokers who are without them. The former have a particular smile when they see a helpless smoker. They approach him kindly and offer him one of the greatest presents, a match. Such people play the mother-child relation.

In 1919, when the Rumanian army temporarily occupied Hungary, hundreds of people who were thought to be communists were rounded up. This meant that whoever was not well-dressed or was loitering or resting in the city parks was suspected, arrested, and, as we heard, shot without any trial. After this nightmare was over, I heard the following story:

A patient, a religious man who was far from being a communist, was arrested with about ten other persons in the city park of Budapest. Two fancy officers, whom the patient thought to be about ten yards from the group, were discussing what should be done with the prisoners. The patient thought that he, along with the others, would be taken away and shot. One of the officers took out a cigarette; but he did not have any matches. The patient, who did, stepped out and gave him a match which was accepted. The officer then made a motion, indicating that the man could leave and go home. After arriving home, the patient shook the whole day, realizing that his life had depended on a cigarette and a match.

It is interesting to note that persons who spend a great deal of money for tobacco take cigarettes from others whenever they have a chance. One would think that they were stingy or greedy people. This is not the case. Many people say that they have a very warm feeling when they know that they are free to reach out and take a cigarette from a table whenever they wish. This behavior must, again, come from the need for the breast.

There is a strong alliance between smokers. Complete strangers feel free to ask for a cigarette from another smoker. They feel that the other fully understands their plight. Smoking is one of the strongest forces of group formation.

Years ago, I had to see a patient who was placed in a private institution located an hour's train ride from New York City. While driving along in a cab toward the station (a small place), I noticed that I was out of cigarettes which I intended to buy at the station. After dismissing the cab, I walked toward the stand in the station and noticed that it was closed. I then asked another cab driver whether there was any place nearby where one could buy some cigarettes. The cabby thought that it would be too risky to go to the place he knew because the train would arrive in a few minutes, so he offered me a pack that was half full. I took one cigarette, but in spite of the fact that I told the man that one cigarette would suffice for the one-hour trip, the driver insisted on giving me what was left in the pack and would not accept any money. I never met this man again; but, as the reader can see, the kindness was not forgotten.

Brill (1922) says:

1. "Neurotic smoking . . . represents a regression to infantile autoerotism . . . its infantile root is thumbsucking" (p. 438).
Is smoking in general a regression to autoerotism? Brill: "It would seem so" (p. 439).
2. ". . . it is my conviction that tobacco, whether indulged in a normal or abnormal sense, is either a continuation of an infantile, autoerotic gratification, or a regression to it" (p. 440).

3. Aggressive men are strong smokers (p. 442).

4. "Most of the fanatical opponents of tobacco that I have known were all bad neurotics" (p. 444).

There are several ways in which people hold the cigarette between the fingers and in the mouth. Some keep it in their mouths all the time, like a pacifier in the mouths of babies. They may dangle it between the lips and draw it back from time to time. The onlooker admires their skill and courage. The greatest acrobats of this kind that I have seen were the Bosnians in Yugoslavia.

In the army, once upon a time, soldiers (and civilians often did the same) rolled their own cigarettes. They carried a bag of tobacco and a pack of cigarette paper in their pockets. There were some masters of smoking who kept tobacco and paper in the same bag. These would reach into their pocket, manipulate for a short time, draw out the rolled cigarette, lick the paper, close it, and light the cigarette, all with one hand.

There are also match-acrobats who, in an emergency, could reach up to another planet and strike a match. And, let's not leave out those who can strike a match in the greatest wind. Such feats prove, more than any other, a man's masculinity. They are Titans, like Prometheus, of whom Freud (1932) writes that he was ". . . a demiurge and creator of man, who brought to mankind the fire, which he stole from the gods hidden in a hollow rod, a fennel-stalk."

And there are the "arsonist candidates" who smoke in bed and fall asleep (like a baby at the breast), or who forget to discard the burning cigarette, or who throw the still smoking match into the wastebasket full of paper, or who burn holes in the tablecloth, ruin woodwork, marble covers, curtains, their own clothes and those of others.

A girl of about thirty declared, among other things, in her first analytic session, that she was a virgin. In the course of the analysis, she related a dream which revealed that she had not told the truth about her virginity. The dream was as follows: "I was standing near a man, conversing. I was wearing a blouse with a white collar. The man was smoking. He burned a hole in my collar with the cigarette." The reader knows what the dream signifies. I told her that I thought she was not a virgin. The poor girl cried and admitted this. She had had an affair with the married man who appeared in the dream. It was this man who had taken away her innocence.

I know one such "arsonist candidate" who has the compulsion to check to see whether the front of his pants is in order, probably because of repressed, exhibitionistic tendencies. He is a smoker. On the cover of each book of matches, there is a warning, "Close cover before striking." The warning intends to prevent an explosion of all the matches caused by carelessly igniting one. Failure to heed the warning can cause, among other disasters, blindness. This man's actions are just the opposite of what he is instructed to do. He turns over the cover so that all the matches are exposed and bare. Then he strikes one.

There are smokers who can strike a match on the surface of an ice-block, or on any other surface, no matter what it may be. They would strike a match on a table cover made of Carrara marble, on a masterpiece of wood, on a stained glass window, on a beautiful mural or on lovely wallpaper. They can light a match by flicking it with the nail of a finger of the same hand in which they hold the match. They can strike it on a thigh which they make solid as a rock or on their shoe soles. Such people would strike a match on Raphael's Madonna. They are like the vandals who stepped on the geometrical circles which Archimedes drew on sand.

Now, we can turn to the *messy smokers* and then to the *ash-acrobats*.

The dread of the housewife is the man who, when smoking, does not care where the ashes fall. He himself is fully covered with ashes, so are the table and the floor around him. Such men are incorrigible. One has to clean after them; they never were "toilet-trained."

Then, there are the ash-acrobats who, intentionally (or "sub-"intentionally) do not discard the ash from the burning cigarette; they keep it as long as possible. They keep the on-looker and, sometimes, the whole family in anxious suspense, wondering, "When? when?—no—not yet. when?" Most of the time, the acrobat wins. When warned, he assumes a non-chalant face, as if to say, "What's this excitement about?" and puts down on the ash tray the undamaged column, in tri-umph.

One such man in analysis revealed that he could not urinate when anybody was present or could hear the splash of urination, even when the door of the bathroom was closed. One of the many motives involved was exhibitionism. As a very small child, his mother praised and admired him for being able to aim the spray of urine straight into the pot. Later, he had to relinquish the habit and repress the strong and ambitious drive; but he could display it with the ash of the cigarette.

Another patient displayed a remarkable skill in flicking off, with a free finger in a "blitz" movement, an infinitesimal amount of ash the moment it became perceptible. She was a woman who suffered great anguish because of her alleged "low" origin, and she desperately tried to fend off the slight-est possibility of being identified as a member of such a group.

Movements with arms and fingers

It may not be an exaggeration to say that knowing every-thing about the expressive movement of human hands and fingers would mean knowing everything about the origin and development of man as an individual and as a social being. What I shall discuss is a very small part of this knowledge, the expressive movements which can be observed and noticed at the present time when people communicate with each other or, at times, when they are alone. We are mainly interested in gestures which accompany or substitute for speech.

A characteristic gesture is that of men who, when meeting or approaching an attractive female, *fix their neckties*. What makes men do this? Most of the time, there are reasons that appear obvious and are immediately accepted. The spontaneous acceptance does not mean that these reasons are wrong. Not at all. For example, sloppiness may be acceptable in children up to a certain age, and in men after a certain age, i.e., old people. A virile male, in order to show his masculinity, has to keep his clothes in good order and fitting by seeing to it, among other things, that his tie or bow is tight, that his trousers are not dangling, and that his buttons and zippers are checked.

The analyst cannot be satisfied with only that much. He is compelled to go further. In the course of analyses, when symbols used in waking life and in dreams are analyzed (and we have a well-worked-out technique for this), we find, besides the obvious, a "deeper," additional meaning. Patients become increasingly convinced of this deeper meaning in the course of their analyses, but most of the readers are not and have not been analyzed. Therefore, with some exceptions, the interpretation *has* elicited and *will* elicit opposition and, perhaps, anger, annoyance, and even disbelief in all things beyond the obvious that analysts claim as valid.

Except at casual social gatherings, ordinarily a man appearing without a necktie or a bow creates the impression that something important is missing. This is because the necktie (or bow) is a phallic symbol. The person who uses it as such is not aware of its meaning. If he were, he would not use it as a symbol because it would be offensive to the user himself as well as to others. For example, many men have a great number of neckties. Many men have a typical dream the content of which is that they have two penises. Girls have "fun" pulling the necktie out of the jacket, vest, or trousers. Females like to buy men neckties. They like to "fix" them on the men, as the following illustration shows.

Long ago, in Hungary, we spent the summer months in a resort place near Budapest. We used the commuters' train to get back and forth to town. One morning, there was a newly-wed couple with us on the train. The young wife who could not part from her husband accompanied him. The husband wore a bow-tie. Twice within one hour, the wife turned to-ward her husband and lovingly fixed his bow. Before going further, the reader must know that, in Hungary, among men, erection is indicated by saying that it "stands"; but the word "stands" is also used to indicate that something "suits him well." Instead of "suit," the expression used is "it stands him well." Now, when the young wife fixed the tie a second time, a male member of the group asked her why she was doing this, whereupon she "innocently" answered that everybody should see that "it stands well." All the men roared with laughter, and she wondered why.

The necktie as a phallic symbol was recognized long ago by several analytic writers, among whom were H. R. (1912) and Hollos (1923).

"Nose-thumbing" and "fica" ("fig")

This chapter completes the chapter dealing with "Sticking out the tongue."

"Nose-thumbing" is done either with the right or with the left hand. The arm is lifted, elbow bent, fingers spread apart, and the thumb is put close to the tip of the nose, so that it touches the nose as if to lengthen the nose with the spread fingers by making the distance between the thumb and the little finger as great as possible. Often it is done simultaneously with sticking out the tongue. Both mean the same; they re-inforce each other. Sometimes, nose-thumbing is done when a person wants to ridicule or to tease another, but it is used mainly to indicate that the other person to whom it is done does not have any power, influence, on the user who does not care; who is, from an emotional point of view, not dependent on the other; cannot be hurt by the other; who does not need him; and for whom the other does not count.

"Nose-thumbing" is used by both sexes against either sex although it is mainly used by males. There does not seem to be much need to introduce the nose as a genital symbol, principally phallic. Probably, in the beginning, it was used as a kind of magic against evil, especially the "evil eye." In our present time, when most people no longer believe in the power of the evil eye, it is used for the purpose as described above. The symbolic meaning is not known to the person.

"Fig" or "fica" is a gesture in which the thumb is placed between the index and middle fingers in such a way that the tip of the thumb sticks out visibly. It symbolizes sexual intercourse; but it is not used consciously for this purpose, as is the rude sign for sexual intercourse in which a ring is formed with thumb and index finger of the left hand (representing the female organs) through which the index finger of the right hand (representing the male organ) is moved so that a rhythmic movement is imitated. Although I have often seen all these gestures, including sticking out the tongue and nose-thumbing, I was not aware that they meant anything more than a desire to taunt somebody; but I did know the meaning of "fica."

In a profound paper, Born (1945) writes, "Another magic means of protection against the 'evil eye' consists of an amulet in the form of sexual organs. The archaic Latin word *fascinum* originally meant the male genitals. Stemming from the same word *fascinum* is the word fascination, which means the capacity of rendering somebody powerless by one's look. To the primitive man, the organs of reproduction evidently appeared more mysterious than anything else, and, consequently, a most formidable magic power was attributed to them. Plutarch makes a significant statement which shed light on the use of phallic amulets. He suggests that amulets ought to protect their owners against the 'evil eye' by directing its attention away from him and toward themselves. For this reason, the representation of the genitals was considered a means to obviate the effect of the evil eye. The spread of Christian morality made the representation of the genitals an offense, so that naturalistic phallic amulets in Christian times were replaced by symbolic forms. The most widespread of these is the *fig* or *fica*, namely, hand with the thumb placed between the index and the third finger, a very old sign for cohabitation."*

Pressing two hands to the temples

Pressing one's head (mainly the two temples) with two hands is probably a movement which everybody has either made himself or observed.

We do this in distress or despair when we feel helpless and seek for a solution. In reporting about the analysis of a dream of one of his patients, Freud (1900) writes, "Whenever his father was tormented by business worries or family difficulties, he had been in the habit of pressing his hands to the sides of his forehead, as though he felt that his head was too wide and wanted to compress it" (p. 427).

A similar gesture is one in which a person, leaning on the table with his elbows, places his head between his two palms. In addition to what was said about pressing the forehead, this gesture can represent sadness, exhaustion, mourning, meditation in distress, and giving up hope for a solution. Besides, both gestures are made when one is tormented by a headache.

Small children, in the same situations, cry, take recourse to thumbsucking or, even, masturbation. Later, under the influence of the knowledge that the head is the instrument of thinking and deciding actions, maturity prompts the use of another organ, the head.

Some people, in despair, especially if the despair is accom-

---

* Quoted by permission from "Fetish, Amulet and Talisman" by Wolfgang Born, Ph.D. in *Ciba Symposia*, Volume 7, Number 7, October, 1945.

panied by anger, hit their heads with their fists. Children throw themselves to the floor and hit their heads so hard that it is frightening. The aim of this distressing action is to "go to pieces" if one cannot eliminate the source of the trouble, which distresses the whole person.

Accompanying writing with tongue and jaws

The use of tongue and jaws simultaneously with activities of the hand has already been described by Darwin (1873), who writes,

> There are other actions which are commonly performed under certain circumstances independently of habit, and which seem to be due to imitation or some sort of sympathy. Thus persons cutting anything with a pair of scissors may be seen to move their jaws simultaneously with the blades of the scissors. Children learning to write often twist about their tongues as their fingers move, in a ridiculous fashion. When a public singer suddenly becomes a little hoarse, many of those present may be heard, as I have been assured by a gentleman on whom I can rely, to clear their throats; but here habit probably comes into play, as we clear our own throats under similar circumstances. The writer has also been told that at leaping matches, as the performer makes his spring, many of the spectators, generally men and boys, move their feet; but there again habit probably comes into play, for it is very doubtful whether women would thus act [p. 34].

To this correct presentation, I can add some observations and comments.

The simultaneous use of the tongue and jaws can sometimes be observed in adults not only at the time of the above-mentioned activities but (as previously mentioned in this book) also during thinking, for example, when somebody tries (though vainly) to imitate with the jaws the form of the letters of the words which are in his mind. One of the first activities performed by everybody is sucking, which is followed, in most persons, by thumb-sucking, and then by the taking of food with the fingers. This succession of prime important actions leaves in the mind indelible fixations which appear simultaneously in the actions under discussion. The tongue is a busy participant in all oral actions.

The simultaneous movement of the observer with a person in action is, in my opinion, due to an identification with him. The observers themselves would like to jump, but have to refrain from doing so; or they think, for example, observing a person jumping onto the steps of an already moving vehicle, that "he" will make it. Thus, magically, they help the person perform his action well and to succeed. The same refers to the identification with the singer. The simultaneous movements of the tongue with the hands in writing or other activities appear in both boys and girls.

Index finger placed alongside the nose

Placing the index finger alongside the nose indicates suspicion. Since man assumed the erect posture, the nose has "lost ground"; but it is still one of the organs which is closely connected with thinking, as recognized long ago by Nietzsche and Freud. Critchley (1939), in his already mentioned book on *The Language of Gestures*, interprets this gesture in the same way.

The connection between suspicion and the olfactory organ, the nose, originates from the fact that man's ability to smell enables him to discover where a smell-provoking stimulus lies hidden without needing to see, hear, touch, or taste it. The stimulus travels through the air to us; and because we are not immediately sure what it is, we become suspicious. For this reason, we use the gesture of putting the index finger to the nose even when we do not want to find out what smells. We would rather find out anything else by thinking. Animals who walk on all fours have retained their olfactory ability;

therefore, they do not need to think. They "think" with their sense of smell.

The gesture of honesty

The sincerity of our feelings and statements is often accompanied by a gesture in which the hand is placed over the region of the heart or over the upper middle part of the chest. The word, "honestly," becomes solemn with this gesture. It is like an oath.

Usually an oath is performed by placing the hand on a holy object like the Bible or by raising the arm. History and anthropology teach us that a long, long time ago the solemnity of a statement was expressed in a different form. The present form, by displacement, is a derivative of the old. We read in Genesis 14:22, of Abraham's oath to the King of Sodom: ". . . I have lift up mine hand unto the Lord . . . that I will not take anything that is thine . . ." The same thing is mentioned in Deuteronomy 32:40. It is as if reaching to heaven where the Lord is thought to be is the equivalent to touching Him. One cannot mislead the Lord; therefore, the sincerity of a statement is made unquestionable.

In addition, the Bible mentions, in two places, that the person making an oath is asked to put his hand on the thigh of the person to whom he makes a promise: (1) Genesis 24:2-3, "And Abraham said unto him . . . servant . . . put thy hand under my thigh . . . and I will make thee swear," and (2) Genesis 47:29, Jacob called upon his son Joseph: " . . . put . . . thy hand under my thigh and . . . bury me not, I pray thee, in Egypt."

On the basis of our knowledge, we must conclude that the phrase, "under my thigh," means the procreative organ, the genitals. The Bible is reluctant to use the word, genitals, bluntly.

To the ancient people, procreation did not mean only a localized and sensual pleasure and gratification. To them, the sex act was the greatest mission entrusted to man by nature. It was the individual's most solemn performance as a member of a group. It was holy.

All present religions try to impress their followers with this holy aspect of the sexual union.

In rituals, one can observe that an individual who has touched a holy object will kiss the hand that has touched that object. When we put a hand over our own chest in order to signify the sincerity of a statement, I believe we intend to touch the other person; but since this habit has been abandoned, we place our hand over our own chests instead. We place it over the region in which we believe the heart to be because this organ is just as important to our lives as are the organs of procreation.

Closing the nostrils with the fingers

Closing the nostrils with the fingers is a gesture of contempt. Both nostrils are pressed together, i.e., closed, in order to convey to the other person that he is a "stinker." It is not meant literally that he is a stinker. The gesture is used both when the person does not smell at all and when he smells good. It indicates, rather, that one does not want the other's company or closeness and that the nature of the latter's conversation stinks.

Once, while walking down the street, I noticed a cute little girl standing on the lawn in front of her home. She was alone. When I passed by, she said, "You are a stinker." I stopped and lifted my arm, smelling myself and saying, "I do not feel that I stink." The girl, who was about five years old, stopped talking, looked puzzled; and I resumed my walk. I had the feeling that the child would make no further use of such comment.

Closing ears with hands
Indication of going to sleep
Listening
Hang yourself

Closing the ears with both hands need not mean a protection against noise. It may indicate, firmly, "I don't want to hear what you say," or "I don't want to hear whatever you say." Listening to a person means that one wants the person or, at least, that one is inclined to hear what he wants to communicate. The same is true of the listening gesture when the external ears are pushed forward, made broader, in order to hear, to listen, to show that one wants very much to pay attention to the communicant. The gesture of "hang yourself" does not need description or interpretation; neither does the gesture which indicates that one wants to go to sleep. We all use them.

Putting the arms akimbo

Putting the arms akimbo is an expressive movement, especially favored by women because it makes them appear cute in the eyes of men.

The two arms are placed on both sides of the body over the crest of the pelvic bone; at the same time, the body is kept erect and firm, and the legs are pressed firmly to the ground and kept slightly apart, to make the appearance of firmness even stronger. The head is lifted. In my opinion, the same intention of showing determination to an action is expressed by males in pulling up their pants; one cannot fight if there is danger of the trousers falling off. A patient told me that if he were attacked, the most helpless position would be to sit on the toilet, pants down, having a bowel movement. We all agree with that.

Men like women to put their arms akimbo and scold them

when the latter are angry. Men find this behavior cute because it displays a good figure to advantage and stimulates the man to subdue the woman sexually because he is still stronger. The state of poise may be somewhat related to this posture (Rangell, 1954).

Crossing the arms over the chest

In old times, teachers often ordered school children to place their arms in the form of number eight in front of their chests. The teacher meant to discipline them to submission to his orders, to prevent their doing anything wrong with their hands which would distract their attention from the teacher. The gesture was a sort of straitjacket. Furthermore, it is a characteristic position of demagogues and dictators. In the latter case, the demagogue indicates that his arms are now resting, but should he unfold them, he would make them hit hard.*

Shaking hands

We accept Hermann's proposition that the main drive carried out by the arms and hands is that of "clinging." The arms, hands, and fingers serve a multitude of other purposes; but all these others are transformations, reactions, substitutes, derivatives of the instinct "to cling."

We were taught that we shake hands to show that we do not harbor evil intentions and that we do not have weapons, i.e., we are friends. "The raising of the hand," says Critchley (1939), "to the forehead—which now constitutes a military salute—was originally a way of demonstrating that the hand

---

* In several instances, the same position is assumed in order to keep warm. While the arms are folded across the chest, the head is drawn down between the lifted shoulders. The posture aims at reducing the surface of the body in order to prevent the loss of body heat. This gesture is often made for psychological and emotional reasons, that is, those who do so have the feeling that they are not or will not be loved.

held no offensive weapon" (p. 12). This is probably true, but more can be said about this subject.

In handshaking, we cling to the other person. The gesture means that we should like to trust each other, as a baby has perfect and complete trust in his mother. Saluting means more than giving honor; it also means that we belong together; that, even if there are differences in rank, in social standing, or the like, we are still equal and we belong together.

There is a right way and a wrong way of handshaking. In the right handshake, the hands of two people are fused and both feel a certain pressure. The same pressure is expected from the other as the first put into it. When the first feels that the latter does not do it, he is let down.

Some individuals want to show off and almost crush the hand they grasp. Some put their hand in that of another who expects to feel some pressure but feels no more than he would in pressing cotton or a caterpillar. The latter is disgusted. The handshake is vapid.

Some extend only their fingers. Again, more was expected, and there is a letdown. The reason for this is, usually, a social anxiety, a fear of contact, which is caused by different complexes.

Some people are ready to meet the possibility that, after the shaking of the hand, the saluting person will touch his arm. At this moment, they will make their arm muscles tight in order to have the other feel how strong they are.

The meaning of the outstretched arms

The arms are stretched out under different emotional conditions. This gesture in man probably serves essentially a purpose similar to that in birds who use their wings for taking off and landing. Man uses his arms for defense, for attack, for balance, for pushing himself forward, for calling attention to himself, for expressing surprise, or victory, or alarm, for blessing and for magic. He drops his arms in a state of despair. He stretches them out in different directions for salute, as in the fascist manner.

The Lord brought the Children of Israel "forth out of Egypt with a mighty hand, and with an outstretched arm" (Deuteronomy 26:8). And again, "And Moses said unto Joshua: Choose us out men, and go out, fight with Amalek; to-morrow, I will stand on the top of the hill with the rod of God in my hand. So Joshua did as Moses had said to him, and fought with Amalek; and Moses, Aaron, and Hur, went up to the top of the hill. And it came to pass, when Moses held up his hand, that Israel prevailed; and when he let down his hand, Amalek prevailed. But Moses' hands were heavy; and they took a stone, and put it under him, and he sat thereon; and Aaron and Hur stayed up his hands, the one on the one side, and the other on the other side; and his hands were very steady until the going down of the sun. And Joshua discomfited Amalek and his people with the edge of the sword." (Exodus 17:9-13) Already, the Talmud wonders how the hand of Moses could cause victory or defeat. The Hertz *Pentateuch* (1938, p. 280) records the comments of theologians. They do not analyze or penetrate the unconscious symbolism of the outstretched arms. Their's are "common-sense" commentaries.

I have stressed the creative-phallic meaning of the arm and of the hand in a study on blessing (1941c). There was a god in ancient times, the god of agriculture, vegetation, and fertility; this god belonged to "The Cult of Sabazios," symbolized by a human arm. On one representation, the god is seen sitting between the thumb and the two other upright fingers, and underneath, in the cavity of the palm, is a mother with her baby. The meaning is that the greatest blessing is the family. The Sabazios hand had a votive and protective significance.

During my adolescent years I was a member of a gang of boys. From those who were already "initiated" in the important issues of life, I learned about a position of the arm which expressed the idea that something (e.g., a woman) was superb. The arm was bent, hand in a fist-position, and often the entire gesture was accompanied by the words, "like steel." This meant power, strength, erection. Should we assume that the politician who raises his arms to greet the audience, who forms the letter "V" with his fingers to celebrate victory; that he who gives the blessing and he who receives it; that the crowd howling with outstretched arms; that the boys expressing their feelings with the arm "like steel"—should we assume that they all have a dim feeling about the meaning of these arm-actions? I would answer in the affirmative.

Crossing the fingers

Finger-crossing, by placing the index finger and the middle finger crosswise, is performed in order to secure success, luck or a favorable outcome of an uncertain and therefore tense situation. It is, furthermore, a magic gesture, a defense against evil, whether that evil comes from within ourselves or from outside.

For example, when somebody goes to take an examination or goes to an important appointment, those who love him cross their fingers, or say, "I cross my fingers. Good luck." It is a primitive feeling of most of us that bad luck comes from evil spirits or from the envy of others.

The fingers are also crossed when we, honest people, think that a "white lie" is inevitable; but because it is still a lie, telling it may have ill effects for the one who tells it. Among other things, the conscience may be angry with the liar and punish him. Again, it is done to avert evil.

In the course of history, the cross acquired a holy meaning. According to Koch (1930), the vertical bar signifies both the heavenly influence on mankind and man's desire for higher things. The horizontal bar represents the evenness of life's events on a single earthly plane. Thus, the cross had significance long before it acquired religious symbolism with the advent of Christianity. As a means for execution, it was used in early days by the Assyrians, Persians, passing to the Greeks and Romans (Funk and Wagnall, 1936).

In ancient times, the vertical line represented the masculine, phallic-generative force; the horizontal line represented femininity, and the crossing of the two lines represented Eros, in the Platonian and Freudian sense, striving for unity, fertility, prosperity, life. Life means maintaining existence, togetherness, love, family, hope—all against destruction and evil.

Once more I return to my native town and to the gang of boys to which I belonged, between six and eight years of age.

Whenever the boys were on the outskirts of the town and no other persons (especially women) were in sight, and a boy stepped aside to urinate, another boy would rush up close to him and start to do the same in such a way that the streams crossed each other. It was a "must" for the second boy to do so. When I asked one of the boys why they did this, he explained that by so doing an enemy would die. (Under the circumstances, what could a member of a gang do but comply?)

Later on, I realized the deep meaning of this "ritual." On the surface, the action appears as something rude or dirty; but even at that time, there was no obscene connotation attached to it and no vulgar words were spoken. It was a serious matter. It represented the unity of the group of youngsters (like mixing the blood of the members for the same purpose), to stand together in danger, and to share goods. It meant brotherhood and love. It was the expression of latent, sublimated homosexuality which is the binding matrix of any kind of association of males.

The members of the gang—never girls—engaged in another strange kind of finger-crossing. On the street (there were only two in the town at that time) we often witnessed the copulation of dogs. Several times we found them locked together. Whenever the dogs engaged in such spectacular activity, and two boys were present, they locked together the index fingers in order (it was understood that it was done for that purpose) that the dogs should not be able to separate. There were cruel scenes which now, after so many years, still make me shudder. The gesture was a kind of magic, probably prompted by envy, followed by cruelty as a regressive reaction to the frustration to which the boys were subjected at that age. Furthermore, it copied, by identification, the copulation.

Forming a ring with the fingers

When the "communicant" conveys information to the "receiver," it often happens that he forms a ring with his thumb and index finger, lifts his hand so that it is visible, and, with this gesture, he indicates that "it is just right" or "perfect" (Ruesch and Kees, 1956, Plate 23).

A ring means that there is no end, it lasts forever. This could be the meaning of the wedding ring.

I am not satisfied with this explanation. Here again, I believe, we see the happiest personal unity, expressed symbolically by the two fingers, that of the mother and child. The gesture is a wish to create every love relationship as "perfect," as "just right," as it was at the beginning of our life with mother. The social movements of our times verify this. Everyone intends to establish security from the cradle to the grave, to establish institutions which will be like a mother's breast from which honey and milk flow into our mouths, to reach the promised land.

Let us hope that we will make true this dream.

To knock on wood for luck

When people converse and somebody reports an event which ended happily and luckily, he looks for some solid matter, preferably wood, so that with the knuckle of the index finger he can knock on it in order to fend off evil which will turn good luck into bad, disaster and a sad end. Again, the idea is that the listener, even if he is a friend or a close relative, might have feelings of envy, against his own will, and that this envy might cause the turn of luck for the worse. Knocking on wood may, therefore, mean that "my luck" is final and all opposition is silenced. In the same way, a chairman silences an audience with his gavel. In addition, the noise of the knocking is supposed to serve the purpose of making the evil disappear.*

"He who laughs at breakfast will cry at supper" comes from the same idea and concern. One should not be conceited over one's good fortune. People grow fearful when one lucky event is followed by many others; a bad turn might come. On the other hand, when one is the victim of a series of unfortunate events, he hopes that, now, a good turn must come, as if a mysterious destiny would need to cause suffering and then to offset the suffering by being good to us. It is not difficult to see that behind this feeling lurks the figure of the powerful father, or both parents, who first punish and then forgive.

People do not like to discuss or to show their good fortune and luck lest they create envy and ill-will against themselves. Employees do not like to show gaiety before the boss for the same reason.

Everywhere we smell danger. From everywhere, evil wishes and actions may work against us. There are forces which want to destroy us and take away what we have. Even

* Additional (oral and other) sources of this magic were found by Fliess (1944).

in the delusion of persecution, there is a small grain of reality on which the psychotic builds up his delusional system. Let us be honest; we *are* jealous; we *are* envious; we *are* able to find joy in the misfortune of others; we *do* look in the newspapers to see how many people younger than ourselves have died. Many doctors have told me, with self-directed distrust, that one of the first things for which they look in their weekly medical journal is the list of deaths; and against their own best will, they feel a sort of gratification when they see that the list is long. Such a list means to them that they have fewer competitors.

It is better not to fool ourselves. It is better to know ourselves in order to be able to take constructive steps toward a change, to establish, in the world, values different from those we now have, and last but not least, to let everybody have the minimum living standard and the minimum security in life.

Remembering, action and finger-snapping

In science, nothing is trivial. A trifle, a gesture, or a simple motion, like snapping of the fingers, may, when devotedly investigated, lead to the clarification of fundamental human phenomena.

Darwin (1873) could, with scientific correctness, trace back expressions of emotions to their very origin. Of finger-snapping, he says:

> various odd little gestures likewise indicate contempt; for instance, *snapping one's fingers*. This, as Mr. Tylor remarks, "is not very intelligible as we generally see it; but when we notice that the same sign made quite gently, as if rolling some tiny object away between the finger and thumb, or the sign of flipping it away with the thumb-nail and forefinger, are usual and well-understood deaf-and-dumb gestures, denoting anything tiny, insignificant, contemptible, it seems as though we had exaggerated and conventionalized a perfectly natural

action, so as to lose sight of its original meaning" [pp. 256-257].

To mention another example, in sneering, in snarling, in the sardonic smile, we draw the corners of the mouth a little backward, thus exposing the canine teeth. According to Darwin, this reveals our animal descent; animals in a threatening mood expose their canine teeth indicating their intention to bite. In human beings this is reduced to a derisive movement of the face (pp. 249-253).

In his description of the mental apparatus, which he considers a "compound instrument," Freud (1900) explains how "memory-traces" of impressions are engraved in this apparatus (pp. 536-542). David Rapaport (1950), presenting a psychoanalytic theory of thinking, found that the process of thinking from a genetic point of view is prompted by "hallucinatory images and ideas of drive objects, or hallucinatory wish fulfillments" (p. 271). The same is proposed in his book, *Emotions and Memory* (1942).

Bertram D. Lewin (1946) has shown that all our dreams take place on a "screen," which is nothing else than the breast on which our head once rested when we were fed and on which, as babies, we fell asleep. No matter what the content of a dream may be, we dream it on the "dream screen," the mother's breast. This means that essentially we have not forgotten the breast.

On the basis of my observations of finger-snapping and particularly on the basis of the circumstances in which in our culture (and as far as I know, in that of America, of Europe, and of China) finger-snapping occurs, I have come to the conclusion that *remembering and taking action is prompted by one of the very first actions and impressions of life: to find the source of food, the nipple, and the suckling.**

---

* Selma Fraiberg (1954), in a beautiful and profound paper, describes another impetus to remembering and to actions—the discovery of the genitals,

Circumstances in which finger-snapping occurs

1. When one is searching for the forgotten or for the solution to a problem and finds it. Often the exclamation added to the finger-snapping is, "I've got it."

2. When one suddenly comes to the realization that one has forgotten something, which means that one has remembered the forgotten. This may be illustrated by a joke: a large audience was chastised by a moral teacher who deplored the low morals of the community. It even happened, according to him, that so-called respectable people had been seen entering or emerging from a house of ill repute. At this point, a certain member of the audience snapped his fingers. The teacher noticed this and later asked the man why he had snapped his fingers, whereupon the man answered, "I remembered that I left my umbrella there."

3. When one wants attention from somebody in order to get something; e.g., service, attention, help; or to do something for others: warn, protect, help.

4. When one wants to stimulate another person to act in behalf of the former or the latter, he encourages him not to be slow but quick, to be swift, to find something, to succeed, to move, to act, to do, and to order. (To snap means to bite. The motion may be accompanied by a smacking of the lips.)

5. Finger-snapping might be done while dancing, to accentuate rhythm.

6. It may have a provocative and challenging connotation when used to put somebody to our service, to make us superior to the other person.

All have a common denominator: to take, to get, to act, to grab, to receive something that one needs, like a gratification or a pleasure.

The clinical picture of finger-snapping

When a person is searching his memory for something which he feels is in his mind or is searching for the solution of a problem, he often gently rubs together the surfaces of the thumb and middle finger, and this may end in finger-snapping if the solution is found suddenly. Some, especially children and adolescents, instead of using the two fingers, lick the upper transition line of the lip, between the skin and mucous membrane. Some use the index or middle finger instead of the tongue. Even the spelling of a word may be accompanied by quietly (and secretly) touching the upper and lower teeth in a certain specific order. Writing, especially by children, is often accompanied by simultaneous movements of the tongue. Chewing the end of a pencil, pen, toothpick (some carry the latter with them the whole day, or at least for hours)—all these "help" in thinking, searching, solving, remembering or carrying out any other action. The use of chewing gum and smoking belongs in this category. Moreover, nail-biting, in a state of tension, is a regressive oral device to facilitate thinking. It is as if the person biting his nail, chewing it as far down as possible, or biting the cuticle at the base of the nail until the flesh bleeds, is seeking a magic and symbolic support for his endeavor. Many spit out or swallow the removed particle as if lending themselves to the illusion that with this the problem is solved. Nail-biting is one of the most absorbing human activities, and persons engaged in it are in a virtual trance, oblivious to anything else around them, like the baby at the breast. It is similar to picking the nose. Some persons cannot rest until they have completely cleaned out all the available territory, almost up to the base of the skull, have removed the tiniest particle, have got between their two fingers the cherished treasure, have played with it for a while, and have finally thrown it away. Some even swallow it. As long as something can be found, such a person persists. Then he stops and waits until a new opportunity arises. The desire that such a new opportunity should arise is always in the mind in a dormant state.

Melitta Schmideberg (1935) says that there are aggressive

elements in nose-picking and thumb-sucking which are more or less concealed by the libidinal factors.

This clinging to a removable part of the body gives strong support to Hermann's theory (1936) on the two fundamental instincts: "to cling—to go: to cling to mother and to go away from her." In infants one can observe a quick movement of the fingers, which is, however, not snapping but a movement that indicates his desire to get the food into his hands quickly. Many persons, while talking or conversing with somebody at the table, collect morsels or any crumbs they can find, make a heap out of the material, form a "mouth" with their fingers and play arduously with their collection. Thumb-sucking in children and putting a finger between the lips in grownups while in the process of thinking, doodling, picking on removable particles of the face, scalp, etc., all have, in my opinion, the same meaning: to re-create the primary pleasurable, life-important experience, the finding of the nipple, and suckling. Whether mother helps or not, the baby searches for the nipple, or for the nipple of the bottle, and snaps it often with a smacking sound. This is repeated in finger-snapping. That the fingers can represent oneself and other persons, I have shown elsewhere when discussing the meaning of the blessing ceremony (1941c). The three fingers used in the blessing ceremony represent the family (as the most blessed unit): father, mother, and child. Similarly, in finger-snapping, the two fingers represent the mother and ourselves (in babyhood) and at the same time the two gums of the baby. The position of the mouth while snapping the fingers is either one in which the lips are pressed tightly together, especially when there is the accompanying feeling of anger or bitterness, or one in which the lips are wide open while the face expresses delight and gratification.

The first problem of a human being (and all other beings) is finding food. Children and animals have a keen memory of places in the house or anywhere else, where they have observed the presence of food. In addition to its self-preservative merits, suckling, and later eating, is accompanied by a strong libidinous feeling. The libidinous-aggressive energy, which is present until death, remains the basic source of all other activities of human beings: working, thinking, searching, remembering and others.

Conclusions

Life begins with breathing, but our postnatal object contact takes place first through food-need and by discovering the breast, the nipple (or the bottle, the former's representative). Dreams of restaurants, advertisements of food and drinks, and the behavior of people in eating places, show that the memory of "the first restaurant" remains indelibly in the mind (Fodor, 1951).

Very few persons can remember the time and act of suckling. The memory is repressed. It has to be repressed because, being such an important and pleasurable experience, without repression it would constantly remain conscious and one would be interested in nothing else. Such a state of mind would endanger the individual's existence. Though repressed, the first action remains as a powerful source of stimuli for all other actions, and creates a constant stimulus for remembering. *Every new experience, discovery and exploration carries with it the first pleasurable and life-securing rhythm of suckling, and, therefore, every remembering, recollection, and action is seeking to rediscover, to repeat, though in vain, the original oral experience* (Schachtel, 1950).

In the course of growing, the child becomes able to take food with hands and fingers. This ability establishes the connection between mouth and fingers (Hoffer, 1949, 1950; Lowenhaupt, 1952). Eventually two fingers (used in snapping) take over the representation of the mother and the baby (and the representation of the two gums of the baby).

Finger-cracking (or knuckle-cracking)

One converses with a person or as an analyst listens to a patient when suddenly, like a bolt from the blue, the speaker cracks his knuckles. The patient can, justly, claim that he does not do it intentionally and that he (women do it as often as men) would like to abstain from doing it; but it is too late. It is a habit. It annoys the doer himself and causes him mental pain because he feels that he is dominated by something over which he has no control.

Long ago, a tall, lean man appeared in my office. He was stern, dry, aloof, and he did not smile at greeting or during the interview. After he was seated, I asked him to tell me what troubled him. He signaled me to watch, lifted his right index finger and bent it.

"What do you mean?" I asked.

"It cracks," he said.

My reaction conveyed puzzlement.

He continued, "That's nothing," and did the same with his wrist.

I showed that I, too, could make a cracking noise by bending my wrist. The cracking noise depends on whether one makes the muscles and ligaments of the wrist taut or allows them to relax. The wrist cracks in the first place but not in the second.

"It cracks here, too," said the man, hitting the top of his head with a sharp crack. "It cracks in my neck."

This I did not reproduce. I had the impression that this was a very serious case. Others in whom this phenomenon could be observed did not come to treatment for this reason. They did not even mention the cracking in the first interview; but we noticed and analyzed the symptom in the course of the analysis. The man here described wanted immediate help which I was unable to furnish. The nature of the analytic treatment was explained to him and the decision as to what to do about it was left up to him. I never saw him again.

The other case was that of a very intelligent, dignified woman who was a chronic knuckle-cracker. During one session of about fifty to fifty-five minutes, she cracked her fingers five or six times. She was quite annoyed by it and suffered mental anguish from the habit. She entered treatment for completely different reasons; but both she and I felt that the cracking was an important phenomenon that must signify the presence of a strong complex. During the course of the treatment, it became clear that she was a very narcissistic and self-centered woman. She demanded absolute attention, and she showed, against her will, strong hostile feelings whenever her husband demonstrated, as a father, affectionate attention to the children whom she loved intensely. This grave conflict in her could be traced back to her childhood.

In the complicated process of her analysis, we could find that when she was frustrated, no matter what or who (husband or children) caused the frustration, aggressive, hostile and murderous impulses were aroused and sought entrance into her consciousness. She repressed them, so that instead of the feelings the cracking appeared.

Murderous impulses, when opposed, as in our refined lady, turn against the person herself. In our case, they appeared in suicidal tendencies, in an impulse to destroy herself. The knuckle-cracking condensed two impulses: to kill the frustrating person with hands and teeth and to destroy herself because of guilt about this desire.

This proposition was confirmed through another case of an analyst-colleague, Dr. George Engel, who kindly permitted the use of the following case about which he wrote in a letter:

A man in analysis who is an inveterate knuckle-cracker commented that he was driving his wife nuts with his knuckle-cracking, but later in the hour mentioned that this thought came into his mind in response to an impulse to crack his knuckles. He then remembered a dream of five or six days earlier. The dream was as follows:

"A big white dog was chasing a cat around. The dog seemed determined and able to catch the cat. I was watching it with blood-thirsty interest. Finally, the dog caught the cat. This was the most fascinating of all, whether the dog would eat the cat right there on the spot. I was spellbound. I watched with a feeling of irresistible curiosity about what the dog would do with the cat. I watched with fascination and horror as to whether the dog would tear him to pieces. The thought was that he would crush up the bones and break them into pieces without puncturing the skin. The dog killed the cat but didn't eat it. It then turned into a man who was standing waiting for the elevator [psychiatric clinic] calmly holding the lifeless body of the cat in his hand."

Playing with the ring on the finger and with the handbag

Because women (there are exceptions) are usually the ones who wear rings, the mannerism of playing with rings can be observed mainly in women.

In this chapter, we deal only with this sort of mannerism when the person using it is unaware of the action. If a lady knows what she is doing, the mannerism is of a different kind, like playing with anything during conversation, in solitude or in private meditation.

The former indicates a conflict, a tension in the person. It expresses a thought which the woman does not like to have, even if the thought contains a wish. In the mannerism, the ring is either made to slide up and down on the finger or transferred from one finger to another several times. There are different drives and thoughts behind this manneristic play.

First of all, the play serves the general purpose of releasing tension, whatever it may be, by a substitutive action similar to the dog's wagging his tail when he has to refrain from an action, and stopping it when he goes ahead.

The sliding of the ring over the finger, besides relieving tension, symbolizes meditations before decision. The removal of the ring from the finger and placing it on the other means a further step in making a decision. The latter action is a trial of the way things would be if the decision were already made.

The problem now is to consider the important thoughts behind this activity. Because the action is performed by women, the thoughts mostly concern troubles with a man, whether it is the husband or some other man. The ring is a symbol of attachment to somebody, in this instance, to the man, represented by the finger. The woman ponders whether she should leave the man and change him for another. The action is full of sexual symbolism. Perhaps, the latter is more evident in the well-known and easily observable play of women with their handbags, which they open and close, open and close, again and again.

It is not necessary for the person who plays with the ring or the handbag to talk or think about the motivations which prompt her activity. She can talk about another problem, thus occupying her mind for the time being. But if there is a more important problem, then the one about which she is speaking is temporarily pushed aside so that the important problem can be used for its own sake.

Confusion around the hands

Many people do not know what to do with their hands in public where they may be seen and observed. It is a great help for them to occupy their hands with different activities, like playing with anything they can grasp; but often this cannot be done because there is no available object or because one is not supposed to do anything at all. In such cases, they are in trouble. They become fidgety and try to hide their hands or, perhaps, bring them into the open, folded.

According to Ferenczi's experiences in such cases, "embarrassed hands" indicate unsuccessfully repressed inclinations to masturbate and only rarely with the suppression of other "bad habits" like nail-biting, nose-picking, scratching oneself, etc. The feeling of anxiety connected with the confusion around the hands, comes, according to Ferenczi (1914c), from exhibitionistic tendencies which are displaced to the uncovered parts of the body like the face and hands.

Ferenczi's findings have been confirmed by many cases. In my opinion, the persistence of the tendency to "bad habits" in many persons is due to traumatic experiences in the primary mother-child relationship, in Hermann's sense, which create feelings of frustration. These feelings are replaced by "bad habits" performed with the hands. After such habits are repressed, they come to the fore in the form of not knowing what to do with the hands, which are the instruments of clinging, security, and knowing where one belongs and what to do.

Manneristic movements with the shoulders

The second part of this book is not a study of gestures in general. It deals only with the manneristic use of the gestures, which are, in the opinion of many scholars before and after Darwin's classical work, innate in all mankind. At their origin, they were useful self-preservative and species-preservative actions. They were handed down to us as an inheritance and appear in a diminutive form.

The primary function of the gestures as well as the meanings which were attached to them in the course of time and individualized by certain persons both overlap with each other. It is impossible to make a sharp division between them.

We are interested in Miller's statement (1950) to the effect that personality and social adaptation of the individual are reflected in the manner and content of his speech.

Exactly the same thing can be said about gestures. The gradual loss of hair and the loss of the jungle (by fire) left the hands without objects to cling to (Hermann). Hermann (1943) refers to Levy-Brühl, who said that "to talk with the hands, in a way, is hand thinking." Also, adds Hermann,

"The hand's relation to the intellect is so strong that it becomes part of it."

The primary gestures change not only for specific purposes of individuals but for the greater good of the group, as shown by Efron's studies (1941) of the gesture behavior of Eastern Jews and Southern Italians in New York City. His book is impressively illustrated by pictures and sketches by Stuyvesant Van Veen.

Not all Jews living in a group gesticulate excessively. Any member of any group can have his own reasons for gesticulation. Moreover, a member of a group characterized by gesticulation must not gesticulate because he belongs to that group. Many members of the same group do not gesticulate. Either they did not do so originally; or, if they did, they have willfully abandoned it for the sake of adaptation to another group.

In gesticulation, not only the hands but the whole body and all its parts are involved. Let us take one example. An Eastern Jew, on a Saturday, is dressed in characteristic attire. His hat is worn far over his forehead; he sticks out his belly, bends backward, and walks in a shuffling manner; his head is up, and his face shows self-content.

What is this? These were poor Jews who lived from hand to mouth, in miserable quarters, faced an insecure future, feared the possibility of a pogrom, and were subjected to all sorts of discrimination. Why, then, did they show such self-content? Why did they talk loudly, and carry their bodies as if they were the most secure of creatures?

They do so *because* they are so insecure. They have to "whistle," so to say, in the dark of their lives, to be loud, to show with their hands, feet, and all the other parts of their bodies that everything is "just" fine.

Darwin (1873, pp. 235, 264-272) speaks about two kinds of "shoulder gestures." One is "showing a cold shoulder"; and the other is the "shrugging of the shoulders" in different situations. "Showing the cold shoulder" was observed by Darwin in sulky children. For example, writes Darwin, "A cross child, sitting on its parent's knee, will lift up the near shoulder, then jerk it away as if from a caress, and afterwards give a backward push away from the offender." We should note that the aim of this movement is to get rid of the "offender."

Darwin enumerates the following reasons for shrugging the shoulders: (a) a man does so when he wishes to "show that he cannot do something, or prevent something's being done"; (b) it accompanies such speeches as, "It was not my fault"; "It is impossible for me to grant this favour"; (c) it expresses patience or the absence of any intention to resist.

To explain the expression of passivity and helplessness with the shrugging of the shoulders, Darwin offers his theory of *the principle of unconscious antithesis* (p. 271), i.e., it is the reverse of bodily expressions of attack (p. 274).

I would like to supplement Darwin's theory. In my opinion, the shrugging of the shoulders, whether it means "showing the cold shoulder" or has any other significance in other situations, wants to express the intention and *the need to get rid of something which is irritating*, like shaking off an annoying bug, like a dog's shaking off water, like a horse's being able to induce quivering motions in parts of the skin which are irritated by an insect, or like a person's shaking off an attacker.

Even when the shoulders express pride, their position means, "I am so much above you that you shouldn't even touch me." To illustrate, I will mention two cases, both of which can be observed in everyday life.

One was the case of a very beautiful four-year-old girl. She was quite aware of her charms and of the irresistible power she had over everybody. She was sitting on the knees of her father, telling some story, in the course of which she raised one shoulder and put her face self-lovingly on it. I believe the gesture seemed to say, "Only I, myself, can know how lovable I am and how to love me."

The other case shows that we analysts are not perfect

either and can be just as manneristic as others. A brilliant colleague, when scheduled to talk at one of the analytic conventions, was seldom seen in the lecture room when *somebody else* was reading a paper. Instead, he walked up and down the corridor, always accompanied by one or more of his admiring pupils. While thus walking, he held his head close to one shoulder (like our charming little girl), dangled his brief case, and hardly touched the floor with his feet. I feel that this colleague was expressing self-content and feeling that he belonged high in the clouds, believing that there should be only one lecture, his, and intimating that nobody could or should get close to him. He acted like the Lord on Mount Sinai: one should admire him, fear him, but never get close to him lest He destroy him.

When a person moves away in order to be called back

The mannerism of moving away in order to be called back is used almost exclusively by women. It is often seen in real life and on the stage. A lady is with her man. She feels hurt and is angry and sulking. Suddenly, she moves away from him, if possible toward a window, with her back to the man whom she otherwise loves and by whom she wants to be loved. She stops there and waits. The man understands this gesture, and goes after her. She shrugs him away; but he insists, is kind to her, and wants to pacify her. In ninety-nine per cent of the cases, reconciliation takes place. He thinks he won. No! She did.

Gait

Every human being has his own particular gait through which he can be characterized and recognized. In this chapter, I would like to mention a few manneristic gaits. There is the gait of self-content which is sloppy, shuffling, waddling like a duck. The person who walks in this manner usually has his belly protruding. His gait shows the contentment of satiety. Then, there is the gait of attractive, young females who, when alone on the street, seem to be competing with the winner of the hundred-yard sprint in the Olympics. The gait indicates that the girls are not on the street because they are streetwalkers. Another manneristic gait is the tip-toeing of the person who wants to indicate that he is always in the clouds, that he is an ethereal person who has no heels or soles (like the analyst-colleague who indicated his self-love through the manneristic movements of his head and shoulders). Finally, there is the tip-toeing gait of those who walk so imperceptibly that others can hardly hear them. The cause of such a gait is the repression of exhibitionistic tendencies.

Summary

This book accentuates the value of analyzing some neglected phenomena of everyday life.

Neuroses consist of subjectively disturbing symptoms, but also of hundreds of other signs: personality characteristics which, because they are common, appear innocuous. I intended to prove that their analysis can be an important part of the "working through" process in therapy. If they are neglected, a valuable opportunity to reach the more fundamental conflicts might be missed. The analysis of mannerisms is a good tool to make the patient aware of, and to soften his resistances against, the perception of unconscious content. This often leads to the core of a neurosis. The "working through" process achieves a profound insight into and understanding of the conflicts which are responsible for the neurosis.

The role which the superego plays in these mannerisms is astounding. The "true" and the "false" superego are in a constant struggle; and if the "false" superego has the dominance, it facilitates and maintains the neurosis and disturbs the attainment of mental and emotional balance. In one way or another, the truth asserts itself.

These findings, applicable to all mankind, rekindle the hope that gradually a universally valid educational therapy can be developed.

Can this be achieved? If the devil is chased out from one place, will he not turn up in another form somewhere else?

We must wait and we shall see. . . .

Bibliography

Abraham, Karl (1911), On the Determining Power of Names. *Clinical Papers and Essays on Psychoanalysis*, 2:31-32. New York: Basic Books, 1955.
—————— (1925), The Influence of Oral Erotism on Character-Formation. *Int. J. Psa.*, 6:254.
Alexander, Franz (1950), The Evolution and Present Trends of Psychoanalysis. *Congrès International de Psychiatrie, Paris 1950*, 5:1-25. Paris: Hermann & Co.
Allport, G. W. & Vernon, P. E. (1933), *Studies in Expressive Movement*. New York: Macmillan, p. viii.
Alrutz, S. (1908), Die Kitzel und Juckempfindungen [On Tickling and Itching]. *Skand. Arch. Physiol.*, 20:371-410. [Richet's comment, according to Altruz, "Chatouillement," Diction de Physiologie par Richet, Paris, Fom. III, pp. 343-344.]
Arlow, Jacob A. (1957), On Smugness. *Int. J. Psa.*, 38:1-8.
Bak, Robert C. (1943), Dissolution of the Ego. *J. Nerv. & Ment. Dis.*, 98:460-461.
—————— (1954), The Schizophrenic Defense against Aggression. *Int. J. Psa.*, 35:129-134.
Barahal, Hyman S. (1940), The Psychopathology of Hair-Plucking. *Psa. Rev.*, 27:291-310.
Basler, A. (1912a), Über den Fusssohlenkitzel [Ticklishness of the Sole]. *Pflügers Arch.*, 148:311-318.
—————— (1912b), Experimentelle Untersuchungen über den Hautkitzel [Experimental Investigation of Skin Ticklishness]. *Pflügers Arch.*, 147:375-392.
Benedek, Therese (1949), The Psychosomatic Implications of the Primary Unit: Mother-Child. *Am. J. Orthopsychiat.*, 19:642-654.
Berg, Charles (1951), *The Unconscious Significance of Hair*. George Allen & Unwin, pp. 1-106.
Bergler, Edmund (1945), Working Through in Psychoanalysis. *Psa. Rev.*, 32:452.
—————— (1947), Specific Types of Resistance in Orally Repressed Neurotics. *Psa. Rev.*, 34:73.
Berne, E. (1953), Concerning the Nature of Communication. *Psychiat. Quart.*, 27:185-198.

Brenman, Margaret (1952), On Teasing and Being Teased. *The Psychoanalytic Study of the Child*, 7:264-285. New York: International Universities Press.

Birdwhistell, Ray L. (1956), Background to Kinesics. *Etc. A Review of General Semantics*, 13:10.

Born, Wolfgang (1945), Fetish, Amulet and Talisman. *Ciba Symposia*, 7:116.

Bose, F., Law, S. & Ganguly, D. (1951), Psychological Study of Language: Preliminary Communication. *Samiksa*, 4:216-229.

Brill, A. A. (1922), Tobacco and the Individual. *Int. J. Psa.*, 3:430-444.

Buch, Max (1909a), Über den Kitzel [On Ticklishness]. *Arch. Physiol*, Leipzig, 33:1-26.

—— (1909b), Die Beziehungen des Kitzels zur Erotik [The Erotic Meaning of Ticklishness]. *Arch. Physiol.*, Leipzig, 33:27-33.

Buxbaum, Edith (1949), The Role of a Second Language in the Formation of Ego and Superego. *Psa. Quart.*, 18:279-289.

Cassirer, Ernst (1946), *Language and Myth*. New York: Dover, p. 84.

Critchley, MacDonald (1939), *The Language of Gesture*. London: Edward Arnold, pp. 11, 121.

Darwin, Charles (1873), *The Expressions of the Emotions in Man and in Animals*. London: Murray.

De Beauvoir, Simone (1953), *The Second Sex*. New York: Knopf.

De Forest, Izette (1954), *The Leaven of Love*. New York: Harper, pp. 28-29.

Deutsch, Helene (1934): Über einen Typus der Pseudoaffektivität ("als ob") [On a Type of Pseudo-Affectivity ("as if")]. *Int. Ztschr. Psa.*, 20:323-335.

Devereux, George (1951), Mohave Indian Verbal and Motor Profanity. *Psychoanalysis and the Social Sciences*, 3:99-127. New York: International Universities Press.

—— (1956), Note on the Feminine Significance of the Eyes. *Bull. Phila. Assn. Psa.*, 6:21.

Diringer, David (1948), *The Alphabet*. New York: Philosophical Library, p. 35.

Efron, David (1941), *Gesture and Environment*. London: King's Crown Press.

Eliasberg, W. (1942), Remarks on the Psychopathology of Pornography. *J. Crim. Psychopathol.*, 3:715-720.

Engel, G. L. (1950), *Fainting, Physiological and Psychological Considerations*. Springfield: Charles C. Thomas, p. 74.

Evans, William N. (1953), Evasive Speech As a Form of Resistance. *Psa. Quart.*, 32:548-560.

Feldman, Sandor S. (1922), Über Erröten [On Blushing]. *Int. Ztschr. Psa.*, 8:14-34.

—— (1926), A Ticroel [On Tic]. *Magyar Orvos*, 17.

—— (1932a), Über das Auslachen [On Ridicule]. *Zbl. Psychother. & ihre Grenzgebiete*, Leipzig, 5:534-539.

—— (1932b), Eine merkwürdige Phobie [A Strange Phobia: Fear of Checking Hat and Coat]. *Psa. Praxis*, 2:96-97.

—— (1941a), A Supplement to Freud's Theory of Wit. *Psa. Rev.*, 28:201-217.

—— (1941b), On Blushing. *Psychiat. Quart.*, 15:249-261.

—— (1941c), The Blessing of the Kohanites. *Am. Imago*, 2:317-318.

—— (1948), Mannerisms of Speech. *Psa. Quart.*, 17:356-367; also in *The Yearbook of Psychoanalysis*, 5:61-71. New York: International Universities Press, 1949.

—— (1949), Fear of Mice. *Psa. Quart.*, 18:227-230.

—— (1956), Crying at the Happy Ending. *J. Am. Psa. Assn.*, 4:477-485

Ferenczi, Sandor (1911), On Obscene Words. *Sex and Psychoanalysis*. New York: Basic Books, 1950, pp. 132-153.

—— (1912), A Case of "Deja Vu." *The Selected Papers of Sandor Ferenczi*, 3:319-321. New York: Basic Books, 1955.

—— (1913), Stages in the Development of the Sense of Reality. *Contributions to Psychoanalysis*. Boston: Badger, 1916.

—— (1914a), Rubbing of the Eyes as a Substitute for Onanism. *Further Contributions to the Theory and Technique of Psycho-Analysis*. London: Hogarth Press, 1926, p. 317.

—— (1914b), Embarrassed Hands. *Further Contributions to the Theory and Technique of Psycho-Analysis*. London: Hogarth Press, 1926, pp. 315-316.

—— (1915a), Talkativeness. *Further Contributions to the Theory and Technique of Psycho-Analysis*. London: Hogarth Press, 1926, p. 252.

—— (1915b), The Analysis of Comparisons. *Further Contributions to the Theory and Technique of Psycho-Analysis*. London: Hogarth Press, 1926, pp. 397-406.

—— (1919), The Technique of Psycho-Analysis. III. "For Example" in Analysis. *Further Contributions to the Theory and Technique of Psycho-Analysis*. London: Hogarth Press, 1926, pp. 184-186.

—— (1924), Thalassa: A Theory of Genitality. *Psa. Quart.*, 2:398, 1933.

—— (1932), On Lamaism and Yoga. *Selected Papers of Sandor Ferenczi*, 3:274. New York: Basic Books, 1955.

Fliess, Robert (1944), Knocking on Wood. *Psa. Quart.*, 13:327-340.

Flugel, J. G. (1925), A Note on the Phallic Significance of the Tongue and of the Speech. *Int. J. Psa.*, 6:209-215.

—— (1954), On Bringing Bad News. *Samiksa*, 7:19-28.

Fodor, N. (1951), Nightmares of Cannibalism. *Am. J. Psychother.*, 5:226.

—————— (1956), *Nomen est Omen. Samiksa*, 10:9-45.

Fraiberg, Selma (1954), Discovery of the Secret Treasure. *The Psychoanalytic Study of the Child*, 9:241. New York: International Universities Press.

Frazer, James G. (1922), *The Golden Bough* (abridged ed. Vol. I). New York: Macmillan, 1954.

Freud, Sigmund (1900), The Interpretation of Dreams. *Standard Edition*, Vols. 3 & 4. London: Hogarth Press, 1953.

—————— (1905a), Wit and Its Relation to the Unconscious. *The Basic Writings of Sigmund Freud*. New York: Random House, 1938, pp. 633-803.

—————— (1905b), Three Essays on the Theory of Sexuality. *Standard Edition*, 7:123-243. London: Hogarth Press, 1953.

—————— (1909), Notes upon a Case of Obsessional Neurosis. *Standard Edition*, 10:153-320. London: Hogarth Press, 1955.

—————— (1913), Observations and Examples from Analytic Practice. *Standard Edition*, 13:193-200. London: Hogarth Press, 1955.

—————— (1914a), Further Recommendations in the Technique of Psycho-Analysis. *Collected Papers*, 2:366-376. London: Hogarth Press, 1955.

—————— (1914b), The Moses of Michelangelo. *Standard Edition*, 13:211-240. London: Hogarth Press, 1955.

—————— (1915), Some Character-Types Met with in Psycho-Analytic Work. *Collected Papers*, 4:318-344. London: Hogarth Press, 1925.

—————— (1916), A Connection Between a Symbol and a Symptom. *Collected Papers*, 2:162-163. London: Hogarth Press, 1924.

—————— (1916/1917), *A General Introduction to Psychoanalysis*. New York: Boni & Liveright, 1920.

—————— (1918), From the History of an Infantile Neurosis. *Standard Edition*, 17:7-122. London: Hogarth Press, 1955.

—————— (1921), Group Psychology and the Analysis of the Ego. *Standard Edition*, 18:69-144. London: Hogarth Press, 1955.

—————— (1925), Negation. *Collected Papers*, 5:181-185. London: Hogarth Press, 1950.

—————— (1930), *Civilization and Its Discontents*. London: Hogarth Press.

—————— (1932), The Acquisition of Power over Fire. *Collected Papers*, 5:288-294. London: Hogarth Press, 1950.

—————— (1937), Analysis Terminable and Interminable. *Collected Papers*, 5:316-357. London: Hogarth Press, 1950.

—————— (1939), *Moses and Monotheism*. New York: Knopf.

Fromm, Erich (1951), *The Forgotten Language*. New York: Rinehart.

Funk & Wagnall (1936), *New Standard Bible Dictionary*. Philadelphia: Blakiston.

Glauber, I. Peter (1944), Speech Characteristics of Psychoneurotic Patients. *J. Speech Disorders*, 9:18-30.

Greenacre, Phyllis (1945), Pathological Weeping. *Psa. Quart.*, 14:62-64.

—— (1955), *Swift and Carroll*. New York: International Universities Press.

Gregory, J. C. (1924), *The Nature of Laughter*. New York: Harcourt, pp. 41-51.

Hall, Stanley & Allin, Arthur (1897), The Psychology of Tickling, Laughter and the Comic. *Am. J. Psychol.*, 14:29.

Hart, Henry H. (1953), The Meaning of Circumstantiality. *Samiksa*, 7:271-284.

Harris, Herbert I. (1957), Telephone Anxiety. *J. Am. Psa. Assn.*, 5:342-347.

Hartmann, Heinz, Kris, Ernst & Loewenstein, Rudolph M. (1949), Notes on the Theory of Aggression. *The Psychoanalytic Study of the Child*, 3/4:9-36. New York: International Universities Press.

Hayakawa, S. I. (1952), Semantics. *Etc. A Review of General Semantics*, 9:243-257.

Heilbrunn, Gert (1955), On Weeping. *Psa. Quart.*, 24:252.

Hermann, Imre (1934a), A Tudattalan es Az Oesztoenoek Oervenyelmelete [The Unconscious and the Whirl Theory of the Instincts]. *Lélekelemzési Tanulmányok*. Budapest: Béla Somló.

—— (1934b), *Die Psychoanalyse als Methode* [*Psychoanalysis as a Method*]. Vienna: Internationaler Psychoanalytischer Verlag.

—— (1936), Sich-Anklammern, Auf-Suche-Gehen [To Cling, To Go Searching]. *Int. Ztschr. Psa.*, 22:349-370.

—— (1940), Studien zur Denkpsychologie [Studies in the Psychology of Thinking]. *Akta Psychol.*, Hague, 5:22-102.

—— (1941), Anklammerung, Feuer und Schamgefühl [Clinging, Fire and Shame]. *Int. Ztschr. Psa. & Imago*, 26:252-274. Abstracted in English: *Int. J. Psa.*, 23:88, 1942.

—— (1943), *The Primordial Instincts of Man* (Hungarian). Budapest: Pantheon.

—— (1949), The Giant Mother. *Psa Rev.*, 36:302-307.

Hertz, J. H., ed. (1938), *The Pentateuch, Hebrew Text*. English Translation and Commentary. London: Soncino Press.

Hoffer, W. (1949), Mouth, Hand and Ego-Integration. *The Psychoanalytic Study of the Child*, 3/4:48-55. New York: International Universities Press.

—— (1950), Development of the Body Ego. *The Psychoanalytic Study of the Child*, 5:18-23. New York: International Universities Press.

Hollos, I. (1923), Schlangen- und Krawattensymbolik [Snake and Tie Symbolism]. *Int. Ztschr. Psa.*, 9:73.

Holstijn, A. J. Westerman (1932), Oral Erotism in Paraphrenia. *Int. J. Psa.*, 15:160-186.

The Holy Scriptures. Philadelphia: Jewish Publication Society of America, 1948, pp. 45-46.

Jacobson, Edith (1946), The Child's Laughter. *The Psychoanalytic Study of the Child*, 2:39-60. New York: International Universities Press.

Jelliffe, S. E. & White, W. A. (1917), *Diseases of the Nervous System.* Philadelphia: Lea & Febiger, pp. 815-823.

Johnson, Wendell (1944), Studies in Language Behavior. *Psychol. Mon.*, No. 56.

Jones, Ernest (1914), The Madonna's Conception Through the Ear. *Essays in Applied Psycho-Analysis*, 2:266-257. London: Hogarth Press, 1941.

——— (1920), A Linguistic Factor in English Characterology. *Essays in Applied Psycho-Analysis*, 1:88-94. London: Hogarth Press, 1951.

Koch, Rudolph (1930), *The Book of Signs.* London: First Edition Club.

Krapf, Eduard (1955), The Choice of Language in Polyglot Psychoanalysis. *Psa. Quart.*, 24:331.

Kris, Ernst (1938), Ego Development and the Comic. *Psychoanalytic Explorations in Art.* New York: International Universities Press, 1952.

——— (1939), Laughter as an Expressive Process. *Int. J. Psa.*, 21:330-331, 1940.

——— & Gombrich, Ernst (1938), The Principles of Caricature. *Brit. J. Med. Psychol.*, 16:319-342.

Kubie, Lawrence S. (1951), The Relationship of Symbolic Function in Language Formation and in Neurosis. *Cybernetics*, ed. Heinz von Foerster. New York: Josiah Macy, Jr., Foundation, pp. 209-235.

Kulovesi, Y. (1939), Die Ausdrucksbewegungen der Bejahung und der Verneinung [The Expressive Movements of Confirmation and Denial]. *Int. Ztschr. Psa.*, 24:446-447.

Lacombe, Pierre (1958), A Special Mechanism of Pathological Weeping. *Psa. Quart.*, 27:246-251.

Lewin, Bertram D. (1946), Sleep, the Mouth and the Dream Screen. *Psa. Quart.*, 15:419-434.

Loewenstein, Rudolph M. (1950), Conflict and Autonomous Ego Development. *The Psychoanalytic Study of the Child*, 5:49-50. New York: International Universities Press.

——— (1956), Some Remarks on the Role of Speech in Psychoanalytic Technique. *Int. J. Psa.*, 37:460-468.

Lorand, Sandor (1929), The Mantle Symbol. *Clinical Studies in Psychoanalysis.* New York: International Universities Press, pp. 25-28.
———— & Feldman, Sandor S. (1955), The Symbolism of Teeth in Dreams. *Int. J. Psa.,* 36:145-161.
Lorenz, Maria (1953), Language as Expressive Behavior. *A.M.A. Arch. Neurol & Psychiat.,* 7:277-285.
———— (1955), Expressive Behavior and Language Patterns. *Psychiatry,* 18:353-366.
Lowenhaupt, E. (1952), A Consideration of Psychic Mechanisms in Vasoplastic Disorders of the Hand. *Psa. Rev.,* 39:329-337.
Marmor, Judd (1958), The Psychodynamics of Realistic Worry. *Psychoanalysis and the Social Sciences,* 5:155-163. New York: International Universities Press.
Masserman, Jules H. (1944), Language Behavior and Dynamic Psychiatry. *Int. J. Psa.,* 25:4-5.
———— (1954), Conceptual Dynamics of Person, Religion and Self. *Psa. Rev.,* 41:311.
Mazzanti, Vincent & Bessell, Harold (1956), Communication Through the Latent Language. *Am. J. Psychother.,* 10:250-260.
Menninger, Karl, A. (1924), Letters of the Alphabet in Psychoanalytic Formation. *Int. J. Psa.,* 5:462-467.
Miller, George A. (1950), *Language and Communication.* New York: McGraw-Hill, pp. 131, 174.
Mitford, Nancy, ed. (1956), *Nobless Oblige.* New York: Harper.
Montagu, M. F. Ashley (1942), On the Physiology and Psychology of Swearing. *Psychiatry,* 5.
———— (1955), Man and Human Nature. *Am. J. Psychiat.,* 112:401-410.
Moro, E. (1918), Das erste Trimenon [The First Trimenon]. *Münch. Med. Wchnschr.,* 65:1149.
Müller, J. (1840), *Handbuch der Physiologie des Menschen [Textbook on the Physiology of Man].* 2:497-498, 1938. (I am indebted to Imre Hermann for calling this reference to my attention.)
Murphy, William F. (1957), A Note on the Significance of Names. *Psa. Quart.,* 26:91-106.
Murray, Elsie (1908), A Qualitative Analysis of Tickling. *Am. J. Psychol.,* 19:322.
Neuman, Stanley (1939), Personal Symbolism in Language Pattern. *Psychiatry,* 2:179-184.
———— & Mather, Vera G. (1938), Analysis of Spoken Language of Patients with Affective Disorders. *Am. J. Psychiat.,* 94:913-942.
Oberndorf, C. P. (1918), Reaction to Personal Names. *Psa. Rev.,* 5:47-52; also in *Int. J. Psa.,* 1:223-230, 1920.

Pederson-Krag, G. (1956), The Use of Metaphors in Analytic Thinking. *Psa. Quart.*, 25:60.
Peto, A. (1946), Weeping and Laughter. *Int. J. Psa.*, 27:129-133.
Pittenger, Robert E. & Smith, Henry Lee (1957), A Basis for the Contributions of Linguistics to Psychiatry. *Psychiatry*, 20.
Ponder, Eric & Kennedy, W. P. (1927), On the Act of Blinking. *Quart. J. Exper. Physiol.*, 18:89-110.
R., H. (1912), Zur Symbolik der Schlange und der Krawatte [On the Symbolism of Snake and Tie]. *Zentralbl. Psa.*, 2:675.
Rangell, Leo (1954), The Psychology of Poise. *Int. J. Psa.*, 35:19.
Rank, Otto (1932), *Art and Artist*. New York: Knopf.
Rapaport, David (1942), *Emotions and Memory*. New York: International Universities Press, sec. ed., 1950, p. 136.
––––– (1950), On the Psychoanalytic Theory of Thinking. In: *Psychoanalytic Psychiatry and Psychology*, ed. Robert P. Knight & Cyrus R. Friedman. New York: International Universities Press, 1954, p. 271.
Reich, Annie (1949), The Structure of the Grotesque-Comic Sublimation. *Bull. Menninger Clin.*, 13:160-171.
Reik, Theodor (1937), *Surprise and the Psychoanalyst*. New York: Dutton, pp. 58-59.
Ruesch, J. (1953), Synopsis of the Theory of Human Communication. *Psychiatry*, 16:231.
––––– (1957), *Disturbed Communication*. New York: Norton, pp. 34-35, 66-69.
––––– & Kees, W. (1956), *Nonverbal Communication*. Berkeley and Los Angeles: University of California Press.
Robinson, Louis (1894), On the Anthropological Significance of Ticklishness. London: *Rep. Brit. Assn. Adv. Sci.*, p. 778.
––––– & Hall, Stanley (1909), mentioned by M. Buch in "Über den Kitzel" [On Tickling]. *Arch. Physiol.*, Leipzig, 33:1-26.
Robitsek, Alfred (1925), Der Kotillon [The Cotillion]. *Int. J. Psa.*, 5:15.
Róheim, Géza (1921), Das Selbst [The Self]. *Imago*, 7:2-3.
––––– (1942), Transition Rites. *Psa. Quart.*, 11:336-374.
Rycroft, Charles (1956), Symbolism and Its Relationship to the Primary and Secondary Processes. *Int. J. Psa.*, 37:137-146.
Sadger, J. (1921), *Die Lehre von den Geschlechtsverirrungen* [On Perversions]. Leipzig: Deuticke, pp. 29-30.
Schachtel, E. G. (1950), On Memory and Childhood Amnesia. In: *A Study of Interpersonal Relations*, ed. P. Mullahy. New York: Hermitage Press.
Schmideberg, Melitta (1935), Bad Habits in Children, Their Development. *Int. J. Psa.*, 16:457.
Seligman, S. (n.d.), *Der böse Blick* [The Evil Eye], 2 Vols. Amonestra Verlag.

Shands, Harley C. (1958), Avoidance of the Particular. Unpublished.

Shapiro, Edward (1926, 1927), Speech As a Personality Trait. *Am. J. Sociol.*, 32:892-905.

Sharpe, Ella Freeman (1940), Psycho-Physical Problems Revealed in Language. *Int. J. Psa.*, 21:204-212.

Sperling, Melitta (1954), The Use of the Hair As a Bisexual Symbol. *Psa. Rev.*, 41:363-365.

Sperling, Samuel J. (1953), On the Psychodynamics of Teasing. *J. Am. Psa. Assn.*, 1:458-483.

Spitz, René A. (1945), Hospitalism. *The Psychoanalytic Study of the Child*, 1:53-74. New York: International Universities Press.

—— (1946), Anaclitic Depression. *The Psychoanalytic Study of the Child*, 2:313-342. New York: International Universities Press.

—— (1957), *No and Yes*. New York: International Universities Press.

—— & Wolf, K. M. (1946), The Smiling Response. *Gen. Psychol. Mon.*, No. 34.

—— —— (1949), Autoerotism. *The Psychoanalytic Study of the Child*, 3/4:85-120. New York: International Universities Press.

Stanley, Hiram M. (1898), Remarks on Tickling and Laughing. *Am. J. Psychol.*, 9:235-240.

Stein, Martin H. (1958), The Cliché. *J. Am. Psa. Assn.*, 6:263-277.

Stekel, W. (1911), Die Verpflichtung des Namens [The Obligation of Names]. *Ztschr. Psychother. & med. Psychol.*, 3.

Sterba, Richard (1942), *Introduction to the Psychoanalytic Theory of Libido*. New York: Nervous and Mental Disease Monographs.

Sternberg, W. (1909), Die Kitzelgefühle [On Ticklishness]. *Zentralbl. Physiol.*, Leipzig, 28:865-869.

—— (1911-1912), Die Physiologie der Kitzelgefühle [The Physiology of Ticklishness]. *Ztschr. Psychol. & Physiol.*, 60:105.

Sugar, N. (1941), Zur Frage der mimischen Bejahung und Verneinung [On the Mimic Process of Confirmation and Negation]. *Int. Ztschr. Psa. & Imago*, 26:81-83.

Szasz, Thomas S. (1955), Entropy, Organization and the Problem of the Economy of Human Relationships. *Int. J. Psa.*, 26:289-297.

—— (1956), Is the Concept of Entropy Relevant to Psychology and Psychiatry? *Psychiatry*, 19:200-202.

—— (1958), Counterphobic Mechanisms in Addiction. *J. Am. Psa. Assn.*, 6:314.

Weiss, J. (1952), Crying at the Happy Ending. *Psa. Rev.*, 39:338.

Wiener, Norbert (1948), *Cybernetics*. New York: Wiley, pp. 19, 26-27.